GOOD HOUSEKEEPING

CREATIVE COOKERY

GOOD HOUSEKEEPING

CREATIVE COOKERY

SUE STYLE

EBURY PRESS
LONDON

Published by Ebury Press
Division of The National Magazine Company Ltd
Colquhoun House
27–37 Broadwick Street
London W1V 1FR

First impression 1988

ISBN 0 85223 785 5

Edited by Veronica Sperling, Helen Dore and Susie Ward
Art Direction by Frank Phillips
Designed by Peter Laws
Photography by James Murphy
Styling by Cathy Sinker
Cookery by Maxine Clark

Filmset by Advanced Filmsetters (Glasgow) Ltd
Printed and bound in Great Britain at the University Press, Cambridge

For Soph and Oliver

champion consumers of pasta, prawns and avocados
and constant encouragers of the maternal efforts

CONTENTS

ACKNOWLEDGEMENTS

I AM INDEBTED . . . to Chefs Robert and Michel Husser of Le
Cerf, Marlenheim; Emile Jung and Fred of Le Crocodile,
Strasbourg; Patrick Labalette of the Hotel Euler, Basel; Michel
Bourdin and Graham Dunton of the Connaught, London; and
Monsieur Marchand, my friendly Alsatian baker over the border
in Hagental-le-Bas. All of them allowed me more than generous
glimpses behind the scenes, and gave unstintingly of their time
and advice. Their approach to the preparation of fine food
inspired the shape of the present book.

. . . to Erica Rokweiler, who read, re-read and read again the
book from its early stages, and generally acted as a skilful,
encouraging and patient midwife throughout the birth pangs.

. . . to my family, who put up with me wonderfully well most of
the time, and never more so than when a deadline loomed.

INTRODUCTION

The self-made cook

The French, with their unerring sense of drama, call my sort of person an *autodidacte* – which sounds quite exciting, but simply means that I never studied cooking, only learnt the hard way, making all the usual mistakes and finding out the whys and wherefores for myself. It wasn't until I started insinuating myself into the kitchens of top chefs and asking them all sorts of terribly obvious questions that it dawned on me that cooking is a sort of game of themes and variations. As I hesitantly inquired about the various dishes on the menu, a pattern of replies began to emerge. The elegant first course? A chilled soup base with ovals of vegetable mousse floated on top, and a few mussels and oysters dotted about. The superb fish entrée? Simply a fish mousseline ('the same as we use for the fish terrines and quenelles, Madame') sandwiched between two thin slices of fish, steamed and sauced. The Gâteau aux Trois Chocolats, surely, must be very complicated? Not really, just a plain sponge, layered with dark, milk and white chocolate mousses...

Back to basics

A vegetable mousse? Fish terrines? Sponge cakes? Chocolate mousse? Even I could make most of these! But I never realized how much I in fact knew, and a whole new world of dishes opened up for me, built on skills I had acquired along the bumpy road, but didn't know how to exploit fully. If you're a wizard at terrines, in other words, or your reputation for sponge cakes has spread far beyond the church bazaar, don't stop there: take these skills a step or two further and you'll be amazed at what you can do with your initial themes by creating clever variations from them.

Themes and their variations

I started to look back over all the dishes I'd done, both at home and at my classes in Switzerland, Mexico and England, and found that most of them could be categorized into one or other of about twenty-five basic cookery themes. Each theme became a chapter, and was given the form of a 'mother recipe' (with detailed notes on techniques), which could be built on to in lots of different directions. Thus the layout is very different from the usual cookbook: instead of being divided into seasons or courses, each chapter may include starters, mains and desserts for various occasions in the calendar, all stemming from the same basic root: the 'mother recipe'.

What's included? What's left out?

The scope is also different from other cookbooks, for three reasons. Firstly, favourite recipes – however delicious – which turned out to be 'dead ends' in terms of possible development were left out; secondly, it's a personal and very catholic selection, based on my own likes (salads, pastry, sauces, fish, lamb, good bread...) and dislikes (deep-frying of anything); and cooking habits built up over several nomadic years, spent variously in Spain, France, Mexico, Switzerland and England: themes and variations in cooking know no frontiers. Thirdly, there are scant instructions for such things as roasting pieces of meat or cooking vegetables correctly, which I'm sure most people know already. This is a book for people who'd like to get beyond the basics, who have already been cooking for a while, but who may lack the imagination and/or courage to branch out a bit and take things a step further.

How to use this book

In each chapter you will find an introduction to the theme, basic snags to watch out for (*Watchpoints*), a bare-bones table of ingredients and instructions on how to use them. It will serve as a sort of refresher course for those who've already been there, or an introduction for newcomers.

Then come the interesting bits: under *Variations*, you will find ideas on how to vary the basic recipe (add a different spice, do it upside down, substitute wine for stock, etc.), while

Further ideas gives suggestions on how to actually use what you've so cleverly constructed. In each case, the quantity in the basic recipe should be enough to enable you to work at least one variation on the theme, so that while you're in the mood, flushed with success, you can press on and let the creative instincts rip – as well as saving time and honing up your skills still further.

'Everyday cooking' and food for children

For all those who are 'not called to the kitchen by the divine inner voice of a Vatel or an Escoffier... but rather... lured there, willy-nilly, by the piping of their husbands' empty stomachs' (M.F.K. Fisher, *The Art of Eating*) – and maybe their children's too – I've included a good number of interesting everyday dishes (not everyday puddings, though – desserts are for high days and holidays). Most of us find dinner party cooking more interesting than the regular production of meals, but man does not live by dinner parties alone and it's much more of a triumph to produce interesting food day in, day out (thereby banishing the concept of 'boring everyday cooking') than to dazzle visiting firemen just a few times a year.

On cooking for children, I think it's

a mistake always to cater down to some supposed level of theirs, different and separate from ours. I'm not sure if it's due to meanness or to an inherent British attitude towards children that we tend to assume that they like bland, tasteless, cheap stodge, eaten in the kitchen with the dogs and the tomato ketchup. I admit it was a bit of a blow to discover quite how much our two enjoy avocados and prawns, and the calm and dignity of the dinner table isn't half shattered by the chatter of tiny but insistent voices of whatever age, but if enjoying delicious food and conversation doesn't begin at home, where will it? Give them the opportunity to try out some of the slightly unusual everyday dishes in the book, and encourage them to be critical – which does not mean tolerating 'Yuck, this is disgusting Mum/Dad,' but expecting a (preferably) polite, considered opinion. Probably the reason we have all put up with such revolting food in England for so long is because for years it was taboo to discuss the contents of the plate at all, whether in criticism or in praise. The next generation's palate is in your tender hands...

Healthy eating

On this vexed question, I prefer to take a 'softly-softly' approach. I think that gripping people (figuratively) by the arm and steering them towards things that are 'good for them' is more likely to send them straight to the nearest McDonalds than to the salad bar. The point, surely, is that food should be good to eat, and a diet of unmitigated bean sprouts with lemon juice, wholemeal pastry which tastes of cardboard, and desserts based on 0 per cent butterfat-content *fromage blanc* and synthetic sugar substitutes is, for me, missing that point. As always, a balance is what's needed: if your everyday diet includes a wide selection of carefully chosen, carefully cooked (if at all), beautifully presented food, served in reasonable quantities, then every now and then you can legitimately permit yourself a splurge and eat something frightfully fattening, creaking with cholesterol and wonderfully wicked – still beautifully presented and still in reasonable quantities.

The taste factor

Finally, on tasting: taste everything, then listen to your taste-buds, look in the larder, think about what might go with what, and develop your own ideas for making your good old basics come to life. I hope you have as much fun as I have had, building on them to make really creative food which is fun to cook, a pleasure to serve and a true joy to eat.

PET HOBBY-HORSES

The metric versus the imperial system

'A pint's a pound the world around,' say the Americans; not so, say the Brits who claim that 'A pint of water weighs a pound and a quarter.' The sheer unadorned simplicity of the metric system, where 1 litre of water weighs 1 kilo whoever you are, comes as a merciful relief to one who, like me, is fundamentally innumerate; even I can manage to count up in 10's and 100's. I realize that it's little help urging people to try and think metric – and not to automatically let the eyes slide over to those comforting but cumbersome pints and ounces – if out in the market your favourite stall-holder would view with deep suspicion a request for a kilo of tomatoes. But it is an easier, more accurate, completely universal system, and more importantly, it is the one with which British children are growing up. I think metrication was first mooted in 1971. Hasn't the transition period gone on a bit?

Spoon measures

All measures are level unless otherwise stated: this means dipping the spoon into the flour/sugar/salt, etc., taking a knife and sweeping off the excess.

Preheating ovens

I am grateful to Ruth Stebler, of the Electricity Board in Zürich, who gave me advice about preheating ovens. Electricity Boards are not known for encouraging their customers to consume less, but the Swiss are notoriously canny, and it turns out that preheating is almost always unnecessary (and extravagant) – so, unless a recipe specifically requires it, assume you don't need to. The exceptions come when the total cooking time is under 15 minutes, or when baking small, butter-laden things like biscuits or pastries which would gently melt and seep, instead of bracing up to the onslaught of heat. Bread positively benefits from the final, gradual increase in heat if put in a cold oven, and soufflés and choux pastry can be treated in the same way with magnificent results. If you have an automatic timer but have hesitated to use it, wondering how to get round the preheating problem, now's the moment to start.

The freezer

I was once asked by a student during a demonstration whether the salad dressing would freeze. Why would she want to freeze it, I wondered vaguely? Before you freeze anything, you might also ask yourself – why? Why not *eat* it while it's good and fresh? Most things deteriorate in the freezer, so I prefer to regard it as an emergency holding store (rather than a dustbin) reserved for high-quality foods which for one reason or another can't be eaten now. Throughout the book, if there's no positive advantage in freezing a dish, I haven't mentioned it.

USEFUL WEAPONS

- FOOD PROCESSOR: for terrines, mousselines, praline, breadcrumbs, etc., but doesn't replace a BLENDER, which makes a finer purée. Also good are STALK BLENDERS (the knife blades are on the end of a plastic 'stalk') for blending ingredients directly in the pan or bowl without tipping into the liquidizer.

- A powerful ELECTRIC MIXER on a stand where the beater revolves around the bowl, not vice-versa, for whole-egg sponges, meringues, sabayons and soufflés.

- NON-STICK (siliconized) BAKING PAPER: for bread, fish terrines, cakes, meringues – anything which might stick or make a mess of the baking sheet.

- DOUGH SCRAPER: a plastic, vaguely half-moon shaped weapon, for lifting out meringue or dough from the bowl and smoothing the tops of cakes, roulades, etc.

- PLANT SPRAYER: for spraying a fine mist of water on breads for a crispy, brown crust; on the baking parchment used for a sponge or meringue which has unaccountably stuck.

- BLOW-TORCH: for caramelizing desserts, searing peppers (spear the pepper on a fork).

THEME 1

MEAT STEWS

beef, lamb, pork, veal and game dressed for dinner

Stew is a sad word, conjuring up the worst sort of nursery meal memories: tough, chewy meat with abundant gristle and fat. The art of creating a good stew is a dying one, as we've all gone increasingly overboard for carefully splayed out splinters of rarely cooked meat; but Granny food is on the way back and anyone who's let their stewing skills lapse should read on.

The rhythm is the same: meat is tossed in seasoned flour, seared for good colour and flavour, set over a bed of vegetables, moistened with stock and wine and given a number of distinctive flavourings. The basic model has Provençal overtones, and could be done with beef, pork, veal or lamb; change the colour of the wine, substitute brown ale or Guinness, use different seasonings and you get a slightly different picture – make up your own model, depending on meat and mood. Variations on the stew theme include the best steak and kidney pie, where the pastry is added later for maximum freshness, a game stew with a herby scone topping, and a veal stew in a puff pastry box.

WATCHPOINTS

Trim the meat very thoroughly of any pieces which you'd rather not meet on your plate – they will not somehow magically melt away in the cooking – and expect to lose up to 200 g (7 oz) per kg (2 lb 2 oz) of meat.

By tossing the meat in seasoned flour before browning it, you not only give good colour and flavour to the sauce, but also the thickening that any self-respecting stew needs. Because it is there from the beginning, well cooked in, there is no danger of a floury feel.

The acidity from the tomatoes in the basic recipe helps to tenderize the meat. Be sure to cook them down to a nice jammy consistency before replacing the meat and liquids.

Do not allow the stew to go above the merest suspicion of a simmer, otherwise the proteins in the meat will toughen rather than soften.

BASIC

MEAT STEW

Serves 6

boneless stewing meat	1.5 kg (3 lb 3 oz)
seasoned plain white flour	a dusting
oil	15–30 ml (1–2 tbsp)
onion, carrot, garlic clove, finely chopped	2 of each
tomatoes, skinned (or canned, with juice)	450 g (1 lb)
stock	about 300 ml ($\frac{1}{2}$ pint)
red wine (Beaujolais Primeur is ideal)	about 300 ml ($\frac{1}{2}$ pint)
salt and pepper	to taste
parsley, thyme and bay leaf	
pieces of orange zest, coriander seeds	2 of each

Pat the meat dry on paper towels (especially if it has been frozen). Toss it in a bag with some seasoned flour to coat very lightly. Tip into a colander and shake off any excess flour.

Heat a light film of oil in a large, heavy frying pan or flameproof casserole into which all the meat will eventually fit and sear a few pieces at a time on both sides. Remove as they are ready, add another film of oil and continue with the rest. After the meat is all browned, add a little more oil if necessary and soften the onion, carrot and garlic without browning. Add the tomatoes and cook over medium-high heat, stirring occasionally until syrupy and thick.

Replace the meat, add the stock and wine which should come almost to the top of the meat – top up if necessary. Season to taste, add the herbs and other flavourings, cover with foil and a lid, bring to the boil, then reduce the heat and simmer very gently on top of the stove or in a 150°C (300°F) mark 3 oven. It's impossible to be rigid about timing, as it varies tremendously according to the type and cut of meat, but it will be somewhere between 1 and 2 hours: lift out a piece after 1½ hours and bite it: when cooked, it should be tender and moist, but not falling apart at the seams.

Remove from the heat and allow to cool. Strain the meat through a colander placed over a bowl, skim off any excess fat and return the de-greased cooking liquid to the pan. Bring it to the boil and check the consistency and seasoning. If it needs further thickening, boil it down hard to reduce. Put the meat back into the sauce and simmer gently for another 20–25 minutes to heat it through and marry up the flavours once more.

Stews, like most of us, mellow with age and are best made 2 or 3 days before needed. Serve with a starch (rice, baked potatoes, gnocchi, etc.) and a crunchy vegetable (broccoli, beans, baby carrots, etc.)

VARIATIONS

● Instead of cubed meat, use a whole piece of braising meat, or chunks of meat on the bone and allow 2 kg (4½ lb) weight.
● Marinate the meat overnight if you wish (especially good for a whole piece) with the onion, carrot, garlic, bouquet garni and wine; drain the meat, reserve the marinade for cooking, pat the meat dry and proceed as usual.
● Vary the meat, using beef, lamb, pork, veal, venison, wild boar, etc.
● Or use joints of chicken (elderly), guinea fowl, pheasant, grouse, pigeon, hare or rabbit and reduce the cooking time to between 1 and 1¼ hours.
● Substitute white for red wine, or use white vermouth, brown ale or Guinness (especially for beef and pork), or cider; vary the stock to match the meat used.
● Use lemon instead of orange peel; a pinch of saffron, cinnamon, curry powder, juniper berries, etc. instead of coriander seeds.
● Take the stew up to the stage where the meat is strained and the sauce thickened and reduced. At this stage, add any of the following:
button onions and mushrooms, lightly sautéed
black or green olives
prunes or dried apricots, soaked and drained
lightly cooked baby carrots, turnips, peas or French beans
sautéed cubes of aubergine or courgette
tinned beans (kidney, flageolet, etc.) or lentils
sautéed rice
then give the stew its final 20/25-minute simmer.

● Following the basic rhythm, you can make any of the following:
Boeuf bourguignon (beef/ red wine/mushrooms/baby onions)
Navarin (lamb/white wine/ carrots/turnips/peas/beans)
Irish pork stew (pork/Guinness/ prunes)
Osso buco (veal shanks/ white wine/lemon peel)
Veal marengo (veal/white wine/ mushrooms)
Civets (game/bacon cubes/ red wine/mushrooms) or invent your own variation.

Further IDEAS

Cover a stew with any of the following and make it into a pie:
puff (p. 88) or shortcrust pastry (p. 81)
a lattice or blobs of choux pastry (p. 98) or mashed potato
a scone mix
a gnocchi topping (p. 99)
Or make puff pastry boxes (*feuilletés* or vol-au-vents, see puff pastry, p. 89) and fill with stew.

Veal Stew in a Puff Box

This dresses up a fairly ordinary stew fit for a dinner party: the pastry is moulded around a foil-wrapped parcel of shredded paper, baked until golden, emptied out and filled with a savoury combination of tender veal, mushrooms, olives and peas.

Serves 6

1 kg (2 lb 2 oz) stewing veal
seasoned plain white flour
2 carrots
2 leeks } **finely chopped together**
1 onion
1 garlic clove, crushed
400 g (14 oz) can peeled tomatoes
300 ml (½ pint) red wine
300 ml (½ pint) veal or chicken stock
salt and pepper
250 g (9 oz) mushrooms, quartered
25 g (1 oz) butter
16 black olives
200 g (7 oz) frozen peas
½ quantity (about 225 g (8 oz)) shortcrust pastry (p. 81)
400 g (14 oz) best puff pastry (p. 88)
1 egg, beaten with a pinch of salt

Trim the veal very carefully (you will end up with about 800 g (1¾ lb)) and cut into cubes. Make a veal stew with the carrots, leeks, onion, garlic, tomatoes, wine, stock and seasonings as described in the basic recipe on pp. 14–15 and allow to simmer until just tender (probably about 1 hour – check to see, and give it a little longer if necessary). Strain the meat, reduce the juices as described in the basic recipe on p. 15 and check the seasoning of the sauce.

Sauter the mushrooms briefly in the butter until just cooked and the juices evaporated. Replace the meat in the sauce and stir in the mushrooms, olives and frozen peas. Set aside for later reheating.

Roll out the shortcrust pastry fairly thickly and use a 25 cm (10 inch) dinner plate as a guide to cut out the pastry base. Lay this on a dampened baking sheet and prick it all over with a fork. Put in the fridge.

To help you shape your puff box, put a piece of foil in a large pudding basin. Fill it generously with narrow strips of tissue paper, then close up the foil over the top of it to make a football shape, firmly packed with tissue paper and nicely domed. Put it in the centre of the chilled pastry base and paint a 2 cm (1 inch) border with water around the edge.

Roll out the puff pastry (for the top) fairly thickly and cut a disc about 35 cm (14 inches) in diameter. Roll it up on the rolling pin, then unravel it carefully over the foil parcel. Try and get rid of wrinkles and folds and press the edges together with the back of a fork. Paint the pastry all over with the egg. Use any leftover scraps of puff pastry to make lattice strips, leaves, crescents, etc. and decorate the box with them; paint again with egg. Put it in the fridge for at least 30 minutes.

Heat the oven to 200°C (400°F) mark 6 and bake the pastry for 25–30 minutes or until golden brown and firm. Using a very sharp knife, preferably serrated, saw off a lid and remove it. Hold the puff box around the top and remove the shredded tissue paper and foil with great care, so as not to do untold damage.

Before serving, heat the puff box gently in a low oven and simmer the stew for a final 20 minutes. Carefully spoon it in and put the lid back on. Serve with any green vegetable.

Make a fairly ordinary
stew fit for a dinner party with Veal
Stew in a Puff Box
(page 16)

*S*weetcorn, egg custard,
pinto beans and a touch of spice turn a basic meat
sauce into Mexican Shepherd's Pie
(page 22)

Minced lamb and
kidneys form the tasty forcemeat surrounding
Stuffed Lamb in a Pastry Case
(page 26)

*C*olourful fish fillets and
their sauce are complemented by green and white
pasta in *Spiral of Sole and Salmon with
Watercress Sauce (page 36)*

Pork Stew with Chillis and Coriander

A colourful dish with distinctly Mexican overtones: pork with a rich tomato sauce, green chillis, black beans and fresh coriander. Substitute parsley for coriander if you don't like it or can't find it.

Serves 6

250 g (9 oz) dried black or pinto beans
1.2 litres (2 pints) water
2 onions, chopped
2 garlic cloves, mashed
30 ml (2 tbsp) lard
1.5 kg (3 lb 3 oz) stewing pork
2 onions, chopped
2 garlic cloves, crushed
450 g (1 lb) beefsteak tomatoes, skinned and chopped, or 400 g (14 oz) can peeled tomatoes
30 ml (2 tbsp) tomato purée
2–3 fresh or canned green chillis, de-seeded and finely chopped
2 slices of pork knuckle with rind
600 ml (1 pint) chicken or vegetable stock
salt and pepper
30–45 ml (2–3 tbsp) finely chopped fresh coriander or parsley
a bunch of radishes, finely chopped

First prepare the beans: cover them with the water (no pre-soaking needed), add 1 onion, 1 garlic clove and 15 ml (1 tbsp) lard (no salt, yet, which would toughen the beans at this stage) and simmer for about $1\frac{1}{2}$ hours.

Trim the pork and cut into cubes. Sear without extra fat (the pork has plenty) or flour (the beans provide the thickening for the sauce), then make a pork stew as described in the basic recipe with the onions, garlic, tomatoes, tomato purée, chillis, pork knuckle and stock. Simmer for about 1 hour – taste for doneness and continue to cook a little longer if necessary.

When the beans have had $1\frac{1}{2}$ hours' cooking, lift out a spoonful and blow on them: the skins should break open and they will be fairly soft and rather tasteless. Heat the remaining lard in a heavy frying pan and fry the remaining onion and garlic until lightly golden. Throw in a good ladleful of beans plus their liquid, and cook, stirring and mashing with a potato masher, until really thick and pasty. Add about 10 ml (2 tsp) salt and then put this paste back into the bean pot. Simmer for about another 30 minutes or until the beans are tender and tasty – check the seasoning, adding more salt if necessary.

Strain the stew, de-grease carefully and boil down the sauce to reduce and thicken as usual. Add the meat to it once more, and stir in about half the beans. Simmer for a final 20 minutes, then sprinkle with fresh coriander or parsley and chopped radishes. (The remaining beans can be served separately, or as a soup for another occasion – dilute with stock as necessary and serve rough, or blended smooth as you prefer.)

Civet of Game with Herby Scone Crust

Any braising cut of game is fine for this rich winter stew with its herby scone topping.

Serves 6

200 g (7 oz) smoked bacon
2 kg (4½ lb) braising game on the bone (e.g. venison shoulder, legs of hare, etc.)
remaining ingredients as in basic meat stew (p. 14)
200 g (7 oz) mushrooms, quartered
25 g (1 oz) butter
salt and pepper

SCONE CRUST
200 g (7 oz) plain flour
5 ml (1 tsp) salt
10 ml (2 tsp) baking powder
25 g (1 oz) butter or margarine
30 ml (2 tbsp) each chopped chives and parsley
about 100 ml (4 fl oz) buttermilk, soured milk, cream or yogurt

Cut the rind off the bacon and set it aside. Cut the bacon into small cubes and put them in a large heavy pan which will take all the meat eventually. Fry gently until the fat runs. Lift the bacon out with a slotted spoon, leaving only a film of fat in the bottom, and set aside.

Chop the game into manageable pieces, toss in seasoned flour and continue as described in the basic recipe on p. 14, adding the reserved bacon cubes and rind to the pan. Simmer the stew for 1½–2 hours, or until tender and melting off the bone. Strain, thicken the sauce and check for seasoning.

Cook the mushrooms in the butter with the salt and pepper over gentle heat with the lid on for a few minutes. Then uncover, raise the heat and cook hard until the juices evaporate and the mushrooms are lightly browned. Put the meat, sauce and mushrooms into an ovenproof dish into which they will just fit with enough room to lay the scone crust on top. (The stew can be prepared ahead up to this point, refrigerated, then reheated in a 200°C (400°F) mark 6 oven to the simmer before covering with the crust.)

For the scone crust, mix or process together briefly the flour, salt, baking powder, butter or margarine and herbs. Add enough buttermilk or alternatives to make a softish dough, halfway between pastry and bread dough.

Roll or pat it out 1 cm (½ inch) thick on a well-floured board (it will be very soft) and cut it to the size of the ovenproof dish with a very sharp knife so as not to press the edges together (which would inhibit rising).

Remove the stew from the oven. Lift the scone crust carefully with floured hands and lay it over the stew. Return it to the oven for about 20 minutes or until well risen and brown on top. Red cabbage with apples and red wine vinegar makes a good accompaniment.

The Best Steak and Kidney Pie

Most people can make good old steak and kidney in their sleep, but it doesn't always occur to them to make a steak and kidney stew first, then add the pastry later as a sort of variation on the theme – it stays much fresher, and this way you can time the preparations in two easy stages. The ideal dish for shooting lunches, church bazaars and visiting foreigners.

Serves 6

1.5 kg (3 lb 3 oz) well-trimmed stewing beef, cut into cubes
250 g (9 oz) lambs' or ox kidneys, trimmed and cubed
seasoned plain white flour
oil or dripping
2 onions, finely chopped
2 carrots, finely chopped
300 ml ($\frac{1}{2}$ pint) beef stock
salt and pepper
1 bouquet garni
300 g (11 oz) puff pastry (p. 88)
1 egg, lightly beaten

Trim the meat and the kidneys very rigorously. You should end up with about 1.4 kg (3 lb) well-trimmed beef and about 200 g (7 oz) kidneys. Flour and sear the meat and kidneys, and soften the onions and carrots as described in the basic recipe on p. 14. Add the stock, salt and pepper to taste and the bouquet garni and simmer very gently on top of the stove or in a 150°C (300°F) mark 2 oven for 1$\frac{1}{2}$–2 hours or until fork tender. Leave to cool.

Roll out the puff pastry to a thickness of 5 mm ($\frac{1}{4}$ inch). Choose any dish which has a good straight rim and a capacity of about 2 litres (3$\frac{1}{4}$ pints). Invert this over the pastry, and using it as a template, cut around it for the lid. Use some of the remaining pastry for strips to go all round the rim of the pie dish. Pour the cool stew into the dish and bury an inverted egg cup or pie funnel in the middle of it to hold up the pastry. Wet the rim of the dish and lay the pastry strips all around it, pressing them together to join as necessary to make a complete band. Brush the top of this also with water. Roll up the pastry for the lid on the rolling pin and let it unravel carefully over the top. Do not stretch or pull it, or it will shrink in the oven. Press the pastry edges together with the back of a fork. Make a hole in the middle for steam and surround this with leaves and decorations made out of any leftover pastry.

Heat the oven to 200°C (400°F) mark 6. Glaze the pie with beaten egg and bake it for about 25 minutes, or until the pastry is golden and the pie hot – stick a skewer into the hole and hold it against your cheek to feel.

T H E M E   2

MEAT SAUCES

for spaghetti, lasagne, moussaka, shepherd's pie et al.

Man does not live by dinner parties alone, and the turn for spaghetti bolognese comes around quite regularly, at least in our family. Since the same meat sauce can be used as the base for moussaka, shepherd's pie or chilli con carne, it seems a good idea to make up a large batch while you're at it (the quantity given will serve up to 12, depending on what you combine it with): use some for now, and freeze some for later use in another guise.

The basic sauce is a beef one, but change the meat, the colour of the wine, and the spices and you can vary the theme for ever, depending on whether you're feeling in an Italian, Indian, Greek, Mexican or French mood.

W A T C H P O I N T S

Try and get your meat freshly minced, before your eyes, otherwise buy it yourself in a piece, trim it carefully and mince or chop it yourself. Don't use any extra fat for browning the meat: between the bacon fat and the meat's own built-in lubrication, you'll have more than enough.

The searing and browning step at the beginning, which calls for brisk heat and a wide shallow pan with a good surface area, is an important first step which will give a rich flavour and colour to the finished sauce. A long, gentle simmer is essential and it is almost impossible to overcook it.

B A S I C
MEAT SAUCE

Makes about 1.5 kg (3 lb 3 oz), enough for 2 main dishes each serving 6–8

bacon diced	100 g (4 oz)
onion, carrot, finely chopped	1 each
garlic, crushed	1 clove
lean beef, freshly minced	1.5 kg (3 lb 3 oz)
canned peeled tomatoes with their liquid or tomatoes, peeled and chopped	400 g (14 oz) 4–5
red wine	300 ml ($\frac{1}{2}$ pint)
beef stock (p. 152)	300 ml ($\frac{1}{2}$ pint)
salt and pepper	to taste
bouquet garni	1
some celery leaves	

Sweat the bacon in a large, wide, heavy casserole until the fat runs. Add the onion, carrot and garlic. Cover and cook slowly until soft – about 10 minutes. Raise the heat and add the minced beef. Fry over high heat, tossing and turning until the meat is crusty and brown in parts.

Add the tomatoes with their juice, the wine, stock, salt, pepper, bouquet garni and celery leaves. Cover, bring to the boil and simmer for $3\frac{1}{2}$–4 hours, until nicely thickened, raising heat and uncovering pan if necessary. Check the seasoning. Serve with pasta, or develop the theme and use as suggested right in other ways.

VARIATIONS

- Instead of beef, use minced lamb or pork, or a mixture.
- Substitute white for red wine or use beer, or skip the wine altogether and use only stock.
- Instead of the bouquet garni, add different herbs and spices according to your own ideas and what's in the cupboard:
curry powder
garam masala
freshly grated ginger
plenty of chopped chillis
fresh coriander
fresh or dried mint, etc.
- Instead of pasta, serve the meat sauce (depending on flavourings) with rice, chapatis or tortillas (p. 109), mashed potatoes or beans.

Further IDEAS

Shepherd's or Cottage Pie: use with a mashed potato topping, or a gnocchi topping (p. 99).

Layered pies (à la moussaka): use with grilled or fried slices of aubergine or courgettes, cooked potatoes, etc.

Lasagne: layer with white or green lasagne sheets (preferably the sort that don't need blanching first), thin béchamel, and a finish of grated cheese or layer with tortillas or chapatis (p. 109).

Use to stuff cooked, hollowed out tomatoes, baked potatoes, courgettes, aubergines, etc.

Chilli con carne: add some chopped green pepper and celery to the onion, and season the sauce with a pinch of cumin seed and chilli powder. 30 minutes before the sauce is ready, add a can or two of beans. Perfect for a teenage buffet with lots of rice.

Polenta Pie

A typical northern Italian dish, super for a warming winter supper. It's really a variation on the lasagne theme and you can substitute lasagne sheets if you prefer.

Serves 4–6

250 ml (9 fl oz) milk
2.5 ml ($\frac{1}{2}$ tsp) salt
150 g (5 oz) medium-fine polenta meal or lasagne sheets
450 ml ($\frac{3}{4}$ pint) light béchamel sauce (p. 152) made with 25 g (1 oz) each butter and plain white flour, 450 ml ($\frac{3}{4}$ pint) milk and seasonings
$\frac{1}{2}$ quantity (about 700 g ($1\frac{1}{2}$ lb)) basic meat sauce (p. 20)
30–45 ml (2–3 tbsp) grated Parmesan

Bring the milk and 450 ml ($\frac{3}{4}$ pint) water with the salt to the boil and tip in the polenta meal. Cook, stirring from time to time, for anything between 2 and 20 minutes (follow the instructions on the packet, as they vary enormously) or until very thick and beginning to come away from the sides of the pan. Tip out onto a board, push the mixture together roughly into a block about 3 cm ($1\frac{1}{2}$ inches) high and leave it to cool. When cool, cut into 1 cm ($\frac{1}{2}$ inch) slices.

(Alternatively cook the lasagne in plenty of boiling salted water, drain and pat dry on paper towels just before using.)

In a large, shallow ovenproof dish, make layers of polenta slices or lasagne sheets, béchamel sauce and meat sauce, finishing with a final layer of polenta or lasagne and béchamel sauce, and a sprinkling of Parmesan. Bake for about 20 minutes at 220°C (425°F) mark 7 until the top is golden brown and the pie hot right through. Serve with lots of salad.

Mexican Shepherd's Pie

The basic meat sauce is given a bit of Mexican flavour and covered with a corny topping instead of mashed potatoes.

Serves 4

½ quantity (about 700 g (1½ lb)) basic meat sauce (p. 20), or its equivalent in leftover minced meat and gravy
Tabasco sauce
400 g (14 oz) can pinto beans, drained
300 g (11 oz) canned or frozen sweetcorn
2 fresh green chillis, de-seeded and finely chopped
1 egg
50 g (2 oz) butter
5 ml (1 tsp) salt

To the basic meat sauce, or minced meat and gravy, add Tabasco to taste, depending on how hot you like it. Add also the pinto beans, and put the mixture into an ovenproof dish. Blend together the sweetcorn, chillis, egg, butter and salt in a liquidizer or food processor and pour this over the top. Bake in a 200°C (400°F) mark 6 oven for about 25 minutes or until the topping is golden brown and puffed up. Serve with salad.

Moussaka

By grilling the aubergine slices and making a topping of yogurt and eggs, you get a lighter, less oily moussaka than the usual fried, white-sauced versions.

Serves 6

2 medium aubergines, sliced and sprinkled with salt
olive oil
½ quantity (about 700 g (1½ lb)) basic meat sauce (p. 20) made with lamb
200 ml (7 fl oz) natural yogurt
2 eggs
15 ml (1 tbsp) plain white flour
salt and pepper
30 ml (2 tbsp) grated Parmesan

Pat the salted aubergines dry with paper towels and brush them lightly with olive oil. Put them briefly under the grill, just enough to lightly brown them; turn once.

Pour one-third of the meat sauce into a large, shallow ovenproof dish, follow with half the aubergine slices, another layer of meat sauce, the rest of the aubergine and a final layer of meat. Liquidize or whisk together the yogurt, eggs, flour, salt, pepper and Parmesan to a smooth custard. Pour it over the top of the moussaka and bake at 180°C (350°F) mark 4 for 20–25 minutes or until the topping is set and golden.

Custard Marrow with Meat Sauce

Custard marrow (or pattypan squash, the creamy white one with the frilly petticoat) makes a good vehicle for a well-flavoured meat sauce.

Serves 4

4 custard marrows, each about 10 cm (4 inches) across
1 shallot, finely chopped
25 g (1 oz) butter
4 eggs
60–75 ml (4–5 tbsp) basic meat sauce (p. 20)
30 ml (2 tbsp) grated Parmesan

Cook the marrow in a large pan of lightly salted water for about 10 minutes or until just tender. Slice off the tops and set these aside. Scoop out the flesh with a teaspoon. Soften the shallot in the butter without browning, then add the marrow flesh and cook hard to evaporate the extra juice.

Add this mixture, with the lightly mixed eggs, to the hot sauce, stirring until the eggs thicken and bind the mixture. Divide it among the marrows, sprinkle with grated Parmesan and bake in a 200°C (400°F) mark 6 oven until golden brown and bubbly. Replace the hats and serve.

All-Purpose Forcemeats

for terrines, casings, sausages and stuffings

You can have a lot of fun with a farce, as the French refer to a forcemeat: an all-purpose, eminently useful meat mixture which may comprise offal, game or poultry as the main protagonist, lean pork for lightness, pork fat for moisture and eggs to bind. Add to this a rich, well-reduced stock and interesting seasonings and you have a simple formula which you can vary almost indefinitely to create your own *terrines maison*.

When you've got a few terrines tucked under your belt, you might like to try moulding the forcemeat in pastry for a *pâté en croûte*. (What *is* a *terrine* and what is a *pâté*? Strictly speaking the former is baked in a dish from which it takes its name; the latter is baked in pastry – pâté (with an accent on the é) = pastried, and the *en croûte* bit is redundant. In practice, things work out rather differently.) Set aside a little forcemeat for shaping into meatballs, sausages or pork pies, or wrap it around a seared piece of meat to give flavour and moisture. Come Christmas, you'll be inventing your own stuffing for this year's turkey, or any other poultry, game or vegetables.

W A T C H P O I N T S

The basic forcemeat features liver as its main flavouring, but other meats can be substituted (see Variations). Pork gives lightness: use a lean cut like boned loin and use the bones for the stock. Many recipes recommend veal instead but I think this adds little (except cost).

Pork back fat, hard and choppable, not flabby, is sometimes difficult to find, but

essential for a good terrine. Do not skimp on the quantity (which in a good forcemeat should constitute up to one-third of the total meats), otherwise your terrine will be dry, dull and difficult when you come to slice it. Avoid salted pork fat, ham fat or salt pork, which would interfere with the balance of seasoning; and bacon, which would interfere with the flavour. Whenever you locate a good source of pork fat,

pounce on it and freeze in 300 g (11 oz) packs for forcemeats. Then chop or process it straight from the freezer (see notes on importance of chilling).

The amount of salt recommended is the standard amount used by French *charcutiers* for pâtés and terrines: 15 g ($\frac{1}{2}$ oz) = 10 ml (2 tsp) per kg (2 lb 2 oz) unsalted meat. Most books (but few chefs or *charcutiers*) are vague about seasoning, and recommend frying a little in the pan before committing the mixture to the terrine, but I don't find this much help, partly because the terrine will almost always be served cold (when the seasonings are muted) and also because a freshly fried piece of forcemeat does not taste the same as a gently baked, cooled and matured one. Trust the scales or your measuring spoon the first time around, then adjust subsequently if you prefer a blander result.

The shallot and garlic are cooked to prolong their life in the terrine; the brandy is flamed to burn away the alcohol, leaving a mellow taste; together with the salt and spices, it acts as a preservative as well as giving flavour, and enables you to keep the terrine for a week to 10 days with good refrigeration.

Stock – unsalted, well-reduced and well-flavoured – is optional but highly desirable: it accentuates the flavour of the terrine and its syrupy consistency gives extra body. Use a pork stock made from the loin bones in the basic recipe; when using any of the alternative meats, make it from their bones (poultry, game, lamb, etc.). (For stocks, see p. 152.)

I find a food processor ideal for making forcemeats. It chops and mixes in one fell swoop, and activates the proteins in the meat which bind them together, without loss of moisture; next best is a very sharp knife. Avoid using a mincer: it squeezes out moisture and is tricky to clean.

The chill factor is very important – if the meat overheats while it is being chopped, it will no longer knit together (making crumbly slices) and may even curdle, which is why butchers add a proportion of chipped ice to meat mixtures when they grind them in their industrial food processors. On your scale and mine, good chilling of all the ingredients and the food processor bowl and blade helps, allowing you to process the meats to the desired consistency without danger.

Caul fat (a lacy web of fat which encloses all sorts of interesting organs inside an animal) is useful – but not essential if you've used a good proportion of fat in the forcemeat – for enclosing terrines to lubricate them while cooking. Soak caul in warm water if necessary to make it pliable. Sheets of pork fat are extremely fatty, so I'm not keen; bacon is absolutely out – unless you want your whole terrine to taste of it.

Terrines are usually baked in the oven in a bain-marie, which gives good gentle all-round heat and keeps them moist. The newspaper sheets help diffuse the heat and prevent excessive shrinkage. Adding just-boiled water to the bain-marie shortens the baking time. Some chefs like to bake terrines at 180°C (350°F) mark 4 – about 1¼ hours for a 1.4 kg (3 lb) terrine; others claim that the longer and slower you cook them, the better they will be: 130°C (250°F) mark ½ for twice as long. Try both and decide what suits you best.

The terrine is done when it feels firm and springy to the touch, not at all squashy or mushy. It should be slightly shrunk from the sides and the juices at most a pale rosy pink. A skewer stuck in the middle will give you a very rough idea – if it is still cold on the cheek, you know the terrine is not ready; if just too warm for comfort, the terrine will probably be done. For retail purposes, butchers take a meat thermometer reading of 65–66°C (150°F); for domestic purposes I find anything between 60 and 65°C (140–150°F) is fine.

Leave plenty of time when planning a terrine: you will need one day for shopping, chopping and marinating, another for cooking and cooling, and then at least 4 days' maturing before the whole thing becomes interesting. Run a knife round the terrine and lift out with a fish slice on to a serving plate.

For a longer wait (10 days–2 weeks), lift it out, scrape off all juices (which would be the first to go off) and freeze them. Replace the terrine in the cleaned out dish, and fill up all the spaces with rendered pork fat or lard – the terrine should be completely covered with fat. Before serving, scrape off excess fat; the reserved juices can be mixed with a little sour cream to serve with the terrine.

Never freeze cooked terrines. They become wet, spongy and really rather nasty. If you must freeze, freeze the raw mixture in its dish, then thaw and bake as usual.

B A S I C

FORCEMEAT

Make about 1 kg (2 lb 2 oz), enough for a 1.4 kg (3 lb) terrine serving 8–10

shallot	1
garlic clove, crushed	1
butter	12 g (scant ½ oz)
cognac (or other spirit)	30 ml (2 tbsp)
liver (pig's, chicken or game; see also Variations)	300 g (11 oz)
lean boneless pork	300 g (11 oz)
pork back fat, unsalted	300 g (11 oz)
well-reduced stock (optional)	100 ml (4 fl oz)
egg	1
salt	15 g (½ oz) = 10 ml (2 tsp)
black pepper, freshly ground	lots
quatre-épices or allspice	2.5 ml (½ tsp)
thyme	1 sprig
bay leaf	2 leaves
caul fat (optional)	

Soften the shallot and garlic in the butter without browning, add the cognac, flame it and then set it aside. Put the food processor bowl, metal blade, the liver, pork, fat and the stock, if used, in the fridge until thoroughly chilled.

Chop the meats and fat to the desired fineness (you may want a mousse-like consistency, or a rough country-style terrine). Work in small batches and be sure the mixture is always very cold throughout the process.

Change over to the plastic blade and work in the stock, if used, egg, salt, pepper, spices, crumbled thyme, and the shallot, garlic and cognac mixture until well-blended and light. (Alternatively, chop the meats finely with a large sharp knife, then beat in the remaining ingredients with a wooden spoon or an electric mixer.) Chill overnight if possible to allow the flavours to blend.

Lay a bay leaf in the bottom of a 1.4 kg (3 lb) terrine and line with caul fat if used. Pack in the prepared, chilled forcemeat, fold the caul fat up and over and trim away any excess. Top with another bay leaf, foil and a lid. Set on doubled sheets of newspaper in a bain-marie and fill with boiling water. Bake at 180°C (350°F) mark 4 for 1¼–1½ hours, or 130°C (250°F) mark ½ for 2½–3 hours (see notes on timing). Leave to cool at room temperature, then chill. If the forcemeat was well chilled at the chopping stage, the terrine will slice nicely when cool and there should be no need to weight it down.

Serve with good chutney, Cumberland sauce, creamed horseradish, pickles, sliced fruit (papayas, kiwis, cranberries, plums), etc. If for a first course, follow with a light fish or vegetable dish; if for a main course, accompany with salads and baked potatoes.

VARIATIONS

● Instead of liver, use any of the following as your main meat flavouring: rabbit, duck, goose, game (furry or feathered), chicken, guinea fowl, pigeon or quail; or lamb or beef.
● *Quatre-épices* can be used for all meats, or substitute:
for game forcemeats: cumin/ juniper
for rabbit, chicken, sweetbreads: nutmeg/cinnamon/ginger
for lamb: cardamom/curry powder
for duck or goose: coriander seeds
● Thyme can be used for all meats, or substitute:
for game forcemeats: sage/ rosemary/marjoram
for lamb forcemeats: rosemary/ mint
for poultry: basil/tarragon/ marjoram
for rabbit: summer savory/thyme
● Instead of cognac or Armagnac, use any of the following:
fortified wine (port, sherry, madeira, etc.)
sweet dessert wine (muscat, marsala, sauternes, monbazillac)
red or white wine
fruit *eau-de-vie* (mirabelle, kirsch, etc.)
● To the finished forcemeat, add any of the following:
shavings of orange peel
whole juniper berries
roasted, skinned hazelnuts
pistachio nuts
strips of main flavouring meat, marinated in the liqueur used for the forcemeat
a truffle or two, finely sliced
diced foie gras
chopped sweated mushrooms
blanched, skinned, chopped sweetbreads
reconstituted (i.e. soaked) dried mushrooms, apricots or prunes
green or pink peppercorns.

Further IDEAS

Instead of making the forcemeat into a terrine, use as follows:

Moulded pâté en croûte: line a loaf tin with greased foil and a layer of spiced shortcrust (p. 81), rolled out rather thickly. Fill with forcemeat (any flavour), top with a rectangle of pastry rolled rather thinner, seal joins with egg. Decorate with spare pastry, make steam holes and keep them open with greased foil funnels. Glaze with egg yolk and bake at 200°C (400°F) mark 6 for about 20 minutes to brown the pastry; then reduce the heat to 180°C (350°F) mark 4 and bake for about 1 hour more (meat thermometer reading: 65–66°C/150°F). Cool it in the tin, then fill up the spaces with aspic if wished (follow the instructions on the packet).

Unmoulded pâté en croûte: shape the forcemeat into a bolster, wrap in spiced shortcrust (p. 81) or brioche (p. 114), seal the joins with egg, glaze it, make steam holes and bake as above.

Sausages: pack the mixture into lambs' casings (tenderest) or pigs' casings (tougher) using a forcing bag and plain nozzle; or roll up in caul fat; or form in foil, chill until firm, then unwrap and grill until golden. Or shape into meatballs and grill or fry.

Stuffed leaves: spread the forcemeat thinly on to blanched cabbage or spinach leaves, roll up and steam for 10 minutes.

Stuffed vegetables: use any of the following as vehicles for the forcemeat and bake until firm:
● cross-sections of an overgrown courgette, seeds removed
● lightly cooked and hollowed out custard marrows, onions, courgettes, etc.
● hollowed-out tomatoes

Stuffed Lamb Fillets in a Pastry Case

Best ends of neck of lamb are boned out, sandwiched with a lamb and kidney forcemeat, with shortcrust pastry underneath and puff on top. Remaining forcemeat is rolled in cabbage leaves, steamed and served as a garnish. Pork tenderloin or fillets of venison can be used instead of lamb, and phyllo pastry (p. 93) instead of puff.

Serves 6–8

2 best ends of neck of lamb, with kidneys if possible, about 700 g (1½ lb) each
1 carrot, chopped
1 small onion, chopped
1 garlic clove, chopped
1 bouquet garni
a few peppercorns
300 ml (½ pint) red wine
¼ quantity (about 200 g (7 oz)) basic forcemeat (p. 24), made with lamb and kidneys instead of liver
salt and pepper
olive oil
150 g (5 oz) shortcrust pastry (p. 81)
250 g (9 oz) puff pastry (p. 88)
1 egg
8 blanched Savoy cabbage leaves

SAUCE
75 ml (5 tbsp) best liver pâté or foie gras
100 ml (4 fl oz) single cream
5 ml (1 tsp) cornflour

Bone out the 2 best ends and discard all skin, fat and membrane to give 2 rather miserable looking fillets, each weighing about 400 g (14 oz), 2 tiny undercuts and the kidneys. Chop up the lamb bones and brown them in a heavy casserole. Add the carrot, onion, garlic, bouquet garni, peppercorns, wine and 1.2 litres (2 pints) water. Simmer gently for 3 hours, then strain and reduce to about 300 ml (½ pint) by fast boiling. Reserve.

Make up the lamb forcemeat as described in the basic recipe on p. 24, using the lamb undercuts and enough kidney in place of the liver to make up the required 300 g (11 oz). Season the lamb fillets and sandwich them with about 200 g (7 oz) forcemeat. Tie together with fine string to make a neat bolster. Heat the oven to 220°C (425°F) mark 7. Season the meat, brush it with olive oil and roast it for 7 minutes. Turn it over and give it another 7 minutes. Remove and cool.

Roll out the shortcrust pastry to a rectangle slightly bigger than the meat and put it on a sheet of non-stick baking paper on a baking sheet. Remove the string carefully and place the meat on top of the shortcrust pastry. Bring the pastry up against the sides of the meat. Roll out the puff pastry for the lid to a rectangle large enough to fit over the entire shooting match. Brush the exposed shortcrust pastry sides with the salted beaten egg and lay the puff pastry over the top. Snuggle the edges in nicely so all is enclosed. Make a trellis with any spare bits of pastry, cut steam holes and prop them open with greased foil chimneys, glaze with remaining egg and chill. (The dish can be prepared a day ahead up to this point. Bring to room temperature before baking.)

Cut the blanched cabbage leaves in half and cut away the hard central rib. Spread them with a thin layer of forcemeat (about 25 g (1 oz) per half leaf) and roll up tightly to a little bolster. Secure with toothpicks and put in a steamer. (Pack any remaining forcemeat into a pâté dish or ramekin and make little pâtés.)

About 45 minutes before you plan to serve the meat, heat the oven to 220°C (425°F) mark 7 and bake for 25 minutes. (The pastry should be golden brown and the lamb slightly pink inside.) Remove from the oven and leave to rest in a warm place for at least 20 minutes.

Meanwhile, steam the cabbage forcemeat parcels for 10 minutes. Make the sauce: liquidize together the remaining stock, liver pâté (or foie gras) and cream. Put them in a pan, whisk them up to a boil, add the cornflour (an insurance policy against curdling) and whisk over gentle heat until of a coating consistency. Check the seasoning.

Carve the lamb en croûte into fairly thick slices, cut each cabbage parcel into 4 or 5 thin slices and splay them around. Serve with the sauce and extra shredded buttered cabbage or fresh broccoli.

26

Rabbit Terrine with Pistachios

Rabbit is stripped off the bones (which are turned into a delectable stock), minced with the usual meats, flavoured with orange zest and given a bit of crunch and colour with some pistachios.

Makes a 1.4 kg (3 lb) terrine giving 16 slices

a 1.4 kg (3 lb) rabbit, skinned and gutted
salt and pepper
45 ml (3 tbsp) mirabelle or other eau-de-vie, or cognac
15 ml (1 tbsp) oil
1 carrot, chopped
1 small onion, chopped
1 bouquet garni
a few peppercorns
1 shallot, finely chopped
1 garlic clove, crushed
12 g (scant ½ oz) butter
300 g (11 oz) lean boneless pork, well-chilled
300 g (11 oz) pork fat, well-chilled
1 egg
5 ml (1 tsp) grated orange zest
15 ml (1 tbsp) chopped fresh thyme
30 ml (2 tbsp) pistachio nuts
a piece of caul fat
1 bay leaf

Remove all the meat from the rabbit, trimming away any sinews, membrane, etc. Cut the saddle fillets into thin strips and the rest of the meat into cubes. Season the fillet strips with salt and pepper and put them in a little dish with 15 ml (1 tbsp) of the mirabelle or other liqueur. Chill them and the cubed rabbit meat.

Chop up the carcass and brown it in the hot oil, then make a stock (p. 152) with the carrot, onion, bouquet garni, peppercorns and 600 ml (1 pint) water. Simmer for 2 hours, strain, return to the pan and boil down hard to reduce to about 100 ml (4 fl oz). Cool, then chill also.

Soften the shallot and garlic in the butter without browning, add the remaining liqueur, flame it, then set aside to cool. Make a forcemeat as described in the basic recipe on p. 24 with the cubed rabbit, pork and pork fat, the chilled stock, egg, 10 ml (2 tsp) salt, pepper, orange zest, thyme and cooled shallot and garlic. (Alternatively chop all the meats and then mix in the rest by hand.) Stir in the pistachios. Chill the mixture for several hours or overnight if possible.

Line a 1.4 kg (3 lb) terrine with the caul fat and put in one third of the rabbit forcemeat. Follow with half the marinated rabbit strips, another third of forcemeat, the remaining rabbit strips and the rest of the forcemeat. Close the caul fat up over the top and trim off any excess. Top with a bay leaf, cover with foil and a lid and bake as usual in a bain-marie at 180°C (350°F) mark 4 for 1¼–1½ hours or until cooked (see Watchpoints on how to tell if the terrine is ready).

Allow to cool at room temperature, then chill and leave for at least 4 days to mature. Serve with mango chutney and a salad of lamb's lettuce and beetroot cubes.

Stuffed Poussins with a Creamy Curry Sauce

Baby chickens are partially boned, filled with forcemeat and braised in a curry-flavoured liquid, which in turn becomes the sauce. Tender pigeons, grouse or quail – though a labour of love – can be used instead of poussins.

Serves 4

$\frac{1}{2}$ **quantity (about 600 g (1$\frac{1}{4}$ lb)) basic forcemeat (p. 24), made with liver**
100 g (4 oz) mushrooms, chopped and sautéed
2 poussins, each about 450 g (1 lb)
salt and pepper
1 carrot, sliced
1 onion, sliced
50 g (2 oz) butter
250 ml (9 fl oz) dry white wine or cider
10 ml (2 tsp) curry powder
1 bouquet garni
250 ml (9 fl oz) chicken stock
45–60 ml (3–4 tbsp) double cream
lemon juice

Make up the full quantity of forcemeat as described in the basic recipe on p. 24 and add the mushrooms. Set aside 600 g (1$\frac{1}{4}$ lb) (about half) for this recipe. (See Further Ideas for suggestions on how to use the rest.)

Make a cut down the line of the breastbone of the poussins and peel back the skin. Cut the breast meat off each side of the breast in one piece, season it with salt and pepper and set it aside. Using poultry shears or a very sharp knife, cut away the whole breast cage leaving only the bone structure on the bottom. Fill the resulting cavity with the forcemeat, lay the breast meat back on top and bring the skin up and over to cover. Stitch with black button thread (easier to see later when you need to pull it out) and pat and push the birds back into a nice busty shape.

In a heavy casserole which will just accommodate the two birds, soften the carrot and onion in the butter until pale golden. Place the poussins on top, add the wine or cider, the curry powder and bouquet garni and enough stock to come about two-thirds of the way up the side of the birds. Cover with foil and a lid and braise gently for about 45 minutes, until the juices run clear when you pierce the leg joint. Lift out the poussins, put them onto a serving dish and leave in a warm place.

Strain (or liquidize, discarding the bouquet garni) the cooking liquid, put it back in the pan and boil it down hard to reduce to about 250 ml (9 fl oz). Whisk in the cream, check the seasoning and sharpen with lemon juice if you wish. Carve the poussins down the breastline, then cut through the bony base with shears. Serve each person half a bird, laid cut side down on warm plates, with some sauce, buttered leeks, or apple slices, and rice (p. 71).

Ballotine of Duck with Green Herby Sauce

A duck is boned out completely and the skin used as a moisturizing and flavour-filled lining for the terrine instead of caul fat.

Gives 16 slices

a 1.5 kg (3 lb 3 oz) duckling
1 carrot, chopped
1 small onion, chopped
1 bouquet garni
a few peppercorns
1 quantity basic forcemeat (p. 24) made with duck instead of liver, duck stock, port and orange zest
salt and pepper
a little extra port
1 bay leaf

SAUCE
a large bunch of parsley, leaves only (use the stalks for the stock)
125 ml (4½ fl oz) good mayonnaise
125 ml (4½ fl oz) double cream

Ask the butcher to bone out the duckling for you; or do it yourself, starting on the underside and working your way round to the breast, using a small sharp knife and keeping as close as possible to the carcass. Don't panic if you puncture the skin as it will all be baked in a terrine so the odd hole won't matter.

Make a rich stock (see p. 152) with the duck bones, carrot, onion, bouquet garni, peppercorns, parsley stalks and 1 litre (1¾ pints) water. Simmer for 2 hours, strain then reduce by hard boiling to about 250 ml (9 fl oz). Set aside 100 ml (4 fl oz) for the forcemeat and 90 ml (6 tbsp) for the herby sauce. Keeping the skin in one piece, remove all the meat you can from the boned duck, weigh out 300 g (11 oz) and use this to make a duck forcemeat following the basic recipe. Cut the rest of the meat into cubes or strips. Season these with salt, pepper and a splash of port.

Put a bay leaf in the bottom of a 1.4 kg (3 lb) terrine or loaf tin, season the duck skin and lay it in. Pack in half the forcemeat, then add the reserved cubes or strips of duck and finally the rest of the forcemeat. Fold the skin up and over to enclose, place the bay leaf on top and cover with foil and a lid if available. Bake in a bain-marie as usual at 180°C (350°F) mark 4 for 1¼–1½ hours (see Watchpoints on how to tell if it is cooked). Allow to cool at room temperature, then chill and keep for at least 4 days.

For the sauce, blend or process together the parsley leaves and reserved stock until smooth and pale green. Then briefly blend in the mayonnaise and cream, and season. Pour a little pool of sauce on to each serving plate and lay a slice or two of ballotine on top.

THEME 4

FISH STEWS

for matelotes, chaudrées, marmites and caldos

Countries all over the world have their fish stews, those with abundant coastlines (France, Spain, Mexico, Portugal) having the best selection, but even the landlocked ones able to boast a few made of freshwater fish. The simplest versions provide a home for all the tiny fish and shellfish which are too humble or bony to merit cooking all on their own, but which in a good variety and in conjunction with interesting herbs and spices make a rich, delicious and economical stew. This approach, however, requires your fellow diners to be fairly blasé about bones, and enthusiastic lickers of fingers. Bearing in mind that most people don't fall into this category, the basic recipe gives both options, fish on the bone or filleted fish, and starts out with a fish stock in which everything later takes a brief simmer, enabling you to time the recipe in two parts.

WATCHPOINTS

For a good fish stock you need heads and bones, so either buy all the fish on the bone and fillet it yourself (or ask the fishmonger to do it for you, provided it's not Friday morning and the shop is full); or – less good – buy ready filleted fish and ask for extra heads and bones for the all-important stock base.

Do not include any skin, as this will discolour the stock.

It is important not to simmer the stock for longer than 30 minutes, otherwise it will be bitter.

Choose as wide a variety of fish as possible and try to get a mixture of fragile, flaky fish – plaice, whiting, grey mullet – which dissolve into the background, medium fish – trout,

lemon sole, rascasse, hake, coley, gurnard, weever, haddock – for bulk, and firm fish – monkfish, sole, turbot, pike, John Dory, dogfish, catfish, eel – for character and staying power.

The stock must be at a rolling boil before the fish goes in, otherwise the temperature drops too quickly and by the time it has regained a boil, the fish is overcooked. Fast boiling also thickens the stew, by emulsifying the oil and the fragile fish pieces into the stock.

For cooking the stew, an asparagus, fish or ham kettle is a tremendously clever idea, but a preserving or large pasta pan with a blanching (or chip) basket also serves.

BASIC

FISH STEW

Serves 6

onion, leek, carrot, celery stick, garlic clove	1 each
oil	30 ml (2 tbsp)
fish trimmings (heads, bones, tails)	about 1 kg (2 lb 2 oz)
dry white wine	250 ml (9 fl oz)
bouquet garni	1
lemon juice and some zest	1 lemon
salt and pepper	to taste
assorted fish on the bone OR filleted weight	2 kg (4½ lb) 1–1.2 kg (about 2½ lb)

Chop the vegetables finely and soften them gently in the oil without browning. Rinse all the fish trimmings well to remove any traces of blood. Put them into a huge, wide pan, add the wine, bouquet garni, lemon juice and a couple of slivers of zest, about 1.5 litres (2½ pints) water, and salt and pepper to taste. Bring to the boil, skim if necessary, and simmer for 30 minutes only.

Strain the stock, pushing down hard on the debris to extract maximum benefit, and return the stock to the pan. Taste for seasoning and flavour – boil down hard if it needs concentrating and adjust the seasoning if necessary. You will need about 1 litre (1¾ pints) well-flavoured, fast boiling fish stock. Put the blanching basket into the pan (or the platform, if using an asparagus, fish or ham kettle).

Cut the fish on the bone into manageable slices, or the filleted fish into good chunks. Keep the different sorts separate. Season them all with salt and pepper and put them into the basket in the fast boiling stock as follows: first the firmest fish (see Watchpoints), then 5 minutes later the medium fish, and 5 minutes after that the flaky, fragile sorts. After a further 5 minutes the cooking time is up: total cooking is 15 minutes only. Do not overcook.

Lift out the basket or platform and put the fish on to a large deep serving dish in a warm place. Check the stock for seasoning and boil down if necessary to reduce and concentrate matters. Pour it over the fish and serve at once in large bowls with plenty of home-made or French bread to mop things up.

VARIATIONS

● Use butter, lard or rendered bacon fat instead of oil.
● Use red wine instead of white, or cider.
● Vary the spices and herbs depending on the emphasis you wish to give your stew: saffron, fennel seeds, tarragon, basil, marjoram, chives, chillis, coriander, etc.
● Instead of all fish, include a proportion of shellfish: rock crabs, mussels, prawns, shrimps, etc. Add for the last 5 minutes of cooking, along with the fragile sorts of fish.
● Thicken the strained stock, if wished, with *beurre manié* (equal quantities of butter and flour worked together to a paste and incorporated in pieces until sauce is thick enough), or cream, or egg yolks and cream, then pour back over the fish.

Further IDEAS

Serve fish stews in ovenproof soup bowls or one large ovenproof dish topped with:
a fish or cheese soufflé mixture (p. 46)
a herby scone crust (see Civet of Game with Herby Scone Crust, p. 18)
rounds of stale French bread rubbed with garlic
a roof of puff pastry (p. 88)

Or simmer some home-made noodles (p. 66), cut into short lengths, in the stew (or use the recipe for pasta sheets spread with fish mousseline, simmered and sliced into the stew).

To the finished stew, add some sliced or quartered sautéed mushrooms or sautéed baby onions.

Individual Fish Stews with a Soufflé Topping

Rescue a little of the cooked fish from the basic stew, mix with some cream and eggs, spread it over the top of individual servings (in ovenproof bowls) and bake until golden.

Serves 8 as a starter

1 quantity basic fish stew made with filleted fish (p. 30)
200 ml (7 fl oz) single cream
50 g (2 oz) fresh white breadcrumbs, soaked in milk
4 eggs, separated
a pinch of salt

Make up the fish stew as described in the basic recipe on p. 30, lift the fish out of the cooking juices and set aside 200 g (7 oz) of it for the soufflé topping. Divide the rest equally among 8 lightly greased ovenproof soup bowls. Boil the juices down really hard to reduce by half, then whisk in all but 60 ml (4 tbsp) of the cream. Check the seasoning and pour the sauce over the fish.

Purée together the reserved cooked fish, breadcrumbs (squeezed out), the reserved cream and the egg yolks. Whisk the egg whites with a pinch of salt until stiff but still creamy and fold them carefully into the fish base. Spread this over the top of the stews and bake at 200°C (400°F) mark 6 for 10–12 minutes, or until the tops are golden and risen.

Fish Stew with Fishy Pasta Spirals

Finely rolled pasta dough is spread with a fish mousseline, rolled up, poached in the stock, then sliced and given a final simmer in the stew at the end.

Serves 8 as a starter
4 as a main course

about 200 g (7 oz) green pasta dough (p. 66)
150 g (5 oz) firm fish fillet (see Watchpoints for suggestions)
a pinch of salt
1 egg white
150 ml ($\frac{1}{4}$ pint) double cream
fish stock
1 quantity basic fish stew made with filleted fish (p. 30)

Make up the pasta dough as described on p. 66 and roll it out very thinly to a large rectangle. Trim all the edges. Blend or process together the fish, salt and egg white until perfectly smooth. Add the cream and process or blend (without overdoing it) until just mixed.

Spread this mixture rather thinly on to the rolled out sheet of dough, roll it up, in a bolster shape, cut it into sausage-sized lengths and wrap them in generously cut foil. Secure the ends with freezer twists, like a Christmas cracker.

Poach these sausages in the simmering stock (see basic recipe, p. 30) or water for 15 minutes. Then unwrap them, cut them into slices 1 cm ($\frac{1}{2}$ inch) thick and add to the simmering fish stew for the last 5 minutes of the cooking time.

Caldo de Pescado

A Mexican fish stew, full of colour and warmth: assorted fish pieces with a rich tomato and chilli broth and complete with fresh tortillas (p. 109) for authenticity.

Serves 6

30 ml (2 tbsp) olive oil
1 onion
2 garlic cloves
3 large tomatoes, roughly chopped
2–3 fresh or canned green chillis, de-seeded and chopped
fish heads and bones
a bunch of coriander
juice of 1 lime and some zest
salt and pepper
2 kg (4½ lb) assorted fish on the bone or 1–1.5 kg (2½ lb) filleted fish
lime wedges, to serve

Make a stock base as described in the basic recipe on p. 30 with the olive oil, onion, garlic, tomatoes, chillis, fish trimmings, coriander stalks (keep the leaves for later), lime juice and zest and about 1.4 litres (2½ pints) water. Simmer for 30 minutes, strain, return the stock to the pan and bring back to a good boil.

Cook the fish in the basket in batches as described in the basic recipe on p. 30, lift it out and keep it warm. Reduce the stock by half over high heat and pour it over the fish. Sprinkle with fresh coriander and serve with plenty of warm tortillas (p. 109). Encourage guests to fill them on the hand with flaked fish, a little sauce and a squeeze of lime, roll them up and eat without further ceremony.

Matelote à l'Alsacienne

Alsace, being a bit short on coastlines, makes its fish stews from freshwater fish and (as you might expect) lots of Alsatian wine. You can cheat on the first count, but the fragrant white wine of the country is a must.

Serves 6

1 quantity basic fish stew (p. 30), using an Alsatian Riesling for the stock and assorted freshwater fish on the bone (trout, salmon, tench, carp, eel, pike, perch, etc.)
250 g (9 oz) mushrooms, quartered
24 baby onions, skinned
25 g (1 oz) butter
2 egg yolks
200 ml (7 fl oz) single cream
chopped parsley, to garnish

Make a fish stock as described in the basic recipe on p. 30, using Riesling for the wine. Make the stew as described on p. 30, using the suggested fish. While it is cooking, fry the mushrooms and onions in the butter until lightly golden and just cooked.

Lift out the fish, put it into a large, deep serving dish with the mushrooms and onions and keep warm. Reduce the stock by half over high heat, then remove from the heat. Whisk together the yolks and cream and whisk them into the stock. Taste for seasoning, pour over fish and vegetables, sprinkle with parsley and serve with home-made noodles (p. 66).

T H E M E   5

FLOURLESS SAUCES

for chicken, meat, game, fish, vegetables or pasta

The flour-based sauces have definitely lost their chic, though béchamel still has its uses (see p. 46), and while a flourless sauce with lashings of enrichment cream or butter may not actually be any better for you, it does give the illusion of being lighter (because it's thinner) and is much, much tastier. The trick is to have an excellent stock (see p. 152) and from then onwards, there's a certain recognizable rhythm about things: the stock is further reduced, given extra character with some good wine, distinctively flavoured, enriched and thickened with cream before the final sharpener of lemon juice is added.

The basic recipe is for a sauce which would go nicely with roast chicken, pasta (which cries out for flourless sauces) or vegetables. From here you can depart into your own variations, depending on what the sauce is intended to accompany.

W A T C H P O I N T S

The stock must be well-flavoured, well-reduced and unsalted in the first instance: a stock made with monosodium glutamate cubes won't do, because their already pronounced saltiness becomes excessive on reduction.

Use a wine which you would ordinarily drink: if it tastes revolting in the glass, it won't improve in the sauce.

There is no danger in boiling the sauce after the cream has gone in, as long as you keep whisking, otherwise – for lack of starch to knit things together – it may separate.

A good tool for flourless sauces, besides a wire whisk, is a 'stalk blender' with which you can blend the sauce in the pan.

B A S I C

FLOURLESS SAUCE

Makes about 300 ml (½ pint)

shallot or onion, finely chopped	15 ml (1 tbsp)
butter	25 g (1 oz)
chicken stock	300 ml (½ pint)
white wine	150 ml (¼ pint)
tarragon	to taste
cream, double, whipping or single	150 ml (¼ pint)
salt and pepper	to taste
lemon juice	to taste

Soften the shallot or onion gently in the butter in a medium saucepan without browning. Stir in the stock, season lightly and allow to reduce by half.

Add the wine and tarragon and allow to reduce again by half. Whisk in the cream and simmer gently for a further 5 minutes. Season to taste with salt and pepper and sharpen as necessary with lemon juice. Strain, if you want a really fine sauce, and serve at once.

If the sauce separates into an oily layer and a vile heap of sediment, whisk it up vigorously with a wire whisk or blender and it will come back together again.

V A R I A T I O N S

● Depending on the final purpose of the sauce, vary the stocks (lamb, beef, game, veal, fish, vegetable) and wines (red wine, port, sherry, madeira, vermouth) or use cider, orange or apple juice.

● Instead of tarragon, use other herbs (basil, chervil, parsley, chives, coriander, thyme, rosemary, mint) or spices (crushed peppercorns, juniper berries, cayenne, curry powder).

● For a sauce with a bit more body, soften some chopped vegetables or fruit with the shallot in the butter (leeks, carrots, garlic (lots), apples, rhubarb, quince), then continue as before.

● Or add some greenery (sorrel, lettuce, parsley, spinach, carrot tops, watercress) to the stock and wine reduction and continue as before.

● For an illusion of a lighter sauce, whip the double or whipping cream before adding it, and whisk it in off the heat; don't boil the sauce any more.

● For a less calorific sauce, substitute any of the following for cream, mixed with a teaspoon of cornflour, whisked in off the heat; don't let the sauce boil:
yogurt (especially Greek)
fromage blanc
quark
sieved cottage cheese

● For an even richer finish, whisk in any of the following to the finished sauce, off the heat, and don't let it boil:
50 g (2 oz) butter
bought liver pâté or foie gras
2 egg yolks

● Instead of a sharpening of lemon juice, use an aromatic vinegar, crushed anchovies or anchovy paste, or interesting mustard.

● Think about your sauce and about what it's to accompany, then check the store cupboard and add any of the following optional extras for a bit of final interest and/or texture:
chopped nuts
seeded grapes
pomegranate seeds
pink or green peppercorns
more finely chopped fresh herbs,
    or a sprinkling of paprika.

Spiral of Sole and Salmon with a Watercress Sauce

Strips of sole are wound around chunks of salmon and served in a bright green sauce. The watercress leaves are puréed raw with the stock, butter and cream to ensure that they keep their colour. Substitute parsley for watercress if you prefer.

Serves 8 as a starter,
4 as a main course

700 g (1½ lb) piece of salmon or sea
trout from the tail end
2 Dover soles, each about 350 g
(12 oz)
a large bunch of watercress or
parsley, 50 g (2 oz)
1 small onion, chopped
1 carrot, chopped
salt and pepper
1 bouquet garni
juice of 1 lemon
50 g (2 oz) butter, softened
150 ml (¼ pint) whipping cream or
single cream

Fillet and skin the salmon. Fillet and skin the soles, reserving all the fish bones.

Strip the leaves from the watercress or parsley and set aside for the sauce. Make a fish stock with the stalks, fish bones, onion, carrot, salt, pepper, bouquet garni and lemon juice, simmering for 25 minutes only.

Cut the salmon fillets into 8 equal fish finger-sized pieces. From each sole you will have 4 half fillets. Lightly season both fish and wind a fillet of sole, skinned side in, around each finger of salmon in a spiral movement. Place in a single layer in a buttered ovenproof dish.

Strain the stock, discarding the debris. Reduce the stock to about 300 ml (½ pint) by fast boiling over a brisk heat. Let it cool a little, otherwise the blender will explode.

Purée the watercress or parsley leaves with the softened butter, warm stock and cream in the blender. Pour into the stock pan, check the seasoning and leave to simmer gently while you cook the fish.

Heat the oven to 200°C (400°F) mark 6 and bake the fish for 6–7 minutes or until just opaque: do not overcook. Tip any juices from the baked fish into the sauce. Cut each spiral into 3 slices and lay them down on hot serving plates. Pour the watercress sauce in a little pool around them. Serve with fresh pasta (p. 66) or baby new potatoes in their skins (naturally).

Lamb with Mint Sauce

Mint is fine with lamb, but in this recipe the sharpness of the dreaded malt vinegar is replaced by yogurt. Substitute rosemary for mint if you prefer.

Serves 6

1.5 kg (3 lb 3 oz) leg of lamb, boned, with bones reserved
3 garlic cloves
1 carrot, roughly chopped
1 onion, roughly chopped
1 celery stick, chopped
1 bouquet garni
salt and pepper
75 g (3 oz) butter
1 shallot, finely chopped
2–3 mint or rosemary sprigs
150 ml ($\frac{1}{4}$ pint) port or red wine
100 ml (4 fl oz) natural yogurt
5 ml (1 tsp) cornflour
extra chopped mint or rosemary leaves, to garnish

Make a good stock out of the lamb bones with one of the garlic cloves, chopped, the carrot, onion, celery, bouquet garni, salt and pepper, and water to cover. Simmer for several hours, then strain and reduce to 300 ml ($\frac{1}{2}$ pint) by fast boiling. Reserve.

Peel one of the remaining garlic cloves and cut it into slivers. Season the lamb, make slits at strategic intervals and insert the garlic slivers. Roll and tie up the lamb and roast it in a 220°C (425°F) mark 7 oven without extra fat (lamb has plenty of its own) for 15 minutes.

Reduce the oven temperature and roast for a further 30 minutes (for slightly pink lamb) or 45 minutes (for well-done lamb). Remove the lamb from the oven and let it rest while you make the sauce.

Pour away all but 5 ml (1 tsp) lamb fat from the roasting pan. Add 25 g (1 oz) of the butter and soften the shallot and the remaining garlic clove, crushed, without browning. Add the lamb stock and any rendered juices from the meat, the mint or rosemary and a little salt and pepper. Reduce by half, then add the port or red wine and reduce again by half.

Strain the sauce and return to the pan. Mix together the yogurt and cornflour and whisk it thoroughly into the sauce. Bring back almost – but not quite – to the boil, whisk in the remaining butter, diced, check the seasoning and sprinkle on the chopped mint or rosemary leaves.

Slice the lamb and serve on heated plates with the sauce, and baked potatoes with garlic butter and brussels sprouts or broccoli.

Marinated Braised Pork with New Wine (Sauser) or Cider Sauce

In both Switzerland and Alsace just over the border from where I live, autumn means *sauser* or *vin bourru*, the still-fermenting must with its fresh, grapey flavour. Cider makes an acceptable substitute in this delicious sauce for a marinated and moistly braised piece of pork.

Serves 4

700 g (1½ lb) boneless pork
salt and pepper
a pinch of *quatre-épices* or allspice
1 garlic clove, mashed
1 bouquet garni
juice of 1 lemon
30 ml (2 tbsp) grapeseed (or other) oil
300 ml (½ pint) well-flavoured veal or chicken stock
1 shallot, finely chopped
a bunch of chervil stalks
25 g (1 oz) butter
150 ml (¼ pint) sauser or medium-dry cider
150 ml (¼ pint) single cream
45 ml (3 tbsp) finely chopped chervil

Put the pork into a non-metal bowl and rub in the salt, pepper, spices and garlic. Add the bouquet garni, splash on the lemon juice and half the oil and leave to marinate for at least 24 hours.

Take the pork out of the marinade and dry it well with paper towels (but reserve any marinating juices). Heat the remaining oil in a flameproof casserole, sear the pork on all sides, then add the stock and simmer very gently on top of the stove or in a 180°C (350°F) mark 4 oven for about 45 minutes. Remove the pork from the cooking juices and let it rest from its labours while you prepare the sauce.

Soften the shallot and chervil stalks in the butter in a medium saucepan without allowing them to brown. Add the pork cooking juices plus any reserved marinade, season lightly and reduce by half. Add the sauser or cider and reduce again by half. Add the cream, season and simmer for a further 5 minutes. Check the seasoning and stir in the chopped chervil.

Slice the pork fairly thickly and pour over the sauce. Serve with crunchily cooked cabbage tossed in butter with apple cubes and plenty of black pepper.

Pheasant with Quince Sauce

An autumnal dish for the opening of the quince (and the shooting) season. The sharpness and slight grittiness of the fruit contrast pleasingly with the rather bland bird (guinea fowl would make a fine substitute).

Serves 4

2 quinces, peeled, cored and sliced
1 shallot, finely chopped
25 g (1 oz) butter
1 pheasant, wrapped in sheets of pork fat or blanched bacon
30–45 ml (2–3 tbsp) quince liqueur or calvados
salt and pepper
1 thyme sprig
150 ml (¼ pint) dry white wine or cider
150 ml (¼ pint) chicken stock
150 ml (¼ pint) double cream or crème fraîche

If using a chicken brick – advisable for pheasants or guinea fowl to counteract dryness – soak it in cold water and drain.

Soften the quince slices and the chopped shallot in the butter without browning, then put them in the chicken brick (or use a heavy casserole) and place the bird on top, breast side down. Pour over the liqueur, season lightly, add the thyme, wine or cider and stock.

Bake for 40 minutes at 180°C (350°F) mark 4 or until the bird is just cooked and the juices from the leg run clear. Remove from the dish and return it to the turned off oven to keep warm.

Fish out the thyme and pour the remaining contents of the dish into a liquidizer. Purée until smooth and tip into a saucepan. Whisk in the cream and allow to reduce by half to about 300 ml (½ pint). Check the seasoning.

Cut the supremes off the breast of the bird and carve in thin slices. Cut the legs in half and cut off the wings. Arrange a selection of breast, leg and wing meat on heated plates, pour some sauce around and serve the rest separately.

Saddle of Hare with a Grapey Sauce

Hare tends to come with rich, dark sauces, but here's a creamy sauce and a grapey finish for a change.

Serves 4

1 shallot or onion, finely chopped
25 g (1 oz) butter
a saddle of hare weighing about
700 g (1½ lb)
8–10 thin rashers unsmoked streaky bacon
salt and pepper
30 ml (2 tbsp) wine vinegar
300 ml (½ pint) game or chicken stock (p. 152)
150 ml (¼ pint) dry white wine
150 ml (¼ pint) double cream
10 ml (2 tsp) coarse-grain mustard
lemon juice to taste
100 g (4 oz) seedless (or seeded) grapes

Soften the shallot or onion in the butter without browning in a shallow, cast-iron dish or roasting pan into which the saddle of hare will just fit.

Wrap the saddle in the bacon rashers and place it on top of the shallots. Season with salt and pepper, sprinkle on the vinegar and roast uncovered in a 190°C (375°F) mark 5 oven for 30 minutes. Remove the hare to a heated serving dish and let it rest at room temperature while you make the sauce.

To the juices in the dish, add the stock and wine. Boil hard to reduce by half, then whisk in the cream and mustard and boil again to reduce once more by half. Check the seasoning, add lemon juice to taste and stir in the grapes.

Discard the bacon, remove the fillets from each side of the saddle of hare, carve them in quite thick slices and reassemble them on the backbone. Pour the sauce and grapes around and serve from the dish.

T H E M E   6

MOUSSELINES

for terrines, quenelles, sausages, stuffings and fillings

In the old days, a mousseline – the basis for quenelles and terrines – was made the hard way: a great deal of pounding over ice, chilling, sieving and more chilling of the main ingredient went on before the addition of a *panade* (for 'lightness' – usually choux pastry or breadcrumbs), whole eggs or egg whites, and finally cream.

In came food processors, out went the pounding and the *panades*, and suddenly everybody had fish terrines and vegetable mosaics on their menus. The basic recipe is for a fish mousseline, but it can also be made with shellfish or white meats. It's a multi-purpose mixture, so when you make your own featherlight mousseline, take it a step further than the usual clichés to make quenelles, sausages, or stuffings for fish, poultry, pasta or pastry.

W A T C H P O I N T S

Perfectly fresh fish has a lot of its own natural gelatine which is needed to knit a mousseline together. If you are not sure about its absolute freshness, add both the egg whites; otherwise one will do. Chill really well before adding the raw unbeaten egg whites and only process until smooth – too violent processing will give a rubbery texture.

Pushing the mixture through a sieve afterwards gives a superfine result but is a real labour of love, therefore optional.

The cream also must be well chilled, otherwise during processing the mixture tends to overheat which vastly increases the chances of its curdling.

Some chefs go as high as twice as much cream as fish, but I think equal quantities is fine. You can get away with less, but the more you use, the more unctuous and (apparently) lighter will be the mousseline.

A food processor is ideal for making mousseline, but another system is to purée the fish in the liquidizer with the whites and seasonings, whip the cream separately and then work it into the fish with a wooden spoon or electric mixer.

FISH MOUSSELINE

Makes 500–600 g (17–21 oz)

fish, skinless and boneless	**300 g (11 oz)**
salt	**to taste (see method)**
egg whites	**1–2**
***quatre-épices* or allspice**	**a pinch**
white pepper	**a pinch**
double cream	**150–300 ml ($\frac{1}{4}$–$\frac{1}{2}$ pint)**
finely chopped herbs (optional)	**to taste**

Roughly chop the fish, put it into a food processor and place in the freezer for 30 minutes. Remove and process with about 5 ml (1 tsp) salt until fairly smooth. (NB: if the mousseline is to be eaten cold (e.g. as a terrine or mousse), it can afford to be quite highly seasoned, but if it is to be used hot (quenelles, sausages, etc.) you may prefer to use less salt.)

With the motor running add the egg whites through the funnel and continue processing until the mixture is just smooth. It will be very stiff and gelatinous. Scrape down the sides of the bowl if necessary and re-process. Add the *quatre-épices* or allspice and pepper and process again. Push through a sieve if you're feeling energetic and want a particularly smooth and velvety result; chill the mixture well.

Start with 150 ml ($\frac{1}{4}$ pint) well-chilled cream and process it in, using a pulsing action. Scrape down the side of the bowl if

*The fine texture and
flavour of chicken is partnered by bright peas and
peppers in Crêpe-Clad Chicken and Basil Terrine
with Summer Vegetables (page 43)*

*S*pinach and Prosciutto
Triple Decker combines three natural companions:
spinach, Italian raw ham and garlic cheese
(page 50)

A brilliant ruby
vegetable soup is given an elegant fillip in Iced
Tomato and Red Pepper Soup with Avocado
Mousse Ovals (page 55)

*T*hese Broccoli Timbales
with a Light Orange Hollandaise look best served
in a simple, pale setting which shows off the pastel
shades (page 58)

necessary, then gradually add the rest of the cream to taste. Do not overmix. Add the herbs if used. Check the seasoning carefully. The mixture should be firm enough to hold its shape on a spoon and will firm up even further when chilled once more.

To make into a simple fish terrine or individual mousses, pack the mousseline into a 700 ml (1¼ pint) terrine (or 6–8 individual moulds or ramekins), cover and bake at 180°C (350°F) mark 4 in a bain-marie for 35–40 minutes (15–18 minutes for individuals) or until just firm and springy. Or use in any of the other ways suggested right.

VARIATIONS

● For fish, use any of the following, depending on availability and your budget: whiting, monkfish, haddock, pike, salmon, pink-fleshed trout. Or use half and half pink and white fish, divide the remaining ingredients between them and make up in two batches, or layer for even more effect.
● Instead of fish, use shellfish, veal, chicken, guinea fowl, pheasant, partridge or quail. Do not use cooked or hot-smoked fish or meat – cooking alters the proteins needed to knit the mixture together.
● Vary the spices – a little horseradish for a bland fish; cayenne, cardamom, ginger or grated orange or lemon zest to cheer up veal or chicken; a smidgen of crushed juniper berries or green peppercorns for game.
● Substitute oil for cream (smoother, but denser); or use half cream and half *fromage blanc* (less calorific, but slightly rubbery).
● For herbs, use dill, basil, chives, tarragon, chervil, etc.
● Add any of the following to the prepared mousseline to give colour and texture:
diced lightly cooked shellfish
sautéed button mushrooms, or soaked dried ones (morels, ceps, etc.)
diced sautéed chicken livers or *foie gras*
whole green peppercorns (freeze-dried or in brine)

Further IDEAS

Quenelles: make up the mousseline in any of its variations and chill well. Shape into ovals with wetted spoons and poach gently for 2–3 minutes in barely simmering stock or salted water. Sauce appropriately (see Flourless Sauces, p. 35 for ideas) and serve.

'*Sausages*': wrap in foil and poach in simmering water for 5–6 minutes or until just firm.

Use as ravioli, tortellini, tortelloni or cappelletti fillings (see Pasta, p. 66).

Wrap in thinly rolled shortcrust or puff pastry, or phyllo, roll up and bake until golden.

Team up a fish, meat or poultry mousseline with a piece of fish, meat or poultry (fillets of fish, slices of pork or veal fillet, chicken/turkey/quail breasts, etc.) and use as follows:
● mounded on top
● sandwiched between 2 pieces
● formed into a nugget with a strip of fish or meat wound round
● filled into a pocket opening cut in a piece of fish or meat.
Steam or bake *en papillote* until the mousseline is firm and the fish or meat cooked.

Souffléd Fish Fillets with an Aniseed Sauce

The fun of this dish is the contrast: salmon or pink trout fillets are cloaked with a mousseline of any white fish (whiting, monkfish, haddock, pike, etc.). and given a bit of 'puff' with extra egg whites; or do it back to front with turbot or monkfish fillets topped with a mousseline of salmon or pink trout.

Serves 8 as a main course

8 boneless steaks or fillets of well-flavoured, interesting fish (see suggestions above), each weighing 150 g (5 oz)
salt and pepper
juice of ½ lemon
1 quantity basic fish mousseline, (p. 40), contrasting in colour with the fillets
2 egg whites
2 shallots, finely chopped
300 ml (½ pint) fish stock
150 ml (¼ pint) dry white wine
a pinch of aniseed
150 ml (¼ pint) double or whipping cream
2 egg yolks
2 tomatoes, skinned, seeded and diced very small, to garnish

Season the fish pieces and sprinkle with the lemon juice.

Make the mousseline as described in the recipe on p. 40, making sure to use fish of a different colour to the fillets. Do not chill it, otherwise the egg whites will be hard to incorporate.

Heat the oven to 200°C (400°F) mark 6. Whisk the egg whites with a pinch of salt until stiff but not dry and fold them carefully into the mousseline. Spread the mixture over the top of the seasoned fish, mounding up slightly.

Sprinkle the shallots in a large, lightly greased ovenproof dish and place the fish on top. Bring the stock and wine to the boil with the pinch of aniseed and pour around the fish. Bake in the hot oven for between 7 and 10 minutes – have a look after 7: the fish should be just firm and opaque and the soufflé mixture a little puffed and lightly golden on top. If the fish is cooked in a ceramic or glass dish, it will take longer than in a cast-iron one, but be careful not to overcook.

When the fish is done, remove it and dish up on to warm plates; keep in a warm place. Strain the cooking liquid into a pan and boil down hard to reduce to about 250 ml (9 fl oz). Whisk in the cream and reduce again to about 250 ml (9 fl oz). Remove from the heat and whisk in the yolks. Reheat gently without boiling.

Serve the fish with a little puddle of sauce poured around and garnish with tomato dice. Plain rice (p. 71) or rice with fish stock (p. 72) goes nicely with this.

Pink and White Fish Bolsters with Leek Sabayon

Fillets of white fish are wrapped around a pink fish mousseline and steamed over a bed of buttery leeks, which in turn become the sauce.

Serves 6 as a starter

½ quantity (about 300 g (11 oz)) basic fish mousseline (p. 40), made with salmon or pink-fleshed trout
3 Dover or lemon soles divided into 12 fillets, each about 50 g (2 oz), skinned
salt and pepper
lemon juice
1 leek, trimmed and finely sliced
1 shallot, finely chopped
25 g (1 oz) butter
30–45 ml (2–3 tbsp) dry vermouth
125 ml (4½ fl oz) fish stock
125 ml (4½ fl oz) double cream
2 egg yolks
30 ml (2 tbsp) cold water

Chill the mousseline well to firm up the mixture.

Season the sole fillets with salt, pepper and lemon juice and put 15 ml (1 tbsp) mousseline on the skinned side of each fillet. Roll up the fillets around the mousseline and lay them down on a piece of greaseproof paper.

In a large wide pan which will take all the fish bolsters in one layer (e.g. a sauteuse), soften the leek and the shallot in the butter very gently without browning. Add the vermouth and stock and lay the fish on top. Cook very gently, covered, for 7–10 minutes or until just cooked – the white fish should be just firm and opaque and the mousseline set and springy to the touch.

Remove carefully and keep warm. Liquidize the leeks and cooking juices with the cream and return to the pan. Boil down hard to reduce to about a teacupful and remove from the heat.

Whisk together the yolks and water until very light, frothy and increased in bulk, then add them gradually to the hot – not boiling – sauce. Check the seasoning. Put two fish bolsters on to each heated plate, pour some sauce around and serve with home-made pasta (p. 66).

Crêpe-clad Chicken and Basil Terrine with Summer Vegetables

Vegetable terrines are usually delightful to look at, but dreary to eat. Here, a chicken mousseline is flavoured with basil and olive oil and tinted pink with a purée of red pepper, then layered in a crêpe-lined terrine with crispy summer vegetables. Splendid for a summer buffet.

Makes a 1 kg (2 lb 2 oz) terrine giving 16 slices

300 g (11 oz) boneless chicken breast, trimmed of all nasties
2 small red peppers, roasted and peeled
5 ml (1 tsp) salt
2 egg whites
a pinch of cayenne or paprika
300 ml ($\frac{1}{2}$ pint) olive oil
15 ml (1 tbsp) chopped basil
50 g (2 oz) mangetout
50 g (2 oz) French beans
50 g (2 oz) courgette
salt and pepper
6 very thin basil-flavoured crêpes (p. 60)

TOMATO COULIS
2 large tomatoes, skinned
salt and pepper
30 ml (2 tbsp) olive oil
15 ml (1 tbsp) red wine vinegar
fresh basil leaves

Make up the mousseline as described in the basic recipe on p. 40, substituting chicken for fish and puréeing it with 1 of the roasted and peeled red peppers before adding the salt, egg whites and cayenne or paprika. Pour the oil in a steady stream through the funnel until just mixed, firm and glossy. Add the chopped basil. Chill the mousseline.

Trim the mangetout and beans, and cut the courgette and remaining pepper into 4 cm (1½ inch) strips about the width of the beans. Cook the courgette strips, mangetout and French beans in lightly boiling salted water for 3–5 minutes – fish them out and taste, they should be crunchier than you would like them if serving as a vegetable. Put in cold water to set the colour.

Line a 1 kg (2 lb 2 oz) loaf tin or terrine with the crêpes. Make a layer of mousseline, then one type of vegetable, more mousseline, another type of vegetable, and so on with successive layers, finishing with mousseline on top. Fold the crêpe ends up and over and cover with foil and/or a lid. Put the whole thing in a roasting tin and fill with boiling water to come two-thirds of the way up the sides of the loaf tin or terrine.

Bake in a 180°C (350°F) mark 4 oven for 50–60 minutes: the top should feel firm and springy and a skewer inserted in the middle will feel uncomfortably warm to the cheek.

Serve with a tomato coulis made by liquidizing the coulis ingredients together.

Seafood Sausages with Sorrel Sauce

The basic mousseline is studded with shrimps, formed into sausages and served with a sorrel (or watercress or spinach) sauce. Be sure to slice and splay out the sausages for serving, as they look a bit menacing crouching whole on the plate.

Serves 8 as a starter,
4 as a main course

1 quantity well-chilled basic fish
mousseline (p. 40) made with
monkfish, about 450 g (1 lb)
giving about 300 g (11 oz) when
filleted
250 g (9 oz) cooked prawns,
unpeeled
1 carrot, chopped
1 small onion, chopped
1 bouquet garni
juice of 1 lemon
15 ml (1 tbsp) snipped chives

SAUCE
1 shallot, finely chopped
50 g (2 oz) butter
100 g (4 oz) trimmed sorrel or
spinach or watercress
250 ml (9 fl oz) fish stock made
from the monkfish bones and
prawn shells
125 ml (4½ fl oz) single cream
5 ml (1 tsp) cornflour
salt and pepper
chervil sprigs

Bone and skin the monkfish and use the flesh to make a mousseline as described in the basic recipe on p. 40.

Peel the prawns. Use the monkfish bones (not the skin, which discolours the stock) and the prawn shells to make a stock with the carrot, onion, bouquet garni, lemon juice and about 600 ml (1 pint) water. Simmer for 25 minutes, strain and return to the pan. Reduce to about 250 ml (9 fl oz) by fast boiling. Reserve.

While the stock is underway, cut 4 pieces of foil, each 20 × 30 cm (8 × 12 inches). Chop the prawns roughly and work them and the chives into the mousseline. Lay 45–60 ml (3–4 tbsp) mousseline (about 150 g (5 oz)) down the middle of each piece of foil, like a sausage. Roll up smoothly and firmly and fix the ends with freezer twists to make a tight bolster. Chill well.

For the sauce, sweat the shallot in the butter gently without browning, add the sorrel or spinach or watercress and allow it to wilt. Add the reserved fish stock and simmer for 5 minutes. Whisk in the cream and cornflour and season to taste. Simmer for 5 minutes more. Put in the blender to smooth out the wrinkles and return to the pan. The whole recipe can be prepared ahead up to this point, ready to proceed just before serving time.

Bring a large wide frying pan of water to a gentle simmer and poach the sausages in the foil for 8–10 minutes – they should feel just firm and springy, not at all squashy or mushy. Stick a skewer into the middle of one of them and hold it against your cheek: it should feel rather warm.

Remove as soon as they are ready, discard the foil and slice the sausages on the bias into 2 cm (¾ inch) slices. Heat serving plates, reheat the sauce and divide it among the plates. Allow one sausage per serving (for mains), or half each (for starters), sliced and splayed out over the sauce, and garnish with the chervil sprigs.

THEME 7

SAVOURY SOUFFLÉS

for soufflés, roulades, spirals and toppings

If you can make a béchamel sauce, know how to beat up egg whites and have a halfway decent oven (invest in an oven thermometer if in doubt), you can make a soufflé. Egg yolks and flavouring are added to the thick sauce base and beaten whites are folded in for lightness and upward thrust.

I seldom use béchamel as a sauce now, preferring flourless reductions, but after many misguided attempts to make soufflés and roulades on a purée base without any flour, culminating in a roulade made only of chopped sautéed mushrooms, yolks and whites, which looked like a dark brown log and tasted of cardboard, I realized the error of my ways. In case you may have lost the knack for a properly made béchamel, there are detailed instructions; the model is for cheese soufflé(s), but you can make vegetable, fish or meat soufflés on the same principle. Bake them in hollowed-out vegetable shells for a change, or bake the mixture flat, fill with something interesting and roll up for a roulade.

WATCHPOINTS

Cooking the roux (flour and butter) for too long and over too high heat will colour it (fine for old-fashioned brown sauce, but not desirable here) and will also impair its thickening qualities. However, cooking it for 2 or 3 minutes over medium heat is necessary to get rid of its slightly gluey, 'floury' texture (neglect of this step is probably what has given all flour-based sauces such a bad name), and also to help the flour and butter disperse more evenly when the milk goes in.

Do not heat the milk before adding it; you dirty another pan and the risk of lumps is increased.

Beat well with a wire whisk to distribute the roux until a boil is reached, then turn down the heat and simmer very gently for 10 minutes to cook the flour before adding the egg yolks and cheese. You can stop the process here: cover the sauce to prevent a skin forming; then reheat the base to tepid to soften it up and make it receptive to the beaten egg whites.

Beat egg whites in a scrupulously clean, preferably metal bowl. A balloon whisk will give the best volume, but an electric mixer with a rotating balloon whisk is fine. If you have the sort of mixer where the bowl rotates around stationary beaters, lift it off the stand, use only one beater and rotate it yourself all around the bowl. Salt gives added stability and volume, enabling you to beat a little longer. Be careful to beat the egg whites only until stiff but still creamy; if they look grainy and gritty, you've gone too far: add another egg white and beat again slowly and carefully until the correctly creamy texture is regained. Start folding in with a metal spoon, then continue with a spatula. Be kind to your carefully beaten egg whites: it's better to have a few splodges of white visible than to overdo it and squash out all their precious air. Extra egg whites give more volume, desirable for a soufflé but not necessary for a roulade (see Variations). If you lose track of how many egg whites you have lurking in fridge or freezer, weigh them – 1 weighs approximately 25 g (1 oz).

For a good rise, soufflé dishes should be filled to just below the rim. Paper collars are unnecessary. Soufflés do not have to be baked at once, or even in a preheated oven – see Holding Techniques.

B A S I C

SAVOURY SOUFFLÉ

Makes a main-dish soufflé for 4 or 8 individual soufflés for starters

butter	25 g (1 oz)
plain white flour	45 ml (3 tbsp)
milk	200 ml (7 fl oz)
well-flavoured grated or crumbled cheese	150 g (5 oz)
egg yolks	4
egg whites	4–6

Melt the butter in a heavy pan. Add the flour and cook over moderate heat, stirring to a smooth, bubbling paste. Remove from the heat and tip on the milk. Return to the heat and bring to the boil, stirring frantically with a wire whisk. Simmer very gently for 10 minutes.

Remove from the heat, stir in the cheese and the egg yolks and season to taste, having regard to the saltiness of the cheese. Cover with clingfilm or a buttered paper if not to be used at once; bring the base to tepid before incorporating the egg whites.

Whisk the whites with a pinch of salt until stiff but not dry and fold 15 ml (1 tbsp) in carefully, using a metal spoon. Fold in the rest with a spatula.

Turn the mixture into a 1.5 litre (2¼ pint) greased soufflé dish or charlotte mould (or 8 × 125 ml (4½ fl oz) greased ramekins). Bake in a 200°C (400°F) mark 6 oven for 25–30 minutes for a large soufflé or 12–15 minutes for ramekins, until well-risen and golden. Give the dish a nudge – the soufflé should be still lightly trembly, but not liquid in the middle.

HOLDING TECHNIQUES

It may be more convenient not to bake soufflés at once, in which case, either:
- leave under the upturned mixing bowl (or washing up bowl – it must cover the soufflé dish completely) for up to an hour before baking;
- or put in the fridge, covered with a plate, for up to 2 hours, then bake;
- or cover with clingfilm and freeze. Remove film and bake from frozen in the usual way, increasing the total baking time by one quarter.

VARIATIONS

• For cheese, use Cheddar, Roquefort, Stilton, goat, Gruyère or a judicious mixture. Avoid Emmental which is tasteless, or Parmesan, which is too strong all on its own, but good in combination with other cheeses or vegetables...
• Instead of cheese, use cooked, puréed vegetables (spinach, rocket, watercress, artichoke hearts, broccoli, fennel, asparagus tips, celery, leeks, cauliflower, parsnips, mushrooms, etc.). Toss the purée with a knob of butter over high heat to dry out really well. Use only well-flavoured vegetables, and sharpen the flavour if necessary with grated Parmesan.

Instead of milk use half milk and half cooking liquid from the vegetables if available.
• Or use finely chopped cooked chicken, ham, game, chicken livers, fish (including smoked), sweetbreads, smoked pork, etc. and use half milk and half stock to match the meat.
• *Emergency soufflé*: substitute a 300 ml (½ pint) can of a top-quality cream soup (lobster bisque, game, etc.) for the béchamel base and flavouring, add yolks and whites (and no extra salt) and bake as before.
• If you increase or decrease the basic recipe, check the following for which size dish or mould to use:

DIAMETER (top)	DEPTH	APPROX. CAPACITY	SERVINGS
Soufflé dishes			
20 cm (8 inch)	9 cm (3½ inch)	2 litres (3½ pints)	6
18 cm (7 inch)	8 cm (3 inch)	1.5 litres (2½ pints)	4–6
16 cm (6 inch)	7 cm (2½ inch)	1 litre (2 pints)	3–4
14 cm (5½ inch)	6 cm (2¼ inch)	600 ml (1 pint)	2–3
Charlotte moulds			
18 cm (7 inch)	10 cm (4 inch)	2 litres (3½ pints)	6
16 cm (6 inch)	9 cm (3 inch)	1.5 litres (2½ pints)	4–6
14 cm (5½ inch)	8 cm (3 inch)	1 litre (2 pints)	3–4
12 cm (4½ inch)	7 cm (2½ inch)	600 ml (1 pint)	2–3

Further IDEAS

Pile soufflé mixtures into cooked, hollowed-out tomatoes, onions or courgettes; or cooked artichokes with some leaves and the choke removed. Bake as for ramekins.
Or layer with:
• lightly poached or soft-boiled eggs
• cooked fish strips or shellfish
• ham strips
• sautéed chicken livers, etc. matching layers with chosen soufflé flavour.
Soufflé toppings: spoon some of the soufflé mixture over a piece of fish, or a bowl of soup in an ovenproof bowl. Bake until golden and billowy and the fish cooked (or the soup hot).
Roulade: line a baking sheet with non-stick baking paper or make a paper roulade case. Spread in soufflé mixture of chosen flavour and bake in the preheated oven for 12–15 minutes until pale gold and just firm. Invert on to a tray lined with a tea-towel and leave to cool.
Fill with a matching or contrasting filling:
• mushroom roulade with creamy walnut filling
• cheese roulade with bacon filling
• shellfish-flavoured roulade with shellfish filling, etc.
Avoid flour-based sauces in the filling, using cream, yogurt or *fromage blanc* instead. Roll up and serve warm or just tepid.
Or bake as for a roulade, then cut into strips and layer with any of the above.

Fennel-souffléd Fish Fillets

Fish fillets (allow 150–200 g (5–7 oz) per person) are seasoned and folded, then cloaked in a fennel soufflé, baked and sauced with a creamy fennel or dill sauce. Serve with a (home-made) pasta or a rice dish flavoured with some extra fish stock.

Serves 6

1 kg (2 lb 2 oz) fillets or boned steaks of fish (lemon or Dover sole or whiting; fresh cod or halibut steaks)
salt and white pepper
juice of $\frac{1}{2}$ lemon
1 fennel bulb, about 225 g (8 oz)
30 g (1 generous oz) butter
green food colouring (optional)
25 g (1 oz) plain white flour
200 ml (7 fl oz) milk and fennel cooking liquid, half and half
2 pinches of fennel seeds
4 eggs, separated
300 ml ($\frac{1}{2}$ pint) fish stock (see p. 152)
150 ml ($\frac{1}{4}$ pint) double cream
fennel, dill or chervil sprigs, to garnish

Season the fish with salt, pepper, and some of the lemon juice. Fold fillets in two and place them (or steaks) well spaced out on a large, lightly buttered ovenproof dish (or 6 individual ones).

Trim the fennel bulb and cut it into quarters. Cook in a little boiling salted water for 10–15 minutes or until just tender. Strain and reserve the cooking liquid.

Liquidize the fennel in a blender or food processor and return to the pan with a knob cut from the butter. Cook over high heat to evaporate excess moisture and add 2–3 drops green food colouring to improve the colour if wished.

Make a béchamel base as described in the basic recipe on p. 46, using half fennel cooking liquid and half milk as your liquid, together with the remaining butter. Add the fennel purée, a pinch of fennel seeds and the egg yolks off the heat, then fold in the carefully beaten egg whites and spoon the mixture over the top of the fish fillets. (Cover loosely with foil if not ready to bake yet, and refrigerate.)

About 15 minutes before serving, heat the oven to 200°C (400°F) mark 6 and bake for 8–10 minutes – the trick is to time things so that the soufflé topping is golden brown and nicely puffed up, and the fish just cooked but still succulent inside.

Make the sauce: put the fish stock and remaining fennel seeds in a small pan and reduce to about 100 ml (4 fl oz). Whisk in the cream and reduce again by half. The sauce should be of a light coating consistency. Strain the sauce, check the seasoning and sharpen with lemon juice if necessary.

Lift the souffléd fish on to warm plates and serve with a pool of sauce poured around and garnished with a sprig of fennel, dill or chervil.

Parsnip, Mushroom and Walnut Spirals

A parsnip roulade spirals creamily around a mushroom and nut filling and comes served in slices with salad.

Serves 6 as a starter

250 g (9 oz) parsnips, trimmed
salt and pepper
25 g (1 oz) butter
25 g (1 oz) plain white flour
200 ml (7 fl oz) milk and parsnip cooking liquid, half and half
pepper
nutmeg
30 ml (2 tbsp) chopped mixed parsley and chives
4 eggs, separated
salad leaves, such as chicory, radiccio, lamb's lettuce, oak-leaf lettuce, etc., to garnish

FILLING

250 g (9 oz) mushrooms, sliced
25 g (1 oz) butter
150 ml ($\frac{1}{4}$ pint) soured cream
50 g (2 oz) shelled walnuts, chopped
150 ml ($\frac{1}{4}$ pint) whipping cream

Line a 20 × 30 cm (8 × 12 inch) baking sheet with non-stick baking paper, or make a 20 × 30 cm (8 × 12 inch) paper roulade case as described in the recipe for Spinach and Prosciutto Triple Decker on p. 50.

Scrub the parsnips well but do not peel them. Cook in a little salted water for about 15 minutes or until just tender.

Drain, reserving the cooking water, rub the skin off the parsnips and purée them in a blender or food processor.

Make a béchamel base as described in the basic recipe on p. 46, using the butter, flour and cooking water as part of the liquid, then stir in the parsnip purée, salt and pepper, nutmeg, herbs and egg yolks. Carefully beat the whites with a pinch of salt and fold them into the base. Spread the mixture into the roulade paper case or baking sheet lined with non-stick baking paper. Bake at 180°C (350°F) mark 4 for about 15 minutes or until just firm. The top should spring back on gentle finger-tip pressure.

Remove from the oven, place a clean tea-towel on top, invert a tray over, turn upside down and leave to cool.

For the filling, cook the mushrooms in a frying pan with the butter, salt and pepper for 5 minutes with the lid on. Remove the lid, raise the heat and continue frying until all the moisture has gone.

Tip into a mixing bowl and add the soured cream and chopped walnuts. Whip the whipping cream into soft peaks and fold it into the mixture. Spread it over the roulade and roll up.

Place the roulade seam-side down on a board, or wrap in foil and chill until serving time. Cut into 1 cm ($\frac{1}{2}$ inch) slices and lay them on individual serving plates. Serve garnished with mixed salad leaves in season.

Courgette Soufflés with a Creamy Garlic Sauce

Here the raw courgettes are grated and salted to remove excessive juice, which is used as part of the liquid for the base. Baked individually and turned out, they sit over a pool of creamy garlic sauce.

Serves 8 as a starter

350 g (12 oz) courgettes, grated
salt and pepper
30 ml (2 tbsp) chopped shallots
2 garlic cloves, crushed
25 g (1 oz) butter
25 g (1 oz) plain white flour
100 ml (4 fl oz) milk
4 egg yolks
30 ml (2 tbsp) grated Parmesan cheese
5 egg whites
300 ml (½ pint) single cream

Grease 8 ramekins or tea-cups (125 ml (4½ fl oz) capacity) and cut little discs of non-stick baking paper to fit the bottoms. Heat the oven to 180°C (350°F) mark 4.

Put the grated courgettes into a colander set over a bowl to catch the juice, sprinkle with 2.5 ml (½ tsp) salt, toss well and leave for about 30 minutes. Squeeze the courgettes out really well to make sure they are quite dry and reserve 100 ml (4 fl oz) of the juice.

Soften the shallot and 1 garlic clove in the butter without browning, add the courgettes and toss them over high heat to make sure all the moisture is evaporated. Sprinkle on the flour and stir well to mix. Add the courgette juice and milk and bring to the boil, stirring. Remove from the heat, stir in the egg yolks and Parmesan. Season to taste with pepper.

Whisk the whites as described on p. 46 and fold them into the warm courgette base. Turn the mixture into the prepared ramekins or tea-cups and bake at 200°C (400°F) mark 6 for 12–14 minutes, or until risen, golden and just firm.

Meanwhile, simmer the cream with the remaining garlic and salt and pepper to taste for 15 minutes. Strain this sauce and keep it warm.

Just before the soufflés are done, divide the sauce equally among 8 heated plates. Remove the soufflés from the oven, slide a knife around the edges and turn them out on to your hand. Peel off the paper and place them, right side up, on top of the sauce. Serve at once.

Spinach and Prosciutto Triple Decker

A spinach soufflé mixture is baked flat, cut into strips and layered with raw ham and garlic cheese.

Serves 6 as a starter

350 g (12 oz) fresh spinach, or
200 g (7 oz) frozen spinach, thawed
25 g (1 oz) butter
a grating of nutmeg
salt and pepper
a pinch of garlic powder or garlic salt
30 ml (2 tbsp) plain white flour
200 ml (7 fl oz) milk
30 ml (2 tbsp) grated Parmesan
4 eggs, separated
30–45 ml (2–3 tbsp) garlic cheese with herbs
4–5 slices best-quality wafer-thin prosciutto
fresh herbs or salad leaves, to garnish

Line a 20 × 30 cm (8 × 12 inch) baking sheet with non-stick baking paper. Or make a roulade case with a 22.5 × 32.5 cm (9 × 13 inch) piece of non-stick baking paper: fold in a 2.5 cm (1 inch) border, clip the corners, overlap and fix with staples. Heat the oven to 200°C (400°F) mark 6.

Cook the fresh spinach in minimal boiling salted water until just tender – 5 or 6 minutes – drain, refresh in cold water and squeeze out really well. (If using frozen spinach just squeeze out excess moisture.)

Chop the spinach finely and toss over moderately high heat in the butter with the nutmeg, salt, pepper and garlic powder or salt until all the moisture is evaporated. Sprinkle on the flour and toss the spinach to make sure it is well mixed. Add the milk and Parmesan and bring to the boil, stirring. Check the seasoning, then remove from the heat and stir in the egg yolks.

Beat the whites with a pinch of salt until stiff but not dry. Fold them carefully into the spinach mixture, spread on the baking sheet or into the paper case and bake for 10 minutes or until just firm and springy. Remove from the oven, place a clean tea-towel on top, invert a tray over, turn upside down and leave to cool.

Cut lengthways into 3 strips, spread 2 of them with the garlic cheese and sandwich with the ham. Assemble to make a 3-layered rectangle. Slice, to show the layers, and serve on individual plates, garnished with a little nest of sharply dressed salad.

Mussel Roulade with Bacon Snippets

The béchamel base is flavoured with the mussel cooking liquid for a roulade, which is filled with the mussels and bacon bits.

Serves 6 –8

1 kg (2 lb 2 oz) mussels in the shell
25 g (1 oz) butter
25 g (1 oz) plain white flour
5 ml (1 tsp) curry powder
200 ml (7 fl oz) mussel liquid and milk, half and half
pepper
4 eggs, separated
200 g (7 oz) smoked streaky bacon, rinded and cubed
45–60 ml (3–4 tbsp) *fromage blanc* or quark
30 ml (2 tbsp) grated Parmesan

Give the mussels a vigorous scrub and discard any which gape open or smell suspicious. Put them into a large saucepan over high heat, cover and cook until they open and release their juice – about 5 minutes – discarding any that do not open. Tip the mussels into a colander lined with muslin, shell them and reserve the juice.

Line a 20 × 30 cm (8 × 12 inch) baking sheet with non-stick baking paper or make a paper roulade case as described left.

Make a béchamel base as described in the basic recipe on p. 46 with the butter, flour, curry powder, mussel liquid and milk. Season with pepper – salt will probably not be necessary. Remove from the heat and add the yolks. Fold in the carefully whisked egg whites as usual and spread on the baking sheet or in the paper case. Bake at 180°C (350°F) mark 4 for 12–15 minutes or until golden brown and just firm to the touch.

Remove from the oven, place a clean tea-towel on top, invert a tray over, turn upside down and leave to cool.

Stew the bacon cubes gently until the fat runs and they are lightly golden. Lift them out of the fat and drain on absorbent paper. Mix with the mussels and *fromage blanc* or quark. Check seasoning.

Trim the edges of the roulade, spread with the filling, roll up and place on a long dish. Sprinkle with the Parmesan and serve with a salad of lamb's lettuce and avocado.

THEME 8

SAVOURY MOUSSES

If the mere mention of gelatine gives you the wobbles, this simple mousse formula may help: sheet or powdered gelatine is dissolved in stock, mixed with the main flavouring ingredient, and lightened and lubricated with a little whipped cream. Gone, thankfully, are the days of those leaden affairs glued together with béchamel and so firmly set with gelatine that the bouncing jaw syndrome was guaranteed.

The basic recipe is for a smoked fish mousse and can be used as is, or flavoured and shaped in plenty of other different ways. You don't have to stick to smoked fish: in fact you can whip up an interesting mousse out of practically anything. Check the store cupboard and freezer, and keep in mind interesting leftovers. (See also pp. 124–127 for sweet mousses.)

WATCHPOINTS

* Gelatine figures:
6 sheets = 10 g = scant ½ oz =
1 UK sachet = 3 level (5 ml)
teaspoons = 1 level (15 ml
tablespoon

15 ml (3 tsp) or 6 sheets of gelatine for this recipe will give a fairly firm set, suitable for mousses which you plan to turn out and slice; 10 ml (2 tsp) or 4 sheets is flying fairly close to the wind and gives a lighter set, suitable for mousses to be served from the dish.

Powdered gelatine should be soaked and then dissolved in the stock; sheet gelatine should be soaked in a bowl of cold water until floppy, then squeezed out and dissolved in the stock.

Do not let gelatine boil, or its setting strength will be impaired; just heat until dissolved and add it, hot, to the main flavouring ingredient in the processor or blender and blend until smooth. This way, you accomplish two tasks in one: chopping or puréeing, but also ensuring that the gelatine is distributed evenly, to avoid any danger of 'jelly babies': lumps or (worse) whole layers of ill-distributed or sunken gelatine. The enrichment, whipped cream, is added to the mixture after it has cooled, otherwise it would liquefy.

BASIC

SAVOURY MOUSSE

Serves 6–8

gelatine, powdered	10–15 ml (2–3 tsp)
or sheets	4–6
stock	300 ml (½ pint)
smoked fish fillet (or see Variations)	300 g (11 oz)
salt and pepper	to taste
lemon or lime juice	to taste
chopped fresh herbs	15 ml (1 tbsp)
double or whipping cream	300 ml (½ pint)

If using powdered gelatine, put the stock in a small pan and sprinkle the gelatine over it. Leave until spongy. If using sheet gelatine, soak the sheets in a large bowl of cold water until floppy, then squeeze them out and discard the water. Dissolve either gelatine over gentle heat in the liquid; do not allow to boil.

Put the main flavouring ingredient in the food processor or blender with salt and pepper to taste, lemon or lime juice and the herbs. Add the hot gelatine mixture and process to the desired consistency. Push through a sieve for a very smooth result.

Cool until just beginning to thicken (put it in the freezer or over ice if you want to speed things up; stir occasionally to prevent uneven thickening), then add the lightly whipped cream. Pour into a serving dish or ramekins and chill until set – at least 4 hours or overnight

VARIATIONS

● Use smoked mackerel, trout,
salmon, kipper, haddock, etc., or
cooked, frozen or tinned shellfish
(prawns, shrimps, crab, lobster,
mussels). Or substitute any of the
following:
2 avocados
cooked, frozen or tinned
   vegetables (asparagus,
   Jerusalem artichokes, artichoke
   hearts, aubergine pulp,
   mushrooms, courgettes,
   spinach, leeks, carrots, etc.)
cooked meat, game or ham
grilled, peeled peppers
● Vary the stock to suit the main
ingredient (fish, shellfish,
chicken, vegetable), and the herbs
also – tarragon for crab, dill for
salmon, coriander for avocados,
etc.
● Use half whipped cream and
half any of the following:
yogurt (especially Greek)
fromage blanc
quark
cottage cheese
a mild mayonnaise

Further IDEAS

Mould the mousse in a terrine,
loaf tin, charlotte mould, ring
mould, cake tin, tea-cups or a pre-
baked pastry case. Or make 2
different flavours of mousse and
layer them in the chosen dish.

   Line the chosen dish with
thinly sliced Parma ham, smoked
salmon, smoked poultry; or
blanched cabbage or spinach
leaves; or very thin herby crêpes
(p. 61).

   Or put the mousse to set in a
bowl, then scoop out nice, neat
ovals with a wet spoon and serve
over a sharp salad dressing
(p. 76); or float them on top of a
chilled soup (vichyssoise,
gazpacho, avocado soup, etc.).

Guinea Fowl Chartreuse

A mousse of leftover guinea fowl
(or any other poultry or game
bird) is moulded in blanched
cabbage leaves. 4 sheets or 10 ml
(2 tsp) of gelatine is enough, as
the guinea fowl and jellied stock
give quite a firm set anyway.

Serves 6–8 as a main course

**10 ml (2 tsp) powdered gelatine or
4 sheets**

**300 ml ($\frac{1}{2}$ pint) guinea fowl stock
(from the bones)**

**300 g (11 oz) cooked guinea fowl,
all skin and bones removed**

150 ml ($\frac{1}{4}$ pint) whipping cream

**150 ml ($\frac{1}{4}$ pint) natural yogurt or
*fromage blanc***

2–3 juniper berries, crushed

8 small blanched cabbage leaves

Make up the guinea fowl mousse
according to the basic recipe on
p. 52 and stir in the juniper
berries.

Line a 1 litre ($1\frac{3}{4}$ pint) charlotte
mould or pudding basin with
blanched cabbage leaves and
pour in the mousse.

Leave to set, then turn out, and
serve with a sharply dressed
cabbage and carrot salad.

Tri-coloured Pepper Mousses

Even if you think you dislike peppers, try these featherlight, mousses, striped red, yellow and green. Serve on a bed of mixed salad with some avocado wedges arranged strategically around.

Serves 6 as a starter

15 ml (3 tsp) powdered gelatine or 6 sheets
300 ml ($\frac{1}{2}$ pint) vegetable or chicken stock
1 red, 1 yellow and 1 green pepper, about 150 g (5 oz) each
salt and pepper
2.5 ml ($\frac{1}{2}$ tsp) cayenne pepper
a drop of green food colouring
1 large coriander sprig, chopped
300 ml ($\frac{1}{2}$ pint) whipping cream
a little vegetable oil
mixed salad, in season

TO GARNISH
1 avocado, cut into wedges
coriander sprigs

Soak and dissolve the gelatine in the stock, as described in the basic recipe on p. 52.

Using the grill, a gas flame or a blow-torch, blister the peppers until quite black all over, then put them into a polythene bag for a few minutes to soften the skin further. Rub off the skin under running water, remove the seeds and chop roughly. Keep the 3 colours separate.

Liquidize the red pepper with a third of the gelatine/stock mixture and season with salt, pepper and cayenne. Set aside in a bowl. Liquidize the green pepper with a drop of green food colouring, the chopped coriander and another third of the gelatine/ stock. Put it into another bowl, then liquidize the yellow pepper with the remaining gelatine/ stock. Season and set aside.

Whip the cream until the beater leaves soft tracks, then divide it equally among the 3 pepper mixtures and fold in.

Oil 6 ramekins or dariole moulds with tasteless oil and divide the red pepper mixture among them. Tap down on your working surface to settle the contents and chill in the fridge until just set. Follow with the green mixture; refrigerate again. Finally add the yellow mixture. Chill in the fridge until 30 minutes before serving.

Run a knife around the edge and give a sharp tap to dislodge each mousse on to a bed of mixed salad, whatever's in season, on individual serving plates. Garnish with some avocado wedges and sprigs of fresh coriander.

Crab and Avocado Mousses

The avocado mousse is covered with the crab to give a two-toned effect, and to avoid the problem of blackening avocado. It makes a rather exotic starter, especially if served in crab shells. Or the mousse may be layered in a 1 kg (2 lb 2 oz) terrine or loaf tin, chilled and turned out on to an oval serving plate, and served with salad.

Serves 8 as a starter

450 g (1 lb) crab, cooked, or 200 g (7 oz) cooked or frozen crabmeat
15 ml (3 tsp) powdered gelatine or 6 sheets
300 ml ($\frac{1}{2}$ pint) crab or chicken stock
salt and pepper
cayenne pepper
150 ml ($\frac{1}{4}$ pint) double cream
150 ml ($\frac{1}{4}$ pint) natural yogurt
1 avocado
lemon or lime juice
a pinch of garlic powder or garlic salt
a little vegetable oil

TO SERVE
mixed salad in season
8 empty crab shells (optional)
chervil, dill or parsley sprigs

If using a whole crab, dissect it and remove all the meat from the body and the claws; set aside the legs for the garnish.

Soak and dissolve the gelatine in the stock, as described in the basic recipe on p. 52. Place the crabmeat in a food processor or blender, season with salt, pepper and cayenne and add half the dissolved gelatine. Blend until smooth, then set aside until cool.

Whip the cream until the beater leaves soft tracks, then fold half of it and half the yogurt into the cooled crab mixture. Leave at room temperature while you make the avocado layer.

Peel and stone the avocado, place in the food processor or blender with the other half of the gelatine, the lemon or lime juice, garlic, salt and pepper to taste. Blend until smooth, then add the remaining whipped cream and yogurt.

Lightly oil 8 ramekins and divide the avocado mousse equally among them. Put in the freezer until set (about 10–15 minutes); then pour over the crab mousse. Chill in the fridge for a few hours or overnight.

To serve, arrange a bed of salad on individual serving plates (or in the crab shells, if available). Dip the ramekins briefly in a sink of hot water to loosen, run a small palette knife around the edge and invert them on to the plates or crab shells. Garnish with the reserved crabs' legs and put a sprig of chervil, dill or parsley on top.

Iced Tomato and Red Pepper Soup with Avocado Mousse Ovals

Ovals of jade-green avocado mousse are floated over bowls of red pepper and tomato soup, for an impressive-looking (but simple) starter.

Serves 8 as a starter

MOUSSE
10 ml (2 tsp) powdered gelatine or 4 sheets
300 ml ($\frac{1}{2}$ pint) chicken stock
2 avocados
salt and pepper
juice of $\frac{1}{2}$ lemon
15 ml (1 tbsp) finely chopped chives or coriander
150 ml ($\frac{1}{4}$ pint) mayonnaise
150 g (5 oz) quark

SOUP
2 red peppers
1 kg (2 lb 2 oz) tomatoes, skinned and roughly chopped
a pinch of sugar
10 ml (2 tsp) tomato purée
a pinch of garlic powder
30 ml (2 tbsp) wine vinegar
60 ml (4 tbsp) olive oil
parsley or coriander sprigs, to garnish

Make the avocado mousse according to the basic recipe on p. 52 and tip into a bowl. Cover with clingfilm and leave in the fridge to set.

To make the soup: using the grill, gas flame or blow-torch (spear the peppers on a fork), grill the peppers until blistered and blackened all over. Put them into a polythene bag and leave for 10 minutes, after which it will be easy to rub off the skins under cold running water.

Put the peppers in a blender or food processor with the tomatoes, sugar, tomato purée, garlic powder, vinegar, oil and salt and pepper to taste. Blend or process until smooth, then push through a sieve. Chill well.

Divide the chilled soup among 8 bowls. Dip a nicely oval spoon in a cup of hot water, scoop out 2 perfect ovals of avocado mousse and slide them on to the chilled soup. Dip the spoon back into the hot water each time to ensure good shapes. Garnish with a sprig of parsley or coriander and serve well chilled.

THEME 9

BAKED CUSTARDS

for timbales, quiches, tarts and puddings

The word 'flan' as used in English has somehow ended up suggesting a sweet or savoury tart, with or without eggs. In France a true *flan* is a custard of eggs, liquids (milk, cream, etc.) and flavouring. Whatever the name, it makes a most useful preparation and the proportions are nice and easy to remember too: for 1 egg you need 100 ml (4 fl oz) milk/cream and 100 g (4 oz) flavouring.

Savoury custards of fish, shellfish, mushrooms or vegetables make elegant starters or accompaniments for a main dish; sweet custards with fruit make soothing puddings. If you tip the flavoured custard into a pastry case, you have a quiche (savoury) or a *tarte* (sweet).

W A T C H P O I N T S

Heating the cream speeds up the baking, but is an optional step. The eggs and cream should be gently whisked and even strained, to give the smoothest results. The main flavouring ingredient can be blended in, or left in whole pieces for a custard with more character.

Always put sheets of newspaper in the bottom of the bain-marie (or baking tin) (stops splashback) and add just-boiled water to come two-thirds of the way up the side of the dish. The slower you bake custards, and the lower the temperature, the less risk of 'cooking' the eggs which gives a gritty custard with excess water floating about on the bottom. With the oven at 150°C (300°F) mark 2 the water will remain well below boiling point (at around 70°C (158°F)).

Some chefs own up to adding a little flour to the *flan* which gives a smoother result and is especially important if used in conjunction with a moist vegetable or juicy fruit, or if you are to bake it in a pastry case, when the juices would seep into the pastry and make it soggy.

B A S I C

BAKED CUSTARD

Makes about 900 ml (1½ pints) custard, serving 4–8

single or double cream	300 ml (½ pint)
eggs	3
salt and pepper	to taste
sugar, herbs or spices	to taste
plain white flour (optional)	15 ml (1 tbsp)
vegetables, fish, meat, etc.	300 g (11 oz)

Bring the cream almost to boiling point, cool a little, then blend or process it briefly together with the eggs, seasonings, sugar, herbs or spices and flour (if used). Blend or stir in the main flavouring ingredient.

Pour into 6–8 greased ramekins, or a 1 litre (1¾ pint) soufflé dish. Bake in a bain-marie at 150°C (300°F) mark 2 until a skewer inserted in the middle comes out clean – about 30 minutes for ramekins, 35–40 minutes for soufflé dishes.

● Instead of all cream, use half cream and half any of the following:
milk (fresh or evaporated)
stock
fromage blanc
quark
yogurt
sour cream
● Instead of 3 eggs, use 2 eggs and 2 yolks for a richer result.
● Use herbs (basil, marjoram, oregano, chives, parsley, thyme, dill etc.) and spices (nutmeg, cinnamon, cayenne, allspice, cumin seed, etc.) with imagination to match the main flavouring.
● Flavour the custard with any of the following:
cooked broccoli, spinach, cauliflower, sprouts, asparagus, parsnips, carrots, etc.
fried aubergines, mushrooms (cultivated or wild), courgettes
sweated onions, leeks, chicory, sorrel
cooked (or smoked, or tinned) fish or shellfish
cooked game, meat, bacon, ham
grated or cubed cheese (50–100 g (2–4 oz) only)
● For sweet custards, omit salt, pepper or herbs and add sugar to taste. Mix or blend in any of the following:
peeled, cored and sliced apples or pears
halved, stoned plums, apricots
cherries, stoned or not as you wish
sliced rhubarb, macerated in sugar overnight (add exuded juices to custard in place of some of the milk)
● Instead of baking custards in ramekins or a soufflé dish, use tea-cups, tartlet tins, shallow dishes, or a charlotte tin, *moule à manquer*, or ring mould.

Tourte of green vegetables: line a greased charlotte mould with blanched spinach or cabbage leaves. Choose several different sorts of blanched green vegetables and instead of blending them in with the other ingredients, layer them in the dish and pour on the custard. Bake as usual in a bain-marie until the custard passes the skewer test.

Quiches and tartes: make a savoury or sweet custard, raid the fridge, garden, freezer or store cupboard (see suggestions left) for interesting solids, bake a pastry case blind and use the following as a rough guide for size and filling needs:

---

20 cm (8 inch) (for 2)

2 eggs
200 ml (7 fl oz) cream
200 g (7 oz) solids

---

25 cm (10 inch) (for 4)

3 eggs
300 ml (½ pint) cream
300 g (11 oz) solids

---

30 cm (12 inch) (for 6)

4 eggs
400 ml (14 fl oz) cream
400 g (14 oz) solids

Scatter the chosen solids over the pastry and pour over custard; or purée them together with the custard. Bake in a 180°C (350°F) mark 4 oven for 25–35 minutes (depending on size), or until set and lightly browned.

Broccoli Timbales with a Light Orange Hollandaise Sauce

Little broccoli custards are unmoulded and surrounded with an orange-flavoured hollandaise.

Serves 8 as a starter

300 g (11 oz) trimmed broccoli
150 ml ($\frac{1}{4}$ pint) chicken stock
150 ml ($\frac{1}{4}$ pint) cream
3 eggs
a grating of nutmeg
salt and pepper
chervil sprigs, to garnish

ORANGE HOLLANDAISE
2 egg yolks
15 ml (1 tbsp) lemon juice
15 ml (1 tbsp) orange juice
a pinch of salt and white pepper
25 g (1 oz) cold butter
a further 70–100 g (3–4 oz) butter, melted
2 egg whites

Cook the broccoli in plenty of boiling salted water until just tender – about 7 minutes. Drain, refresh under cold water to set the colour, and put into the blender.

Heat the stock with the cream and add to the blender with the eggs and seasonings. Blend until quite smooth.

Cut discs of non-stick baking paper and put in the bottom of 8 well-greased ramekins (125 ml ($4\frac{1}{2}$ fl oz) capacity). Pour in the custard and bake as described in the basic recipe on p. 56 in a bain-marie at 150°C (300°F) mark 2 until they pass the skewer test (about 35 minutes).

Put the yolks for the sauce in a metal bowl over hot, almost simmering, water. Beat them until thick and sticky, then whisk in the lemon and orange juice, salt and white pepper. Gradually whisk in the cold butter, bit by bit, then follow with the melted butter, added in a steady stream. By the time all is added, you should have a rich, creamy emulsion. Check the seasoning.

Just before serving beat the egg whites with a pinch of salt until stiff but still creamy and fold them carefully into the warm sauce. Turn out the broccoli custards, pour a little sauce around, garnish with chervil sprigs and serve the rest of the sauce separately.

Chanterelle Custards

Cooked (or canned, at a pinch) chanterelles are baked in a creamy savoury custard, for an unusual first course, or as the accompaniment for game.

Serves 8 as a starter or accompaniment

400 g (14 oz) cooked or canned chanterelles
150 ml ($\frac{1}{4}$ pint) game or chicken stock
150 ml ($\frac{1}{4}$ pint) single or double cream
3 eggs
15 ml (1 tbsp) chopped chives
salt and pepper

Grease 8 ramekins (125 ml ($4\frac{1}{2}$ fl oz) capacity) and put a little disc of non-stick baking paper in the bottom of each. Divide the chanterelles among the ramekins.

Heat the stock with the cream and use to make a custard with the eggs, chives, salt and pepper. Pour it over the chanterelles.

Bake as described in the basic recipe on p. 56 in a bain-marie at 150°C (300°F) mark 2 until they pass the skewer test (about 35 minutes). Leave to cool for a few minutes, then slide a knife round the edges, turn out the custards, remove the lining paper and serve either as a first course, with a little creamy game sauce (see Flourless Sauces, p. 35) or as the accompaniment for a game dish.

Spinach and Sweetcorn Quiche with a Touch of Horseradish

Green spinach and yellow sweetcorn makes an interesting quiche filling.

Serves 2

¼ quantity (100 g (4 oz)) shortcrust pastry (p. 81)

100 g (4 oz) fresh spinach *or* 50 g (2 oz) frozen spinach, thawed

2 eggs

5 ml (1 tsp) creamed horseradish

200 ml (7 fl oz) single or double cream or quark

100 g (4 oz) canned or frozen sweetcorn

salt and pepper

25 g (1 oz) cheese, diced

Roll out the pastry thinly to fit a 20 cm (8 inch) quiche tin and bake blind. Cook the spinach in plenty of boiling salted water for 5–6 minutes. Drain, refresh under cold water to set the colour and squeeze dry by handfuls. Chop finely (or put in the processor).

Blend or process together the eggs, horseradish, cream or quark and spinach. Stir in the sweetcorn, season to taste and pour into the pastry shell. Scatter over the cubes of cheese and bake at 180°C (350°F) mark 4 for 25–30 minutes or until golden brown and set. Serve with a salad.

Alsatian Plum Flans

A bit like clafoutis, only with much less flour. Nice with a blob of cinnamon flavoured ice cream on top.

Serves 6

150 ml (¼ pint) milk

150 ml (¼ pint) cream

3 eggs

a pinch of ground cinnamon

30 ml (2 tbsp) sugar

15 ml (1 tbsp) plain white flour

30 ml (2 tbsp) pflümli (plum eau-de-vie), kirsch or other liqueur

450 g (1 lb) plums

Heat the milk with the cream and blend it together with the eggs, cinnamon, sugar, flour and liqueur. Lightly grease 6 × 11 cm (4 inch) shallow ovenproof dishes (or use ramekins).

Halve and stone the plums and arrange them, cut side downwards, in the dishes. Pour over the custard and bake at 150°C (300°F) mark 2 for about 25 minutes or until set and golden.

Black Cherry Tart with Lemon Yogurt Custard

Ground nuts on the bottom of the pastry case give a nice flavour and a bit of crunch, as well as serving as a waterproof layer.

Serves 4

150 g (5 oz) shortcrust pastry (p. 81)

30 ml (2 tbsp) breadcrumbs or ground hazelnuts

200 g (7 oz) stoned black cherries

1 egg

2 egg yolks

200 ml (7 fl oz) lemon yogurt

15 ml (1 tbsp) plain white flour

30 ml (2 tbsp) soft light brown sugar

Heat the oven to 180°C (350°F) mark 4. Roll out the pastry and use to line a 20 cm (8 inch) quiche tin. Sprinkle the breadcrumbs or nuts over the base. Arrange the cherries on top.

Make a custard as described in the basic recipe on p. 56 with the egg, yolks, yogurt, flour and sugar and pour it over the cherries. Bake in the preheated oven for 25–30 minutes or until the custard is set and the pastry golden.

THEME 10

CRÊPE BATTERS

for lacy pancakes, battered puddings, pies and galettes

Although it's fun to make your Mardi sinfully Gras, it's a pity to confine yourself to a once-yearly feast of pancakes with lemon and sugar: the basic batter (milk, water, plain flour and eggs) can be made more interesting by varying the liquids, using different sorts of flour, and by adding oils, herbs or spices, while fillings can encompass anything from shellfish to starfruit.

Nor is the batter uniquely destined for the crêpe pan: the same mixture with a few more eggs makes the lightest Yorkshire puddings imaginable, a more than passable Toad in the Hole, *Moules dans le Houle* (a sort of Mariner's Toad), Clafoutis, ice cream cones and galettes galore.

WATCHPOINTS

A blender, processor or electric mixer makes light work of blending the liquids, flour and eggs to a smooth cream (and of chopping any herbs you may care to add in the process) but gets the gluten (the element in flour which gives it its elasticity) rather over-excited. Hyper-active gluten gives tough results, so it's always better to rest the batter for an hour or so before using.

Crêpe pans need only be wiped out with a piece of oiled absorbent paper before you begin; thereafter no further oil or butter is necessary: the fat in the mixture is enough. Heat the pan really well before you start: splash some water in it – it should hop about in extreme agitation and disappear in a flash. If too hot, however, the batter turns to scrambled eggs in the bottom instead of spreading about evenly – it takes a couple of crêpes to get the heat right, so first attempts are usually only fit for the dog, and just when you get really good, the batter is all finished. Such is life.

BASIC

CRÊPE BATTER

Makes about 16 crêpes

water	125 ml (4½ fl oz)
milk	125 ml (4½ fl oz)
plain white flour	100 g (4 oz)
oil or melted butter	30 ml (2 tbsp)
eggs	2
salt	a pinch

Place all the ingredients in the order listed in a liquidizer, food processor or electric mixer and blend until quite smooth. Scrape down and re-blend if necessary. Leave the batter to rest for about 1 hour before using; it will keep for 3–4 days in the fridge. Whisk up again briefly before using.

Brush out a small, heavy frying pan of the diameter you wish for your crêpes with a smidgen of oil and heat it steadily. Pour in a small amount of batter – enough just to film the bottom – any excess swilling about should immediately be tipped back into the jug. There should be a definitely protesting sizzle as the batter first goes in.

Cook until the underside is golden and the crêpe can easily be lifted. Toss (nonchalantly) or turn (gingerly, with a spatula) to cook the second side. Stack up as the crêpes are ready. If you don't get at least 16 crêpes 15 cm (6 inches) in diameter out of this amount, you are making them too thick.

They can be frozen filled (see Further Ideas), or unfilled (in batches of 8–10), whichever you find most convenient, but they're nicer fresh from the pan/oven.

- *Savoury* batter: substitute stock for water.
- Choose yogurt, *fromage blanc*, quark, or cottage cheese instead of milk for a thicker result (more like drop scones), using plain white flour only.
- Instead of all white flour, use two-thirds white and one-third wholemeal, buckwheat, fine oatmeal, chickpea flour, etc.
- Use different oils: walnut, hazelnut, olive, etc. in the batter and add plenty of freshly chopped herbs to match the crêpe filling (e.g. dill/smoked salmon, tarragon/chicken, basil/meat with tomato sauce, coriander/chicken and guacamole, etc.). Or flavour with garlic, celery or herbal salts, cayenne, etc.
- *Sweet crêpes*: substitute orange or apple juice for water and sweeten if wished with sugar or honey to taste.
- Use almond or hazelnut oil or melted butter; flavour with almond essence, cinnamon, nutmeg, lemon or orange zest, orange flower water, liqueurs, etc.

Fill savoury crêpes with cooked diced/shredded meat (chicken, ham, game, veal, chicken livers, etc.) or fish or shellfish; or vegetables (asparagus, broccoli, mushrooms, spinach, etc.) in a light sauce; sprinkle with more sauce or grated cheese and heat through in a 180°C (350°F) mark 4 oven.

Crêpe cakes: make normal-sized or tiny crêpes, layer with selected fillings (ham and horseradish, spinach and ricotta or cottage cheese, mushrooms and quark, etc.) in a soufflé dish/charlotte mould or ramekins (for individual crêpe cakes). Bake in a bain-marie at 180°C (350°F) mark 4 until hot. Turn out and serve with tomato sauce (p. 149).

Bite-sized cocktail crêpes: 5–6 tiny ones to the pan. Daub with:
- soured cream and lumpfish roe
- taramasalata
- guacamole (p. 112)
- *fromage blanc* and a halved cherry tomato (cut side down)

Savoury galettes: make the basic savoury batter with yogurt and stir in about 100 g (4 oz) of any of the following:
- sweetcorn (canned or frozen)
- chopped or grated celery, celeriac, onion, carrot, etc.
- chopped ham, prosciutto, etc.
- grilled, peeled peppers, diced
- cooked, chopped spinach
- raw courgettes, grated, salted and squeezed.

Sweet galettes: make sweet batter with yogurt and add 100 g (4 oz) of any of the following:
- cubed, sautéed apple or pear
- stoned, chopped plums, apricots, cherries, peaches
- blackberries, raspberries, etc.

Make galettes about the size and thickness of drop scones (American pancakes) and fry them in a little hot oil or clarified butter, turning once when they are golden. Serve savoury ones as accompaniments to meat (sweetcorn with chicken or duck, spinach or courgette with lamb, etc.) and sweet ones with ice cream or vanilla sauce (p. 138).

Yorkshire puddings: use the basic savoury batter (makes 24 individuals): halve everything in the recipe except the eggs and make up as usual. Heat the oven to 220°C (425°F) mark 7, brush 2 × 12-hole bun tins with a little oil and heat them in the oven until smoking. Fill the holes two-thirds full and bake for 10–12 minutes or until well risen.

Toad in the Hole: make the basic batter as usual and add 2 more eggs. Heat a lightly oiled roasting pan in a 220°C (425°F) mark 7 oven until smoking, pour in the batter, scatter sausages (and maybe chunks of bacon and a few mushrooms) on top and bake for 30–35 minutes or until golden brown and well risen.

Fill sweet crêpes with mincemeat, pastry cream or crème Chiboust (p. 139), fresh fruit and whipped cream. Bake until hot through and flame with liqueur if wished.

Clafoutis: add 2 more eggs and a little sugar to the basic butter and preheat the oven as above. Grease an ovenproof dish (or individual ones), pour in the batter, scatter stoned fruit (plums, apricots, peaches, cherries) on top, sprinkle with icing sugar and bake for 12–15 minutes (individuals) or 30–35 minutes for a big dish.

Broccoli and Prosciutto Parcels

Thin herby crêpes are lined with prosciutto, filled with broccoli and served with an orange sauce.

Serves 4 as a starter

1 quantity basic crêpe batter with herbs (pp. 60–1)
8 broccoli spears (about 300 g (11 oz))
1 orange
8 slices raw ham, prosciutto-style
150 ml (¼ pint) single cream
a little instant-blending cornflour (optional)

Make up the batter as described on p. 60, allow to rest, then make 8 very thin crêpes in the usual way. Trim the broccoli spears, remove the leaves and peel the stalks. Take fine strips of zest from the orange with a julienne knife or potato peeler. Cook the broccoli and zest in boiling salted water for 4–5 minutes or until the broccoli is just tender. Drain and refresh the broccoli and zest in cold water. Reserve about 300 ml (½ pint) of the broccoli stock.

Lay a slice of ham on each crêpe, top with a piece of broccoli, fold over the ends of the crêpe to make a parcel and place them all seam-side down in a lightly buttered ovenproof dish.

Put the crêpes in a 180°C (350°F) mark 4 oven to heat through gently (about 15 minutes, no more) while you prepare the sauce: reduce the stock by half. Add the reserved orange peel, cream and orange juice and reduce again by half. Taste carefully for seasoning and thicken if wished with a little instant-blending cornflour. Serve poured over the hot pancakes, on hot plates.

Saffron Seafood Crêpes

The saffron-flavoured mussel liquid is used to flavour the crêpes, which are filled with mussels, mushrooms and crunchy vegetables.

Serves 8 as a starter, 4 as a main course

1 kg (2 lb 2 oz) mussels in the shell, to give about 400 g (14 oz) shelled
150 ml (¼ pint) dry white wine
a sprig each of thyme and parsley
1 bay leaf
1 shallot, chopped
1 garlic clove
1 envelope powdered saffron or 2 pinches threads, soaked in boiling water and strained
1 quantity basic savoury crêpe batter (p. 60), using mussel stock/milk as liquid
1 carrot, cut into 2.5 cm (1 inch) matchsticks
1 leek, cut into 2.5 cm (1 inch) matchsticks
250 g (9 oz) button mushrooms
250 ml (9 fl oz) double or whipping cream
instant-blending cornflour (optional)

Scrub the mussels well and remove any which smell suspicious or persistently refuse to close when tapped smartly on the head.

Bring to the boil in a large pan the wine, herbs, shallot, garlic and saffron liquid. Throw in the cleaned mussels, clap on the lid and steam them open (about 5 minutes.) Remove them with a slotted spoon and slip them out of their shells, discarding any that have not opened. Set them aside. Strain the mussel stock through a piece of muslin to eliminate sand and use 125 ml (4½ fl oz) of it in the basic crêpe batter.

Make up the batter as described on p. 60, allow to rest, then make 16–18 very thin crêpes about 15 cm (6 inches) in diameter in the usual way.

Put the remaining stock back into the pan and bring to the simmer. Throw in the carrot, leek and mushrooms and simmer for just 5 minutes – do not overcook: the vegetables should retain some character. Remove them with a slotted spoon to join the mussels and set aside about a cupful of stock (freeze the rest). Whisk in the cream and reduce by half. The sauce should be of a lightly coating consistency. Thicken with a little instant-blending cornflour if wished.

Put about 30 ml (2 tbsp) of mussel filling in each crêpe, moisten with a little sauce, roll up tightly and lay in an ovenproof dish. Sprinkle on any remaining sauce and bake in a 180°C (350°F) mark 4 oven for about 15 minutes. Cover with foil if the pancakes begin to curl up and harden before they are hot through. Serve the rest of the sauce separately, poured in a little golden pool beside the pancakes, and garnish with greenery.

Moules in the Ho(u)le

No reason why Toad should have a monopoly: mussels, monkfish and bacon cubes are scattered over a mussely batter and baked till golden brown. Good for a supper dish. Individual ones baked in cast-iron or ovenproof dishes are also nice as a first course.

Serves 4 as a main course

450 g (1 lb) mussels in the shell, to give about 200 g (7 oz) shelled
1 quantity basic savoury crêpe batter (p. 60), using mussel stock/milk as liquid
2 eggs
100 g (4 oz) bacon in the piece, rind removed and cut into cubes
15 ml (1 tbsp) oil
150 g (5 oz) filleted, trimmed monkfish, cut into cubes

Clean the mussels as in the previous recipe and steam them open in a heavy pan without extra liquid. Remove from their shells, discarding any that have not opened, and set aside. Strain the mussel stock through a piece of muslin and measure out 125 ml (4½ fl oz). Make up the crêpe batter as described on p. 60, using the mussel stock instead of water and adding no salt. Whisk in also the extra eggs.

Heat the oven to 220°C (425°F) mark 7. Put the trimmed, cubed bacon in a heavy roasting pan and bake in the oven until it is golden and crusty, the fat rendered and the pan good and hot – 5–10 minutes. Pour in the batter, dot the mussels and monkfish chunks around it and return to the oven for 25–30 minutes, or until golden brown and billowy. Serve with a tomato and onion salad.

Honeyed Pear Sorbet with Crêpe Cones and Chocolate Sauce

A nicely sharp sorbet of pears, lemon juice and honey sits inside crisp crêpe cones, all served on a dark pool of chocolate sauce. Substitute a bought ice cream or sorbet if you prefer.

Serves 6

4 pears, about 450 g (1 lb)
juice of 1 lemon
75 ml (5 tbsp) clear honey
2 egg whites
1 quantity basic crêpe batter (p. 60)
melted butter
150 g (5 oz) plain chocolate
300 ml (½ pint) water
50 g (2 oz) sugar
150 ml (¼ pint) single cream

Peel, core and chop the pears. Stew them with the lemon juice and 60 ml (4 tbsp) honey until soft. Purée until smooth and freeze to a mush; tip into a food processor and process to a smooth snow with the egg whites (alternatively whisk the whites to soft peaks and beat them into the half-frozen purée). Return to the freezer until firm.

Make up the batter as described on p. 60, adding the remaining honey, allow to rest, then make 12 very thin crêpes in the usual way – there will be more than you need, so use any extra for another recipe. As the crêpes are ready, place brown side down on a board. Fold them in half, then in half again, making a cone shape. Scrumple up a ball of foil and post it inside to prop the whole thing open. Brush the exterior of the cone with melted butter, place on a baking sheet and bake in a 200°C (400°F) mark 6 oven for 3–4 minutes or until golden brown and crispy enough to hold its shape. Continue with the remaining pancakes until done, setting them aside on a rack to cool as you work.

Make the chocolate sauce: melt the chocolate in the water with the sugar, then boil for 10 minutes or until syrupy and somewhat reduced. Cool. Stir in the cream to give a light coating consistency.

Scoop out balls of sorbet and fill each cone. Put 2 on each plate and surround with chocolate sauce. A little additional sliced fresh pear, sprinkled with lemon juice and icing sugar, makes a nice garnish.

Orange Macaroon Crêpe Parcels with Fruit Filling

The slightly crunchy, orange-flavoured batter encloses fresh fruit and comes with a flaming finish.

Serves 4

½ quantity basic sweet crêpe batter (p. 60)
60 ml (4 tbsp) orange liqueur
30 ml (2 tbsp) sugar
15 ml (1 tbsp) macaroon crumbs or powdered praline
2 bananas
2 slices pineapple
60 ml (4 tbsp) marmalade

Make up the batter as described on p. 60, allow to rest, then add 30 ml (2 tbsp) of the liqueur (keep the rest for flaming the crêpes later), sugar and macaroon crumbs or powdered praline just before making into 8 lacy crêpes. Set aside.

Slice the bananas fairly thickly on the slant. Quarter the pineapple slices. Divide the fruit among the crêpes, adding a dab of marmalade to each. Fold into 4 like a handkerchief. Put in a heavy ovenproof dish and give them about 10 minutes in a 220°C (425°F) mark 7 oven.

Heat the reserved liqueur in a ladle, pour it over the crêpes and set alight. Serve with ice cream.

A slightly crunchy
pancake is a superb foil to soft exotic fruits in
Orange Macaroon Crêpe Parcels with Fruit Filling
(page 64)

*An imaginative
variation on more common seafood pasta dishes is
Mushroom and Mussel Lasagne with Saffron
Sauce (page 70)*

A creamy rice ring forms
the base to a circlet of overlapping shellfish in
Avocado and Prawn Risotto
(page 74)

This beautiful star-
shaped Winter Warm Salad of Belgian Endive and
Fish is a symphony of calculated contrasts
(page 79)

PASTA

for home-made noodles, tortellini, ravioli, cannelloni, lasagne

Although opinions are sharply divided as to whether or not it was Marco Polo who introduced pasta to Italy after a spell in the East, the Italians have for years topped all the leagues as consumers of pasta – some 32 kg (65 lb) per head per year on average. But more recently, creative cooks the world over have adopted it and made much of it, and there's no reason why you shouldn't be one of them.

The standard formula is simply eggs and best-quality hard wheat flour, with a little oil for extra suppleness. Ribbon noodles are a good place to begin to get your confidence going, but the fun really comes when you start to create your own dishes by flavouring, shaping and filling the pasta in lots of different ways (without perhaps going to such extremes as black spaghetti coloured with squid ink, or chocolate vermicelli for dessert). Don't let anyone tell you that you need complicated gadgetry and machinery: a big working space, a large rolling pin and good tummy muscles are all that's required.

WATCHPOINTS

The best pasta is made from high-protein durum wheat flour, with plenty of gluten to give it the correct chewiness and desirable body. If you can't get this flour, or strong bread flour, then it's a good idea to use a little very finely ground semolina (*semolina di grano duro* – fine meal from durum wheat) as part of your flour total.

The standard proportions (1 egg to every 100 g (4 oz) flour) are only a guide, and will vary a bit depending on the type of flour and the size of the eggs: you may need to add a little more oil or water to get the correct consistency for the dough; or conversely to add sprinkles of flour as necessary to achieve the same end.

Mixing by hand can be done quickly and simply, but it's less messy in a food processor or electric mixer.

Don't try to roll out the dough immediately after it has been mixed and kneaded, otherwise it will be impossibly jumpy and elastic.

B A S I C

PASTA DOUGH

Makes about 450 g (1 lb), enough for noodles for 4

plain white flour	250 g (9 oz)
fine semolina	50 g (2 oz)
salt	5 ml (1 tsp)
eggs	3
oil	5–10 ml (1–2 tsp)

Using either an electric mixer and dough hook, or a food processor, or a bowl and plenty of elbow grease, mix or process together the flour, semolina and salt. Add the beaten eggs and just enough oil to bind the whole thing to a stiff ball of dough, a bit like bread dough only firmer. Knead very vigorously (4–5 minutes in the mixer or food processor, 10 minutes by hand) until smooth, supple and no longer sticky to the hand. Like bread dough, the more you knead, the better it will be. Wrap it in clingfilm and give it a rest for at least an hour to give the gluten a bit of a break.

To roll pasta by hand, cut the ball of dough in half, flour a large board and use a long, well-floured rolling pin or a smooth, straight broom handle. Roll out each piece to a large, thin, even rectangle. Sprinkle the rolled out sheet with flour and fold over and over on itself like a flattened Swiss roll. Cut the roll into slices as narrow or as wide as you wish, slip the handle of a wooden spoon through the slices, give it a bit of a shake and they should all fall off, nicely separated and opened up. Sprinkle them with flour and leave them to dry out a bit.

To roll pasta using a machine, slice the dough into 4–6 pieces. Dust the pieces with flour and flatten them out to the width of the rollers. Feed them through the machine rollers starting at the widest setting and working up to the finest. If they get unmanageably long, cut them in two. Hang the sheets over a broom handle suspended between two chairs and leave to dry out a little. They should be supple but not sticky, nor should they be allowed to dry out too much or you won't be able to feed them through the rollers. Keep an eye on them. Feed the pasta sheets through the cutting rollers (you may have several width options). If the rollers do not cut right the way through, the sheets are not quite dry enough. Wait a few minutes and try again. If too dry and brittle, they will crack; spray with water, rest a bit and try again.

The pasta can be cooked immediately, or kept in the fridge for 3–4 days, or allowed to dry out until brittle, when it will keep for several weeks; or it can be frozen. To cook, use masses of fast boiling water with salt or a stock cube and a little oil. Impossible to be rigid about timing, but freshly made pasta cooks very quickly: start testing after 3 minutes: it should be just soft, but still nicely chewy.

Serve with any flourless sauce (pp. 34–5), or cream, butter, *fromage blanc*, or grated cheese, or herbs. Or mix with strips of crunchily cooked vegetables cut the same width as your pasta.

V A R I A T I O N S

● Instead of plain white flour and semolina, use strong flour if available; or substitute 100 g (4 oz) of any of the following for the same amount of plain flour: wholemeal, buckwheat, rye flour or cornmeal.

● Instead of whole eggs, use any of the following, keeping in mind the required consistency (see Watchpoints):
only yolks (up to 7) for an amazingly rich yellow dough
only whites (3–4) for a low cholesterol version

● *Herby pasta:* mix 30–45 ml (2–3 tbsp) finely chopped fresh herbs (especially basil or chervil) with the eggs and add to the basic recipe.

● *Saffron pasta:* use 1 envelope powdered saffron (or 5 ml (1 tsp) saffron threads) soaked in 30 ml (2 tbsp) boiling water (remove the threads if used) in place of 1 of the eggs.

● *Pink pasta:* use 30 ml (2 tbsp) tomato purée in place of 1 of the eggs.

● Or flavour and colour pasta using about 100 g (4 oz) of any of the following puréed with only 1 egg (omit the other 2):
cooked spinach (buy/pick 200 g (7 oz))
grilled and peeled (or tinned) red, green or yellow pepper
cooked beetroot, Jerusalem artichokes, parsnips, carrots, etc.

Ravioli: roll out the pasta to very thin sheets. Place teaspoon-sized fillings (mousseline (p. 40), cooked spinach and ricotta, stiff vegetable purée with Parmesan, cooked or tinned mussels, oysters, etc.) well spaced apart on half the dough sheets. Moisten the dough around the filling, lay a second sheet over and press down into the valleys to seal well. Use a scone or biscuit cutter to cut out round or square ravioli, or use a sharp knife or pasta wheel.

Tortellini or cappelletti: roll out the dough very thinly, stamp out circles or squares, place a teaspoon of filling (same ideas as for ravioli) to one side of the circle, moisten edges and fold over like a turnover. Turn up a cuff around the outside edge and bring the points around to meet each other. Pinch them together to form a little 3-cornered hat.

Cook all ravioli, tortellini or cappelletti in plenty of boiling, salted water (or add a stock cube), or (for a small amount) steam them. Timing: between 5 and 8 minutes – keep testing, as for all pastas.

Lasagne or cannelloni sheets: cut the rolled out dough into strips approximately 15 × 10 cm (4 × 5 inches). Blanch 3–4 sheets at a time in lightly boiling, oiled and salted water and lift out as soon as they are floppy. Drop them in a sink or bowl full of cold water, then drain and pat dry on tea-towels just before using. Layer the sheets (lasagne) or fill and roll them up (cannelloni), using meat sauce, vegetables or shellfish in a creamy sauce, etc. Bake in a 200°C (400°F) mark 6 oven until hot and bubbly (about 20 minutes).

Green Pepper Pasta Salad with Avocado, Courgette and Almonds

Noodles are flavoured with green pepper, cut into short lengths, cooked and tossed with avocado, courgette strips, toasted almonds and basil or chives.

Serves 4 as a starter

1 green pepper, about 150 g (5 oz)
1 egg
250 g (9 oz) plain white flour
50 g (2 oz) fine semolina
5 ml (1 tsp) salt
olive oil
1 medium courgette, cut into strips
about 300 ml (½ pint) basic salad dressing with yogurt (p. 76)
1 avocado
1 large 'beefsteak' tomato
50 g (2 oz) flaked almonds
30 ml (2 tbsp) finely chopped basil or chives

Sear the pepper all over using a grill, gas flame or blowtorch, put into a polythene bag and leave for 10 minutes, then peel under running water and remove the stalk and seeds. Put the flesh into the food processor with the egg. Process to a smooth purée. Add the flour, semolina, salt and just enough oil to make a firm dough as described in the basic recipe on p. 66. Rest the dough.

Cut the dough in half and use half (about 250 g (9 oz) to make noodles for this recipe. Use the rest for another recipe (or freeze for a later use). Roll the dough out very thinly to a large rectangle. Cut noodles as directed on p. 66, then cut them into 6 cm (2½ inch) lengths.

Cook the noodles and courgette strips in plenty of boiling water with a stock cube added for about 3 minutes or until just tender. Drain and toss immediately in a large mixing bowl with enough dressing to coat them. Arrange on a serving dish.

Peel and stone the avocado. Cut it and the tomato into 8 segments. Toss each carefully in some more dressing in the mixing bowl and arrange them alternately on top of the noodles and courgettes. Grill or lightly fry the almonds and toss them over, with the basil or chives. Serve at once.

Salmon Ravioli with Spicy Tomato Sauce

Tomato-flavoured pasta dough is filled with salmon mousseline and served with a creamy, spicy tomato sauce.

Serves 8 as a starter, 4 as a main course

1 quantity basic pasta dough (p. 66) coloured pink with tomato purée
250 g (9 oz) fresh salmon fillet
4 ml ($\frac{3}{4}$ tsp) salt
a pinch of mixed spice
1 egg
150 ml ($\frac{1}{4}$ pint) double cream
1 shallot, finely chopped
15 ml (1 tbsp) oil
1 green chilli, de-seeded and finely chopped
3 large tomatoes, skinned and diced or a 400 g (14 oz) can peeled tomatoes
1 garlic clove, crushed
salt and pepper
200 ml (7 fl oz) double or soured cream
150 ml ($\frac{1}{4}$ pint) well-flavoured fish or chicken stock

Make up the pasta dough as described in the basic recipe on p. 66, using 30 ml (2 tbsp) tomato purée in place of 1 of the eggs and mix as described to a firm dough. Rest the dough while you prepare the filling and the sauce.

Purée together the salmon fillet, salt, mixed spice and egg in a food processor or blender until perfectly smooth. Then blend in the cream briefly, in short bursts. Do not overprocess or you risk curdling it. Chill the mixture.

Soften the shallot in the oil over medium heat without browning. Add the chilli, tomatoes and garlic, season with salt and pepper and cook over gentle heat until the juices render. Raise the heat and drive off excess moisture. Turn into a blender or food processor with the cream and stock. Purée until smooth. Sieve, then return to the pan and simmer gently while you prepare the pasta.

Roll out the dough by hand (2 sheets) or by machine (4 sheets) as directed in the basic recipe on p. 66. Take teaspoons of the well-chilled filling and place little mounds all over one of the prepared pasta sheets, well spaced apart. Brush a little water in between the mounds and lay a second pasta sheet on top. Press down between the mounds to create valleys and cut around with a 6 cm ($2\frac{1}{2}$ inch) scone or biscuit cutter or a floured glass. (Repeat the process with the other 2 sheets if you have cut the pasta on the machine.) There will be quite a lot of waste dough from the valleys. Reshape it into a ball, moistening if necessary, and recycle it into noodles.

Bring a large pan of water to the boil and add 15 ml (1 tbsp) salt. Cook the ravioli for about 7 minutes, calculating from the time they float to the surface. Drain on paper towels, then serve with the sauce, either on individual serving plates or in a large dish. A little sprig of dill or chervil on top adds a certain something.

Cannelloni with Bacon and Leeks with Ana's Walnut Sauce

Ana was responsible for my first nervous steps into the world of home-made pasta: here is a delicious dish using her superb sauce of garlic, wine, cream and walnuts. Omit the bacon, if you wish, for an unusual vegetarian dish.

Serves 4–6

1 quantity plain or green basic pasta dough (p. 66)
225 g (8 oz) streaky bacon, rinded and cubed, or lardons
25 g (1 oz) butter
1 kg (2 lb 2 oz) leeks, about 5, trimmed, washed and sliced
salt and pepper
freshly grated nutmeg
1 egg
60–75 ml (4–5 tbsp) quark or
fromage blanc

SAUCE
2 garlic cloves, peeled
30 ml (2 tbsp) oil
100 g (4 oz) ground walnuts or hazelnuts, or a mixture
200 ml (7 fl oz) dry white wine
200 ml (7 fl oz) top of the milk or very thin cream
25 g (1 oz) grated Parmesan
water or stock

Make up the dough (plain, or with 100 g (4 oz) cooked spinach or peeled green pepper in place of 2 of the eggs) as described in the basic recipe on p. 66. Use half the dough for this recipe (make noodles or another shape with the rest, or freeze for later use).

After the resting period, roll out the dough as thinly as you can by hand (or to the finest setting with the pasta machine) and cut sheets 15 × 10 cm (6 × 4 inches). Blanch them in boiling salted water and drop them into a sink or bowl full of cold water.

Fry the bacon bits over high heat until the fat runs. Remove them and tip off most of the excess fat, leaving about 15 ml (1 tbsp). Add the butter, leeks, salt, pepper and nutmeg and cook over gentle heat without allowing the leeks to brown. Stir the bacon bits back into the pan and remove from the heat. Add the egg and quark or *fromage blanc*. Check the seasoning and allow to cool a little.

Drain the pasta sheets on tea-towels and place a generous tablespoon of filling at one end of each sheet. Roll up cigarwise and place in a large, lightly buttered ovenproof dish which will accommodate all the cannelloni in one layer – you should have about 32 of them, so you'll need a generous dish, or even two. Bake the cannelloni in a 180°C (350°F) mark 4 oven for 20 minutes, and in the meantime make the sauce.

Fry the garlic cloves in the hot oil until golden. Discard them and add the walnuts or hazelnuts to the pan. Stir over moderate heat, then moisten with the wine and cream and simmer for 15 minutes, stirring occasionally. Add the Parmesan and dilute with stock or water if necessary to a thick coating consistency.

When the cannelloni have had their 20 minutes, pour over the sauce and bake them for a further 5–10 minutes or until golden brown and bubbly. Stick a skewer into the middle and it should feel uncomfortably hot to the cheek.

Mushroom and Mussel Lasagne with Saffron Sauce

Instead of layering your lasagne with meat sauce and béchamel, try this version with mushrooms, mussels and a light saffrony sauce for a change.

Serves 4–6

1 quantity basic pasta dough (p. 66) flavoured with saffron
2 kg (4¼ lb) mussels, cleaned, to give 450 g (1 lb) shelled
2 garlic cloves, crushed
25 g (1 oz) butter
250 g (9 oz) mushrooms, quartered
salt and pepper
10 ml (2 tsp) plain white flour
45–60 ml (3–4 tbsp) double or soured cream
2 carrots, cut into matchstick strips and blanched
lemon juice
45–60 ml (3–4 tbsp) *fromage blanc* or quark

SAUCE

250 ml (9 fl oz) reserved mussel juices
1 envelope saffron powder or 5 ml (1 tsp) saffron threads
150 ml (¼ pint) dry white wine
200 ml (7 fl oz) double cream
a little instant blending cornflour (optional)

Make up the dough as described in the basic recipe on p. 66, using 1 envelope saffron powder soaked in 30 ml (2 tbsp) boiling water in place of 1 of the eggs. Set aside one-third of the dough for this recipe (make noodles or some other shape with the rest, or freeze for a later use).

Rest the dough, then roll out as thinly as you can by hand (or to the finest setting with the pasta machine) and cut sheets about 15 × 10 cm (5 × 4 inches). Blanch them in boiling salted water and drop them into a sink or bowl full of cold water.

Scrub the mussels thoroughly and discard any which refuse to open. Put them into a large pan and cook over lively heat until they open: shell them and reserve, discarding any that have not opened. Strain the cooking juices through a piece of muslin and reserve.

Soften the garlic in the butter, add the mushrooms and pepper to taste and cook over moderate heat with the lid on until the juices render. Uncover, raise the heat and cook until the liquid is almost evaporated. Stir in the flour and cook for a couple of minutes before adding about 125 ml (4½ fl oz) of the reserved mussel juices. Bring to the boil, add the cream, blanched carrots and lemon juice to taste. Then add all this to the reserved mussels.

For the sauce, bring the remaining mussel juices to the boil. Soak the saffron powder or threads in some of the hot juices until fragrant and yellow (then discard the threads if used) and add the saffron liquid and white wine to the pan. Reduce to about 300 ml (½ pint) and then whisk in the cream. Continue to cook, stirring, until reduced to the desired consistency – if necessary, thicken with instant-blending cornflour. Check the seasoning and sharpen with drops of lemon juice as necessary.

Drain the pasta sheets on tea-towels. Put a little of the saffron sauce in the bottom of a large, lightly buttered ovenproof dish and lay one of the pasta sheets on top. Add a layer of the mussel mixture. Continue layering, finishing with a layer of sauce and the *fromage blanc* or quark. Bake in a 200°C (400°F) mark 6 oven until the top is golden and bubbly and a skewer stuck in the middle feels rather warm to the cheek.

RICE

I have a publishing friend who talks witheringly of the sort of dinner parties (nowadays, surely, mercifully rare) where 'dead chicken 'n' rice' is on the menu. Leaving aside the dead chickens, anything more tedious than plain boiled white rice is hard to imagine. In this version, the rice is first fried with a little onion and garlic and then given as much stock as it can gobble up in the time that it takes for it to cook to a nicely chewy and interesting texture (i.e. *al dente*). I hope this chapter will help you if you're one of those people who hanker after fluffy pilaffs or creamy risottos, but are afraid that anything more taxing than your usual methods may land you with inadvertent rice pudding.

W A T C H P O I N T S

The basic recipe is for long-grain rice. Other varieties of rice can be used (see Variations), but while the cooking times and the method may vary slightly, the ratio of stock to rice remains the same: provided there are no other moisture-inducing ingredients in the dish (as in Paella, for instance, see recipe on p. 73) rice will absorb between $2\frac{1}{2}$ and 3 times its own weight in stock.

NB: bear in mind that 1 l water or stock weighs 1 kg; 750 g = 750 ml. Therefore it is possible to calculate how much stock a given amount of rice will absorb by multiplying the weight of the rice by $2\frac{1}{2}$ or 3. Thus 300 g of rice needs between 750 g (or ml) and 900 g (or ml) stock. It's less straightforward using the imperial system since the relationship between oz and pints is not immediately obvious.

BASIC

RICE

Serves 4–6

onion, finely chopped	1
garlic clove, mashed	1
oil, clarified butter, lard or dripping	15 ml (1 tbsp)
long-grain rice	300 g (11 oz)
stock	750–900 ml ($1\frac{1}{4}$–$1\frac{1}{2}$ pints)
salt and pepper	to taste

In a heavy flameproof casserole, fry the onion and garlic gently in the fat until golden and fragrant. Add the rice and fry for 5 minutes, stirring from time to time. Add 750 ml ($1\frac{1}{4}$ pints) of the stock, with salt and pepper to taste, cover and cook over moderate heat. Have a look after about 15 minutes: the stock should have disappeared, the rice grains will be fluffy and separate, and little holes will have appeared all over the surface. Taste: it should be cooked, but still bite-y (*al dente*). If definitely still a little hard, add the remaining stock. Cook for a final 4–5 minutes. Check the seasoning, fork up and serve hot with sauced dishes where a blotter is needed; or cold in salads.

VARIATIONS

● With the onion and garlic, soften any of the following: cubes or strips of red, green or yellow peppers
trimmed, chopped chicken livers
thinly sliced leeks, carrots, celery, celeriac, fennel, etc.
sliced or quartered mushrooms
● Instead of long-grain, use brown rice: proceed in exactly the same way, but increase the cooking time to 35–40 minutes. Brown rice continues to have quite a chewy, nutty texture, even when fully cooked.
● *Risotto*: use Italian round-grain rice (e.g. Arborio or Vialone). Don't cover the pan and stir 2 or 3 times during cooking. Check for doneness as usual, adding the remaining stock if necessary. Continue stirring for the last 5 minutes, when rice is most apt to stick. Instead of being fluffy and separate, the grains will be deliciously gooey and sticky.
● Vary the stock depending on what you plan to serve the rice with: chicken, beef, veal, fish; or use half stock and half wine, as in Italian 'black' risotto, which uses Barolo and stock for a deep purplish result; or Anton Mosimann's champagne risotto...
● Blend into the stock any of the following, reducing the stock, if necessary, to take account of their moisture:
a grilled, peeled pepper, any colour
skinned, seeded tomato flesh
herbs
saffron

FURTHER IDEAS

To make your rice into more of a main dish, prepare it as described in the basic recipe and stir in any of the following optional goodies 5 minutes before cooking time is up:
● frozen or canned corn kernels
● chopped herbs
● chopped nuts or raisins
● chopped cooked meat, vegetables, fish or shellfish
● thin strips of omelette
● grated cheese
● chopped hard-boiled eggs
● fried tofu cubes
● avocado cubes.
    Mould cooked rice into greased ramekins, dariole moulds, timbales, ring moulds, etc., packing down well. Reheat if necessary in a bain-marie in a 180°C (350°F) mark 4 oven and turn out to serve.
    Spread cold cooked rice on to crêpes, smoked salmon, raw ham, air-dried beef, etc., roll up and chill; cut in slices and serve as appetizers.
    Stuffed vegetables: use to stuff grilled and peeled peppers, tomatoes, etc.

Prosciutto and Brown Rice Salad

A slightly Japanese-inspired supper dish or starter, brown rice is spread on to the prosciutto (instead of seaweed), rolled up, sliced and served with a salad.

*Serves 6 as a starter,
4 as a main course*

400 g (14 oz) cooked brown rice (made from 100 g (4 oz) raw rice, or one-third of basic recipe, p. 71)
8 slices (100 g (4 oz)) prosciutto
4 tomatoes, thinly sliced
sharply dressed mixed salad leaves, oak-leaf, lamb's lettuce, radicchio
slivers of Gruyère
fresh herbs to taste

Cook the rice as described in the basic recipe on p. 71 and season it well while still warm. Cool, then spread about 30 ml (2 tbsp) rice on to each of the prosciutto slices in quite a thin layer and roll them up tightly.

Using an extremely sharp knife, slice the rolls into 5–6 pieces and lay them out around a serving plate. Inside this ring, put a ring of sliced, dressed tomatoes. In the middle put a mound of dressed mixed salad leaves. Arrange the Gruyère slivers on top and scatter fresh herbs over.

Paella

The normal quantity of stock is considerably reduced in this famous rice dish, to take account of the moisture in the fish and shellfish.

Serves 8 with 2nd helpings

a 250 g (9 oz) piece of streaky bacon
450 g (1 lb) chorizos or pork sausages, sliced
salt and pepper
8–10 chicken pieces
2 squid, about 450 g (1 lb), cleaned and cut into rings
1 large onion, chopped
1 garlic clove, mashed
1 green pepper, de-seeded and chopped
750 g (1½ lb) short-grain risotto rice
450 g (1 lb) firm fish, filleted, skinned and cubed
10 prawns, raw or cooked and unpeeled
450 g (1 lb) mussels in the shell or 200 g (7 oz) frozen or brine-bottled mussels
750 ml–1 litre (1¼–1¾ pints) fish or chicken stock
1 envelope powdered saffron or 1 pinch saffron threads
200 g (7 oz) frozen peas
100 g (4 oz) green or black olives

In a *paellera* (40 cm (16 inch) diameter), huge frying pan or other large shallow recipient, cook the bacon and chorizos or sausages until the fat runs. Lift them out with a slotted spoon and drain on paper towels. Tip off most of the fat. Season the chicken pieces and fry them in the remaining fat until lightly golden. Remove, then follow with the seasoned squid rings. Remove to join the chicken and soften the onion, garlic and green pepper without browning, adding oil if necessary to film the bottom of the pan. Add the rice with 5 ml (1 tsp) salt and fry well, stirring and turning until well coated with oil (about 10 minutes).

Bury the bacon, chorizo, chicken, squid, fish, raw prawns (cooked ones should go in later), and mussels in the shell (frozen/bottled go in later also) into the rice, pushing them down well. Heat the stock and dissolve the saffron in a little of it. Strain if using threads and pour 500 ml (about 16 fl oz) of the stock over the *paella*. It should just cover the ingredients. Season carefully with salt and pepper and then either simmer over gentle, even heat or bake in a 180°C (350°F) mark 4 oven, uncovered, for 20–25 minutes.

Add the cooked prawns and frozen/bottled mussels, if used, the peas and olives and continue to cook until all the stock is absorbed and the rice tender – about another 10 minutes, making 30–35 minutes in all.

Taste the rice and tip the pan to see the state of the stock in the bottom. It is not unknown for the rice to be still slightly hard and all the stock evaporated, in which case add more stock and continue cooking; if, on the other hand, the fish and shellfish have released more juice than you'd bargained for, and the rice is tender when there is still a lot of liquid about, pour it off and put the *paella* back on the heat for a few minutes, stirring, to evaporate any excess. Serve with a sharply dressed green salad.

Avocado and Prawn Risotto

A response to a request for a dish containing 2 of my children's favourite foods, this creamy risotto is packed into a ring mould, turned out and decorated with alternating avocado segments and prawns.

Serves 4 as a main course or 6 as a starter

1 onion, finely chopped
1 garlic clove, crushed
oil
300 g (11 oz) short-grain risotto rice
900 ml (1½ pints) chicken stock
salt and pepper
8 prawns, raw and unpeeled
1 avocado
lemon juice

Soften the onion and garlic in 30 ml (2 tbsp) oil without browning, then fry the rice for 5–10 minutes, stirring. Add the stock and prepare a risotto in the usual way, stirring from time to time, until the stock is absorbed and the rice creamily cooked.

Check the seasoning, remove the rice from the heat and turn it into a lightly greased 1.25 litre (2 pint) ring mould, packing in well to firm up. Cover with foil and leave in a warm place until ready to serve (or allow to cool and reheat in a bain-marie at 180°C (350°F) mark 4 for 20–25 minutes or until warm through).

Toss the unpeeled prawns briefly in hot oil until pink and just cooked – 3–4 minutes. Halve and stone the avocado, cut in 8 segments and peel away the skin. Turn out the rice, garnish with alternate slices of avocado and prawns, squeezed with a little lemon juice.

Crown of Long-Grain and Wild Rice

Uncle Ben's packets of long-grain with wild rice are tremendously convenient, but are improved by the addition of a few vegetables and the use of only half the sachet of rather violent herbs and spices that comes in the packet.

Serves 4–6 as an accompaniment

1 carrot, finely chopped
a small piece of celeriac (about 50 g (2 oz)), peeled and chopped
1 leek, finely sliced
25 g (1 oz) butter
1 packet (170 g (6 oz)) Uncle Ben's long-grain with wild rice
150 ml (¼ pint) dry white wine
350–400 ml (12–14 fl oz) water

Soften the carrot, celeriac and leek in the butter without browning. Stir in both sorts of rice and fry gently for 5 minutes. Add the wine, 350 ml (12 fl oz) of the water and half the sachet of herbs and spices. Cover the pan and cook for 15 minutes; taste for doneness and add the remaining 50 ml (2 fl oz) water if necessary. Cook for a further 5 minutes.

Turn the rice into a greased or non-stick 1.25 litre (2 pint) ring mould, and press it down well to firm it in. Cover with foil and leave in a warm place until ready to serve. (For a longer wait, allow the rice to cool, then refrigerate; reheat in a bain-marie at 180°C (350°F) mark 4 for 20–30 minutes or until it feels really hot.)

Turn the rice out on to a round dish and fill the crown with watercress or parsley, or more buttered carrots, celery and leeks. Serve as an accompaniment to duck, chicken or red meats.

THEME 13

SALADS AND DRESSINGS

The British used to be funny about salads. There was a time
when people would mutter apologetically about 'rabbit's food',
as they piled, unlovingly, the limp lettuce leaves, watery
tomatoes, unswallowable hard-boiled eggs and cucumber
chunks into a rather small bowl and set it on the table with
vague murmurings about it being 'healthy' and 'good for you'. A
bottle of euphemistically named salad cream would lurk nearby.
But that's all changed now, and the fact that salads are 'healthy'
and 'good for you' (the very words are a calculated turn-off) is
just a bonus: the main point is that they should look tempting
and taste delicious, made from ingredients bought (or grown)
with care and imagination, tossed generously with lots of
delicious dressing in a huge bowl, and served with a flourish.

WATCHPOINTS

Use plenty of imagination in choosing and using different oils and vinegars (malt is out). The basic recipe gives a fairly thick, creamy dressing (but with no cream), emulsified in the liquidizer to form something getting towards a mayonnaise. Its thickness is a result of the combined activity of the oil, vinegar, mustard, egg and yogurt. Omit the egg and yogurt and you get more of a straight vinaigrette.

Make up a large quantity of dressing once in a while and keep it in the fridge so that each time you want a salad (every day?) you don't have to fiddle about with sticky jars and tablespoons of this and that.

Use imagination also in the ingredients for salads, especially in the leaves department: oak leaf, radicchio, corn salad (lamb's lettuce), chicory, sugarloaf, Chinese leaves, endive, sorrel or young spinach, etc. Wash and dry them in a salad spinner, or put them in a tea-towel, dash out into the garden and whirl them around your head like a dervish. Or, more conveniently, use the bags of mixed, ready washed saladstuffs – increasingly easy to find nowadays.

WATCHPOINTS

Crunchy ingredients like carrots, apples, celery, celeriac, nuts, bacon and cucumber give a bit of texture to a leafy salad, or combined with soft ones like potatoes, beetroot, avocado. Avoid raw onion or garlic in salads, and grill and skin peppers before using them, for improved colour and digestibility.

To avoid the beautiful symmetry of your carefully arranged salad being lost in the tossing, put a good amount of dressing in a large mixing bowl, and dress each different type of ingredient separately. Then arrange them in the serving bowl or dish: no more disturbances necessary, and especially good for things like avocado which tends to get lost and bruised in the mêlée.

BASIC

SALAD DRESSING

Makes about 500 ml (18 fl oz)

salt	5 ml (1 tsp)
pepper, freshly ground	lots
mustard	5 ml (1 tsp)
oil	300 ml ($\frac{1}{2}$ pint)
vinegar	120 ml (4 fl oz)
herbs	lots
honey	5 ml (1 tsp)
natural yogurt (optional)	30 ml (2 tbsp)
egg, raw (optional)	1

Put all the ingredients together in a liquidizer and blend until smooth. Thin down with water or stock if it is too thick for your liking – but don't add more vinegar or oil, as this will disturb the proportions. Used generously on salads every day, this amount should last you about a week, kept in a screwtop jar in the fridge.

VARIATIONS

● Use different salts (herbal, celery or garlic) instead of ordinary salt, and different coloured peppercorns (green, pink or a mixture), always freshly ground.
● Vary the mustards: English, herby, Dijon, Meaux, etc.
● For oils, use a mixture of one of the blander salad oils (soya, sunflower) and one of the characterful ones (olive, walnut, hazelnut, grapeseed, etc.).
● Avoid malt vinegar like the plague, and use any of the many vinegars now available: cider, red or white wine, sherry, fruit, herb, home-made; or use lemon or lime juice, or a proportion of orange juice with the vinegar.
● Vary the herbs throughout the year and to match the salad, from chives through thyme, tarragon, basil, mint, chervil to parsley – and even dried herbs in the winter.
● For an alternative sweetener to honey, use brown or white sugar, or omit it altogether.
● Instead of yogurt, use *fromage blanc*, quark or cottage cheese for the same, nicely sharp, uncloying effect. For a richer result, use cream, cream cheese, blue cheese or other cheeses. Or skip it altogether if you prefer a clear dressing.
● Use only raw egg white (instead of a whole egg) for a very thick, low-cholesterol dressing which can be used instead of mayonnaise. Or use a hard-boiled egg for a slightly different texture.

Further IDEAS

When composing the ingredients for your salad, have in mind a balance of colours:
- green (all sorts of lettuce, corn salad, spinach, sorrel, peppers, beans, broccoli, sprouts, watercress, cress)
- red (radicchio, tomatoes, beetroot, radishes, peppers)
- orange (carrots, tangerines, oranges)
- yellow (peppers, yolks of hard-boiled eggs)
- white (chicory, celery, celeriac, cauliflower, white radish)
Balance textures too:
- crunchy (iceberg lettuce, cucumber, apple, walnuts, peanuts, pomegranate seeds)
- soft (potato, avocado, beetroot, hard-boiled eggs, quail's eggs, Jerusalem artichokes, tinned beans, sweetcorn, cheese cubes)
Match and contrast flavours:
- sharp (lemon/lime/grapefruit segments, sorrel, redcurrants)
- bitter (chicory, endive, fennel, dandelion leaves)
- sweet (apples, tangerines, oranges, grapes, melon) and then make up your own combinations.
Over the top of a dressed salad you might like to scatter:
- crisply fried bacon or nuts
- sautéed slivers of fish, poultry, sweetbreads, mushrooms (cultivated or wild)
- edible flowers (nasturtium, chives, etc.)
- fresh chopped or torn herbs

SOME FAVOURITE COMBINATIONS

Baby beetroot, cubed goat cheese, walnuts and chives
Potatoes and sautéed bacon
Crunchy cooked sprouts, raw mushrooms and sautéed bacon
Melon, tomato and cucumber with mint
Flageolet, kidney and pinto beans with chopped radishes, red onion, avocado and fresh coriander
Celery, apple and walnut
Chicory and tangerine

Spring Salad with Asparagus and Bacon

The first of the asparagus is always rather expensive, so use it sparingly, the tips in the salad and the tails in the dressing.

Serves 6 as a starter

12 asparagus spears, trimmed and cooked
½ quantity (about 300 ml (½ pint)) basic salad dressing (p. 76)
1 shallot, finely chopped
selected interesting saladstuffs (oak-leaf, dandelion leaves, chicory, heart of lettuce, etc.)
100 g (4 oz) Gruyère, cut into fine strips
100 g (4 oz) smoked, rindless streaky bacon, diced
4–5 chive flowers

Cut the top 10 cm (4 inches) off the cooked asparagus spears and set them aside. Put the tail ends in the liquidizer with the dressing and the shallot and blend until smooth. Sieve if necessary.

In a mixing bowl, toss the different saladstuffs separately in the dressing, then arrange them nicely on a large, flat dish. Toss the asparagus spears and the cheese strips also in the dressing and arrange them on top. Fry the bacon dice briefly without any extra fat until crusty and golden and toss them over the salad at the last moment with their fat. Strew the chive flowers over everything and serve at once.

Summer Salad of Marinated Fish

The fish is 'cooked' in the lime juice and served with avocado, red onion (less pungent than ordinary, especially when soaked in cold water) and lime segments.

Serves 6 as a starter

600 g (1¼ lb) assorted fresh fish fillets, e.g. mackerel, whiting, sole, trout, skin removed
juice of 2 limes
salt and pepper
about 150 ml (¼ pint) basic salad dressing (p. 76)
1 avocado, peeled, stoned and cut into 8 segments
½ red onion, sliced wafer-thin and soaked in cold water
1 lime, peeled and cut into segments
2 tomatoes, skinned, seeded and diced
30 ml (2 tbsp) chopped fresh herbs

Cut all the fish into strips about 1 × 3 cm (½ × 1¼ inches), toss in a bowl with the lime juice, salt and pepper and leave to marinate for 15 minutes (longer if you prefer and have the time).

Toss the fish in the dressing in a large mixing bowl and arrange it like the spokes of a wheel on a large round plate. Turn the avocado segments carefully in the dressing and interleave them with the fish pieces. Garnish the salad with the onion, lime segments, diced tomato and herbs.

Autumn Salad with Smoked Chicken and Pears

Choose pinky-brown salads like oak-leaf, lollo rosso and radicchio, mix them with assorted greenery and pear slices and toss over some sautéed smoked chicken at the end.

Serves 6 as a starter

about 450 g (1 lb) assorted pink and green saladstuffs
about 150 ml (¼ pint) basic salad dressing (p. 76) with lots of chives
2 large, ripe pears, peeled, cored and thinly sliced
5 ml (1 tsp) walnut oil
the breast meat from a small smoked chicken, skinned and finely sliced
8 walnut halves
60 ml (4 tbsp) red wine vinegar

Wash and dry the saladstuffs. Put the dressing into a large mixing bowl and toss the pink varieties in it. Shake off excess dressing and arrange them on individual serving plates. Do the same with the green sorts and the pear slices.

Heat the oil in a non-stick pan and fry the chicken slices very briefly, toss them over the salads and dot the walnuts around. Deglaze the pan with the vinegar and pour it over; serve at once.

Winter Warm Salad of Chicory and Fish

A beautiful, star-shaped salad of delicious contrasts: on top of the slightly bitter chicory leaves sits a sweetly dressed warm fish salad, topped with soured cream and lumpfish roe.

Serves 6 as a starter

3 limes or 2 lemons
2 large heads chicory (to give about 30 leaves)
about 150 ml ($\frac{1}{4}$ pint) basic salad dressing (p. 76) made with lime or lemon juice instead of vinegar
450 g (1 lb) mackerel or firm white fish fillets, skinned
salt and pepper
little oil for frying
juice of 2 blood oranges
60–75 ml (4–5 tbsp) soured cream
50 g (2 oz) lumpfish roe
coriander, chervil or parsley sprigs, to garnish

Take long fine strips from the rind of the limes or lemons with a potato peeler or *julienne* knife and simmer for 1 minute in boiling water. Set them aside.

Dip the chicory leaves into the dressing and arrange them, 5 to each individual serving plate, in star formation.

Cut the fish into thin strips and season lightly with salt and pepper. Fry in a non-stick pan with a little oil over high heat for 1–2 minutes until just seized and barely opaque. Distribute the fish among the 6 plates, placing it in a little nest in the centre of the chicory leaves.

Deglaze the pan with the blood orange juice (or substitute red wine vinegar), swirl it around and pour over the fish. Moisten with the remaining dressing, top each salad with a blob of soured cream and a little lumpfish roe. Scatter the reserved blanched lime or lemon peel over the salad and garnish with the herbs.

THEME 14

SHORTCRUST PASTRIES

savoury and sweet for amuse-gueules, *quiches, pies, tart(let)s, wrap-ups and turnovers*

The simplest pastry, shortcrust or *pâte brisée*, has approximately twice as much flour as fat, a little salt, plus the minimum liquid – and the minimum manhandling – possible to bind the whole business together. Perhaps it's all the complicated names and the surrounding mystique that sends even accomplished cooks scurrying to the supermarket shelves for ready-made pastry, so to simplify matters – and encourage you to branch out beyond the bought variety – this chapter thinks in terms of a plain shortcrust as the basic, with other options (more fat, eggs, egg yolks, increased sugar, etc.) coming as variations on the theme. Try varying the flours, fats or liquids, and adding spices and herbs, and you will have something much more original and delicious than anything out of a packet. Once you've mastered plain pastry in all its many variations, you might like to have a go at puff pastry (p. 88).

WATCHPOINTS

Chill all ingredients well, starting with yourself. If you're new to pastry, start with the least quantity of fat and then, as you get braver, work up towards the maximum amount. Many books tell you to start by mixing the fat with the flour until it resembles fine breadcrumbs. Don't. If you overwork it with your hot little hands at this stage you will get porridge, not fine breadcrumbs, and your pastry will be tough; a rough mixing is enough at this stage, as more thorough blending comes later.

Always chill pastry for at least 1 hour to relax the gluten before rolling out. Pastry should be a delicate vehicle for a delicious filling, not a sledge-hammer blow to the palate and waistline, so concentrate on rolling it out very thinly and use the least you can get away with. Chill once more after rolling and shaping, otherwise it will shrink in the baking.

The amount of liquid needed will vary depending on the type of flour, whether you have used the full amount of butter, its consistency, the temperature of the kitchen and other variables. The point is to add the minimum necessary to draw the dough together into a rough ball. Work quickly on the 'smearing' of the pastry (which accomplishes the final mixing of fat with flour and gives a flaky effect) and banish from your head any idea of kneading, which gets the gluten in the flour excited and would make the pastry tough.

SHORTCRUST PASTRY

Makes about 450 g (1 lb)

unsalted butter	125–175 g (4½–6 oz)
plain white flour	250 g (9 oz)
salt	2.5 ml (½ tsp)
iced water	45–60 ml (3–4 tbsp)

Cut or mix the fat into the dry ingredients with knives, a pastry blender or your fingertips. Do not overwork: there will still be some quite large bits of fat in evidence which is as it should be. Add the iced liquid bit by bit, just enough to enable you to press and draw together the mixture into a lump.

Put the dough on a cool work surface, close to you, and using the heel of your hand, push and smear it, bit by messy bit, away from you. Work fast so that it does not soften. You will end up with rather a ragged pile of dough at the other end of the work surface. Scrape it all together with a dough scraper or spatula, form it into a ball again and sprinkle on a dusting of flour.

To increase the flaky effect, halfway towards a puff pastry, give the pastry several sharp karate chops with the side of your hand to flatten it out a bit, fold it in two and repeat the process. Wrap in foil and chill for at least an hour before using.

(Alternatively, cut or mix in the fat with the food processor, add the liquid through the funnel and process a few seconds more, just long enough to bind together the dough; omit the smearing step, bash and fold for the optional flaky effect and chill.)

Flour the board and rolling pin well. Beat the chilled pastry with the pin to get it going in the right direction, then roll it out thinly, always away from you and always rotating the pastry a little to get an even shape and to make sure it's not irrevocably stuck to the board. Cut or shape it as required and chill again before using.

Pastry freezes well, but as it is the rolling, shaping and chilling which takes time, not the initial making of the dough, I think it makes more sense to freeze the ready-shaped or filled dough.

Bake all shortcrust pastries in a preheated 200°C (400°F) mark 6 oven.

Savoury pastry
● Instead of all plain white flour, use up to one-third wholemeal flour, oatmeal, or ground walnuts.
● Instead of all butter, use half butter and half margarine, white vegetable shortening, lard, cream cheese or blue cheese.
● Flavour with fresh herbs (parsley, basil, dill, chives, etc.) or spices (cayenne, garlic powder, allspice, saffron, curry) or grated cheese.
● Instead of iced water, use its equivalent (45–60 ml (3–4 tbsp)) of egg, egg yolks, egg whites, white wine, lemon juice or stock.

Sweet pastry
● Instead of all flour, use up to one-third ground almonds or hazelnuts.
● Add sugar to taste – up to 6 tbsp.
● Instead of all butter, use half butter and half margarine or white vegetable shortening.
● Flavour with spices (nutmeg, cinnamon, allspice) or grated orange or lemon zest.
● Instead of iced water use its equivalent (45–60 ml (3–4 tbsp) of egg, egg yolks, egg whites, white wine, lemon, orange or apple juice.

Savoury pastry: make up basic savoury pastry (or any of the variations) and use as follows:

Spirals: roll out the pastry thinly to a large rectangle and spread with a filling such as:
- cream cheese with herbs
- pesto
- cottage cheese mashed or processed with walnuts, herbs and oil
- smoked fish or sardines mashed or processed with cottage or cream cheese
- yeast extract and cream cheese
- chutney mashed or processed with butter or cream cheese
Roll up like a Swiss roll, slice 1 cm ($\frac{1}{2}$ inch) thick, lay the slices on a greased baking sheet, rest, then bake for about 10 minutes or until golden.

Savoury tartlets: cut out rounds with a scone cutter and lay them in mince pie tins. Fill with something like:
- sautéed bacon, apple and walnuts
- diced fish or shellfish in a light sauce
- duxelles and cream cheese
- chopped cooked chicken, avocado and quark
- chopped sautéed vegetables with egg
- cubes of Camembert and a smoked mussel or oyster, etc.
Wet edges of pastry cases, top with a second round of pastry, pressing to seal, brush with beaten egg and rest. Then bake for about 15 minutes or until golden and crusty.

4-cornered parcels: cut small squares of pastry, put 15 ml (1 tbsp) of filling (same as left, or your own ideas) on each one, bring up the corners and press edges together to make parcels. Place on a greased baking sheet, brush with beaten egg, rest, then bake for 10–15 minutes until golden.

Mini-turnovers: cut out rounds with a small scone cutter, place some filling to one side, wet edges, fold pastry over and press edges together to make turnovers. Paint with beaten egg and bake for 10–15 minutes or until golden.

Quiches: bake the pastry case blind, or lay it over a greased, inverted quiche tin or tartlet tins and press it well against the sides; bake upside down, ease it off the tin(s) when firm and set on a foil-lined baking sheet. Fill shells with:
- any savoury custard (pp. 56–7)
- cooked vegetables, fish, meat in a sauce with eggs
- thick tomato sauce (p. 149) with whole eggs and yolks
- thick cheese sauce with eggs, etc.
Return to the oven for 25–30 minutes or until the filling is set and the pastry firm.
To avoid baking pastry blind for quiches or tarts, paint with any of the following:
- egg white
- mustard
- chutney
- breadcrumbs
Then fill and bake on a well-heated baking sheet, or use only bottom heat if you have this option.

Pies (covered): roll out 2 discs of savoury pastry, any flavour, line a quiche tin with one of them and fill with:
- forcemeat (p. 24)
- leftover cheese cubes, cream and egg
- cooked vegetables, meat, fish in a sauce, etc.
Cover with the other pastry disc, wet edges and seal, make a steam hole and bake until the filling is cooked and the pastry golden.

Wrap-ups: use an eggbound pastry for extra strength and wrap it round a piece of seared meat (fillet of pork, lamb or beef; chicken breast or turkey breast; boned fowl, etc.) or a forcemeat (p. 24); bake at 200°C (400°F) mark 6 until the pastry is golden and the meat cooked.

Sweet pastry

Fruit tarts (large or individual): make up sweet pastry (plain or in any of its variations), bake blind or upside down, fill with pastry cream (p. 139) and cover with:

- strawberries, grapes, bananas, kiwis, raspberries, oranges
- poached apples, peaches, pears, plums, cherries
- canned apricots, lychees, mango slices, guavas, pineapple

Paint the finished tarts with warm apricot or redcurrant jelly; or sprinkle with icing sugar and caramelize briefly under the grill.

Fruit tarts with a cream and egg finish: bake blind or upside down and fill with:

- sautéed, poached or raw apples
- poached pears
- halved, stoned plums, apricots, damsons, greengages
- sliced rhubarb
- blackberries, bilberries, cherries, gooseberries, redcurrants

Pour over sweet custard with added fruit and bake until set and the fruit cooked.

To avoid baking pastry blind for tarts, paint/spread the bottom with any of the following:

- egg white
- breadcrumbs or stale brioche or sponge cake crumbs
- jelly or sieved jam
- ground hazelnuts, almonds or walnuts

Covered tartlets: roll out pastry very thinly, stamp out discs and put them in bun or muffin tins. Fill with mincemeat, cooked or tinned fruit, jam, etc., top with pastry lids, snip holes for steam, brush with milk or egg and bake until golden.

Herby Cylinders with Bacon and Apple

Herby pastry is cut into strips, wound around foil-encased Smartie tubes, baked and filled with a crunchy filling. Fun to make and impossibly fragile to eat.

Makes 8

½ **quantity (about 225 g (8 oz))
basic shortcrust pastry (p. 81)
with egg and herbs**
1 egg, beaten
**30–45 ml (2–3 tbsp) sesame or
poppy seeds**
**100 g (4 oz) thin streaky bacon,
rinded and diced small**
**1 tasty dessert apple, cored and
cubed small**
**45 ml (3 tbsp) *fromage blanc* or
quark**
**30 ml (2 tbsp) finely chopped
walnuts**
salt and pepper
a pinch of cayenne pepper

Make up the pastry as described in the basic recipe on p. 81, using egg instead of iced water and adding chopped fresh herbs. Chill well.

Preheat the oven to 200°C (400°F) mark 6. Roll out the pastry to a very long, thin rectangle about 45 × 24 cm (18 × 12 inches). Trim all the edges. Cut into eight 45 × 3 cm (18 × 1½ inch) strips.

Enclose 4 empty Smartie tubes in foil and grease well. Wind a strip of pastry around each in a spiral motion, overlapping the edges of the strip a little. (Do this in 2 batches, unless you're particularly flush for Smartie tubes.) Brush liberally with beaten egg and place on a greased baking sheet. Sprinkle with sesame or poppy seeds and bake until golden brown and firm. Twist the pastry carefully off the tubes and cool. Make the other 4 cylinders in the same way.

Fry the diced bacon without any extra fat until crisp. Mix with the apple, *fromage blanc* or quark, walnuts and seasonings and poke this mixture with a teaspoon gently down the prepared herby cylinders. Serve on a bed of lettuce leaves.

Mussel Morsels

Little parcels of smoked mussels
and Camembert to go with
drinks.

Makes 12 mouthfuls

½ quantity (about 225 g (8 oz))
basic shortcrust pastry (p. 81),
with cayenne
100 g (4 oz) can smoked mussels,
drained
1 Camembert or Caprice des
Dieux cheese, cut into 12 cubes
1 egg, lightly beaten

Preheat the oven to 200°C (400°F)
mark 6. Roll out the pastry thinly
to a large rectangle and cut into
12 equal squares.

On each square put 2 mussels
and a cube of cheese. Bring up all
4 corners to make a parcel and
pinch the edges together. Glaze
with beaten egg and bake for
10–12 minutes or until piping hot
and golden.

Upside Down Cox's Apple Hearts with Orange Pastry

Well-flavoured apple slices are
tossed in butter and sugar and
baked under a thin layer of
orange pastry.

Serves 6

½ quantity (about 225 g (8 oz))
basic sweet shortcrust pastry
(p. 81) made with a scraping of
orange zest and orange juice
6 Cox's Orange Pippin apples
(about 450 g (1 lb))
juice of ½ lemon
50 g (2 oz) granulated sugar
25 g (1 oz) butter
juice of 1 orange
15–30 ml (1–2 tbsp) Calvados or
orange liqueur
150 ml (¼ pint) single cream

Make up the pastry as described
in the basic recipe on p. 81. Chill
well, then roll out fairly thinly.
Choose heart-shaped or round
tartlet tins, or individual quiche
dishes, and use one of them as a
template to cut out 6 pastry tops.
Put the tops in the fridge on a
baking sheet to firm up.

Peel and core the apples, slice
and mix with the lemon juice and
sugar. Fry briskly in the butter
until just tender but still
characterful. Divide the mixture
among the 6 baking dishes.
Return the pan to the heat,
bubble up the orange juice and
liqueur, whisk in the cream and
allow to reduce a little.

Heat the oven to 200°C (400°F)
mark 6. Spoon the reduced juices
over the apples, top with the
chilled pastry pieces and bake for
10–12 minutes – just long enough
for the pastry to colour lightly.
Unmould the hearts (or tarts)
upside down on to the plates and
serve with ice cream or whipped
cream.

Spinach and Salmon Turnover

With emergency rations from the store cupboard and freezer, plus your own homemade pastry, this makes a rather good supper dish.

Serves 4

½ quantity (about 225 g (8 oz)) basic shortcrust pastry (p. 81) with salmon juice and dill
225 g (8 oz) can salmon
1 onion, finely chopped
25 g (1 oz) butter
300 g (11 oz) frozen spinach
15 ml (1 tbsp) plain white flour
300 ml (½ pint) milk and juice from canned salmon
salt and pepper
freshly grated nutmeg
30 ml (2 tbsp) grated Parmesan
2 eggs

Make up the pastry as described in the basic recipe on p. 81, using some of the juice from the canned salmon as your liquid and flavouring it with dill. Chill well. Put the rest of the salmon juice in a measuring jug.

Soften the onion in the butter without browning. Add the well squeezed out chopped spinach and cook for 5 minutes to evaporate any excess moisture. Stir in the flour and toss over moderate heat for a few minutes to make sure it is well mixed and cooked in.

To the salmon juice in the jug, add enough milk to make 300 ml (½ pint). Add this to the spinach, season with salt, pepper and nutmeg and bring to the boil, stirring. Simmer for about 5 minutes. Remove any itinerant bones or nasties from the salmon, break it up and add to the pan with the cheese and one of the eggs. Check the seasoning and allow to cool.

Roll out the pastry fairly thinly to a rectangle about 30 × 45 cm (12 × 18 inches). Line a baking sheet with non-stick baking paper and lay the pastry on top. Spread the filling over to one side of the pastry, leaving a 2.5 cm (1 inch) border all around. Paint the border with water. Using the baking paper to help you, lift the unspread edge of the pastry up and over the filling to enclose completely. Seal the edges with the side of your finger or a fork, and then fold them up against the turnover for extra anti-leak security.

Decorate with any leftover pastry scraps, paint with the second egg, lightly beaten, and cut two little steam escape holes. (The turnover can be prepared ahead up to this point and refrigerated.)

Heat the oven to 200°C (400°F) mark 6 and bake the turnover for 35–40 minutes or until golden brown. A bowl of soured cream or *fromage blanc* with chopped dill can be served to accompany.

Scalloped Mushroom Tartlets

The pastry is formed on scallop shells, filled with mushrooms and given a lid. Inverted, the ribs of the shells make a nice pattern.

Serves 4 as a main course

½ quantity (about 225 g (8 oz)) basic pastry (p. 81)
8 bacon rashers, rinded and snipped into pieces
1 garlic clove, crushed
250 g (9 oz) mushrooms, chopped
salt and pepper
15 ml (1 tbsp) mixed chopped parsley and chives
60 ml (4 tbsp) chopped walnuts
90 ml (6 tbsp) double cream or *fromage blanc*

Make up the pastry as described in the basic recipe on p. 81. Chill well.

Fry the diced bacon without extra fat until just browned and the fat rendered. Tip off any excess fat and add the garlic. Cook gently until soft but not brown. Add the mushrooms, very little salt and pepper, and the parsley and chives. Cover and cook gently for 10 minutes until the mushroom juices are rendered.

Uncover and cook fast until the juices evaporate. Add the walnuts and stir-fry for a couple of minutes, then add the cream. Bubble up and simmer for a while until thickened. Taste for seasoning and set aside until cold.

Preheat the oven to 200°C (400°F) mark 6. Lightly grease 4 scallop shells (or use individual quiche dishes or ramekins). Roll out the pastry thinly and cut into 4 equal squares about 18 cm (7 inches) each. Lay the pastry squares over the shells, pressing well into the ridges. There will be a generous border of pastry all around. Spoon in the cooled filling. Bring the pastry edges up and over the filling, brush with cold water and press them together to seal into the semblance of a parcel.

Bake for 10–15 minutes or until the pastry is golden and crusty. Remove from the oven, flip them over and return to the oven for a further 5 minutes to finish the cooking and ensure the underside of the pastry is cooked. Serve direct from the shell with good chutney and a salad.

Green Spirals with Walnuts, Rocket and Basil

Savoury pastry is spread with a sort of rocket and basil pesto, rolled up, sliced and baked until golden-brown.

Makes about 30 mouthfuls

½ quantity (about 225 g (8 oz)) basic shortcrust pastry (p. 81)
25 g (1 oz) shelled walnuts or pecans
3 garlic cloves, mashed
a large bunch of rocket leaves
60 ml (4 tbsp) chopped basil
75 ml (5 tbsp) olive oil
juice of 1 lemon
125 g (4½ oz) cottage cheese

Make the pastry as described in the basic recipe on p. 81. Chill well.

Preheat the oven to 200°C (400°F) mark 6. Blend or process together all the remaining ingredients to a smooth, green ointment.

Roll out the pastry to a large, fairly thin sheet about 30 × 40 cm (12 × 16 inches) and spread it with 45–60 ml (3–4 tbsp) of the green paste. Roll it up like a Swiss roll into a bolster 40 cm (16 inches) long and about 3 cm (1½ inches) wide. Cut it into 1 cm (½ inch) slices and lay them on a greased baking sheet. Bake for 10 minutes in the preheated oven until golden and fragrant. Any remaining paste can be used as a dip or as a sauce for spaghetti.

Leek and Smoked Mackerel Upside Down Tart

Remember Tarte Tatin? Here's a savoury version, with a fishy leek filling and the pastry baked on top, so it stays nice and crisp.

Serves 6

3 leeks, about 300 g (11 oz) trimmed weight, sliced finely
25 g (1 oz) butter
salt and pepper
150 ml (¼ pint) water
100 g (4 oz) smoked mackerel fillet
150 ml (¼ pint) double cream
150 g (5 oz) quark
2 eggs
2 egg yolks
¼ quantity (about 100 g (4 oz)) basic shortcrust pastry (p. 81) made with egg white and herbs

Stew the sliced leeks with the butter, seasoning and water for 10 minutes. Raise the heat and cook hard to drive off the moisture. Cool.

Skin the mackerel and remove any bones. Flake the fish into a bowl or food processor, and mix with the cream, quark, eggs, yolks and salt and pepper to taste.

Butter a 22 cm (9 inch) *moule à manquer* or cake tin and lay a disc of greaseproof paper on the bottom. Put in the leeks and pour on the fish mixture. Roll out the pastry to a round the size of the tin and lay it on top. Bake at 200°C (400°F) mark 6 for 30–35 minutes or until the pastry is golden. Slip a knife around the edge, turn out on to a heated serving plate and remove the paper. Serve with a sharp, crunchy salad.

THEME 15

PUFF PASTRIES

for boxes, bases, layers and houses to put things in

Real puff pastry is a miracle of lightness which literally melts in your mouth. An initial rough dough is made from flour, water and very little butter. Later up to the same weight of butter as flour is built into the basic dough, and distributed by a series of rolls and turns. It helps to get plenty of practice (as does the pastry chef who taught me at Le Cerf in Marlenheim, who makes about 30 kg (60 lb) a week), but an expert Swiss baker in one's village, or a dangerously convenient source of Bird's Eye frozen puff pastry sheets, tends to work against this. However, the kick you get from seeing your own home-made sheets billowing about in the oven is undeniable, so here is how.

WATCHPOINTS

The chill factor is as important for puff pastry as for other pastries, so work on a marble or stainless steel surface if possible, chill the water and the butter really well before starting, and give the pastry plenty of chilling all along.

The lemon juice or vinegar counteracts some of the elasticity in the flour; however, it is important not to knead the initial flour/water/butter mixture more than very briefly, or it will become impossibly elastic and jumpy, and hard to roll out. Start with the least amount of butter and graduate later to equal weights of butter and flour, for the lightest, flakiest result.

Roll out puff pastry rather thick (5 mm/¼ inch) if you want a good rise (eg for feuilletés), and trim all around the edges before cutting to shape – an untrimmed edge will rise unevenly.

Roll out puff pastry thinly (2 mm/ ⅛ inch) where a rise is not needed (eg for millefeuilles), and prick all over with a fork to prevent rising. Recycled leftover pastry is ideal for this purpose.

Cut the pastry with an extremely sharp knife or cutter, otherwise you will squash the edges together and prevent them from rising; also, when glazing with egg yolk, do not let the egg dribble down the sides or the pastry will be glued to the baking sheet and likewise prevented from rising. The salt with the egg yolk helps to give an even better colour and the glaze can be done well ahead and the pastry refrigerated. Brush or spray the baking sheets with water (the steam helps to make the pastry rise) but do not grease them – the pastry has enough built-in fat of its own not to stick

BASIC

PUFF PASTRY

Makes about 575 g (1¼ lb)

plain white flour	250 g (9 oz)
salt	2.5 ml (½ tsp)
butter	25 g (1 oz)
iced water	125 ml (4½ fl oz)
vinegar or lemon juice	5 ml (1 tsp)
unsalted butter	175–250 g (6–9 oz)
egg yolk + pinch of salt	

Get everything really cool (including yourself) before you start. In a large mixing bowl, or in the food processor bowl, mix together the flour, salt and the first butter. Add the iced water and vinegar bit by bit to give a rough dough which will just hold together. Do not overwork. Roll it into a ball, cut a deep cross in it and put it, loosely covered, into the fridge for at least 30 minutes.

Beat out the large piece of butter with a rolling pin to about a 10 cm (4 inch) square. Take the dough out of the fridge – where you made the cuts, it should have opened out like four petals of a flower. Extend each of these 'petals' with the palm of your hand, then use a rolling pin to roll them outwards to give the dough the shape of a rough cross. Put the beaten-out butter in the middle, close up the arms of the cross over the top of it to make a parcel, sealing the joins with water, and chill once more for 30 minutes.

Beat the dough out a bit to get it going in the right direction, then roll it out to a rectangle.

Divide it mentally in three equal parts, fold the short edge closest to you towards the middle and the short edge farthest away from you over the top of it, so that you have folded it in three like a business letter. Then give it a turn through 90 degrees so that it looks like an unopened book (one turn). Roll it out again to a rectangle, fold it once more in three, turn and put it to chill again (two turns).

After an hour or so, roll it, fold it and turn it twice more, giving a total of 4 turns. Wrap it in greaseproof paper and chill it until needed. Roll out to the desired thickness, depending on its use (see Beyond the Basics), glaze with beaten egg yolk and chill again – 10 minutes in the freezer if you want to speed things up, anything from 30 minutes to 24 hours in the fridge.

Bake all puff pastries in a preheated 220°C (425°F) mark 7 oven.

Further IDEAS

Feuilletés or *puff pastry containers*:
Roll out pastry 5 mm ($\frac{1}{4}$ inch) thick and cut out:
- triangles
- circles
- scallops
- pear shapes
- tear drops
- fish shapes etc

Put on a dampened baking sheet, glaze with beaten egg yolks, and bake for 10–15 minutes or until golden brown and mightily risen. Cool, split in half horizontally, remove any raw pastry, fill with any of the following and serve at once:
- fish and shellfish in a creamy sauce
- game in a port sauce
- snails in garlic butter
- sweetbreads and/or mushrooms in a creamy sauce
- poached fruit cloaked in a sabayon (p. 133), etc.

Vol-au-vents: cut rings from thickly rolled pastry and bases from thinly rolled – make them mouthful-sized for nibbles, up to pie-sized for tarts. Glaze with beaten egg, superimpose rings on to bases and bake until golden brown. Fillings as above.

Millefeuilles: roll out rather thin – 2 mm ($\frac{1}{8}$ inch). Prick with a fork to prevent rising and bake for 10–15 minutes or until golden brown and dry. Remove, cut strips of the size you wish, and layer with:
- salmon and mushrooms in a light sauce
- a strong cheese sauce lightened with beaten egg whites
- a savoury mousse (p. 52)

or:
- *Crème Chiboust* (p. 139)
- sweetened *fromage blanc* and fruit
- a fruit mousse (p. 124), etc.

Cheese, poppyseed or sesame twists: roll thinly and cut into 10 × 1 cm (4 × $\frac{1}{2}$ inch) strips. Paint with egg, sprinkle with Parmesan, poppy seeds or sesame seeds and twist into barley sugar spirals. Bake until golden brown.

Fish or cheese rolls: roll thinly and cut into strips about 8 cm (3 inches) wide. Make any of the following fillings:
- fish mousseline (p. 40)
- stiff cheese sauce lightened with beaten egg whites
- leftover bits of hard cheese mashed to a paste with cream and chopped walnuts

Form them into sausage shapes down the length of the pastry strips, roll up, seal joins with water, glaze with beaten egg and bake until golden brown. Serve sliced with drinks.

Puff pastry discs (for ice cream, mousses, etc.): roll very thinly, cut out discs 10 cm (4 inches) in diameter, put on a dampened baking sheet, prick all over with a fork and sprinkle with icing sugar. Bake for 10 minutes or until golden and crispy.

Puff Pastry Poissons with Monkfish and Mushrooms

Fish pastry shapes baked and filled with the fish mixture make an elegant first course.

Serves 6 as a first course

575 g (1 lb 4 oz) puff pastry (p. 88)
1 egg yolk beaten with a pinch of salt
100 g (4 oz) bacon, rinded and diced small
25 g (1 oz) butter
1 small onion or shallot, finely chopped
250 g (9 oz) mushrooms, quartered
salt and pepper
juice of ½ lemon
250 g (9 oz) boneless monkfish, cubed
125 ml (4½ fl oz) dry white wine
250 ml (9 fl oz) fish stock
5–10 ml (1–2 tsp) tomato purée
125 ml (4½ fl oz) double cream
15 ml (1 tbsp) each finely chopped parsley and chervil
sprigs of chervil, to garnish

Roll out the pastry 5 mm (¼ inch) thick – do not skimp on the thickness, otherwise the pastry will not rise. Cut out 6 fish shapes, each measuring about 16 cm (6¼ inches) from nose to tail and 11 cm (4¼ inches) wide. (There will be quite a lot of waste: piece together and layer any leftovers, press them into a semblance of order, chill and use as in any of the Further Ideas, p. 89.)

Place the fish pastries on a dampened baking sheet and brush with the beaten egg yolk, taking great care not to let it dribble down the sides. Chill as described on p. 89. Then heat the oven to 220°C (425°F) mark 7 and bake them for about 10 minutes or until nicely golden. Remove them from the oven and carefully split then in half horizontally. Discard any uncooked pastry, and keep the pastry *poissons* warm.

Sweat the bacon in a heavy frying pan until the fat runs. Discard the fat (which would add nothing to the finished dish) and put in the butter. Soften the onion or shallot without browning, add the mushrooms, salt, pepper and some of the lemon juice, cover and sweat for 2–3 minutes. Remove the lid and cook hard to evaporate the juices. Season the monkfish pieces with salt, pepper and lemon juice and add them to the mushrooms. Toss over moderate heat, shaking and stirring them for 2–3 minutes until just cooked and opaque. Lift them out and keep them warm.

Add the wine and the fish stock to the pan and allow to reduce by half. Whisk in the tomato purée and cream and reduce again by half. Check the seasoning, stir in the reserved fish and mushrooms and the herbs.

Spoon some of this filling over the bottom halves of the pastry *poissons*, top with the pastry lid and serve any extra sauce around the edge. Garnish with chervil sprigs.

Tartelettes Flambées

Puff pastry is rolled out very thinly, stamped out in circles, spread with *fromage blanc* or quark and cream, sprinkled with bacon slivers and onion and baked until bubbly. An excellent way to use up leftover pastry.

Makes about 36 mouthfuls to go with drinks

150 g (5 oz) puff pastry (p. 88)

150 g (5 oz) *fromage blanc* or quark

45 ml (3 tbsp) double cream

a pinch of salt

2 egg yolks

50 g (2 oz) smoked streaky bacon, rinded

1 onion

Roll out the puff pastry very thinly and cut out 36 discs about 4 cm (1½ inches) in diameter with a scone cutter or floured glass. Put on a heavy, dampened baking sheet. Mix together the *fromage blanc* or quark, cream, salt and egg yolks and daub a little of this mixture on each of the discs. Cut the bacon in very tiny strips and chop the onion very finely. Scatter them over the top of the pastries and chill until ready to bake (or freeze).

Heat the oven to 220°C (425°F) mark 7 and bake the pastries for about 7 minutes or until golden brown and bubbly – lift them up to make sure that the underside of the pastry is nice and golden. Serve piping hot on a napkin-lined tray.

Ragoût of Game and Mushrooms in a Pear-Shaped Pastry Case

Pear-shaped pastry cases filled with strips of tender game and mushrooms in a buttery port sauce. A lovely autumn starter. Spiced pears, made by simmering peeled pears in red wine, spices, salt, pepper and a pinch of sugar, go nicely with it.

Serves 6 as a starter

250 g (9 oz) puff pastry (p. 88)

1 egg yolk, beaten with a pinch of salt

300 g (11 oz) strips of tender game (venison, pheasant, grouse, hare, wild duck, etc.)

75 g (3 oz) butter

1 shallot, finely chopped

250 g (9 oz) mushrooms (cultivated or wild), sliced

salt and pepper

125 ml (4½ fl oz) port or red wine

125 ml (4½ fl oz) best game stock

5 ml (1 tsp) redcurrant jelly

Roll out the pastry rather thinly to a large rectangle. Cut out 8 pear shapes, each about 11 cm (4½ inches) long and 7.5 cm (3 inches) wide (reassemble scraps as described on p. 90 and keep for another use). Put the pear pastries on a dampened baking sheet, criss-cross 4 of them with the point of a sharp knife, glaze with the salted egg yolk and chill as described on p. 89.

Heat the oven to 220°C (425°F) mark 7 and bake the pastries for about 10 minutes or until golden brown and risen. Put them on heated plates in the turned off oven to keep warm.

Pat the game strips dry. Heat 25 g (1 oz) butter and toss the strips over high heat for 2 minutes only. Remove them and keep warm. Lower the heat and soften the shallot gently without browning. Add the mushrooms, salt and pepper, cover and cook gently until the juices are rendered.

Remove the lid, raise the heat and cook hard until the juices evaporate. Put the mushrooms aside with the meat. Deglaze the pan with the port or wine, stock and redcurrant jelly and allow to reduce by half. Remove from the heat and whisk in the remaining butter. Put the meat and mushrooms back in briefly to marry up the flavours and to heat through.

Spoon a bit of filling on to each of the plain pastries, and sit the criss-crossed one on top, or to one side.

Salmon and Mushroom Millefeuille

Adapted from an idea of Emile Jung's at Le Crocodile, where they do something similar for buffets, thin sheets of freshly baked puff pastry are layered with finely sliced cooked salmon and duxelles. The dish can be served at room temperature, or gently reheated to tepid. A bowl of *fromage blanc* with some chopped chives or dill makes a nice accompaniment.

*Serves 6–8 as a starter,
4 as a main course*

250 g (9 oz) best puff pastry (p. 88)
300 g (11 oz) fillet of salmon
salt and pepper
1 shallot or spring onion, finely chopped
25 g (1 oz) butter
450 g (1 lb) mushrooms, finely chopped
a little lemon juice to taste
30–45 ml (2–3 tbsp) double cream

Roll out the puff pastry as thinly as possible to a large rectangle and trim all the edges. Put it on a dampened baking sheet, prick it all over with a fork to prevent it rising and put it in the fridge or freezer for 10 minutes.

Heat the oven to 220°C (425°F) mark 7 and bake the chilled pastry for about 10 minutes or until golden brown and dry.

Line a heavy baking sheet with buttered foil. Cut the salmon into very thin slices (5 mm ($\frac{1}{4}$ inch)) and lay the slices on the sheet. Season with salt and pepper and bake in the hot oven for 3 minutes only. The salmon should be barely opaque. Remove from the oven and set aside.

Sweat the shallot or spring onion in the butter; add the mushrooms, a squeeze of lemon juice and salt and pepper. Cover and cook for about 5 minutes until the juices render, then raise the heat and cook hard to evaporate the juices. It is important that the mixture is fairly dry. Stir in the cream, cook a bit more to amalgamate and set aside.

Divide the pastry sheet into 3 equal strips. Place one of them on a serving dish, spread it with half the mushrooms and lift half the fish on to it with a fish slice. Follow with a second layer of pastry, more mushrooms and more fish. Finally top with the last piece of pastry. Press any crumbs into the sides. Serve at room temperature, or reheat gently in a 160°C (325°F) mark 3 oven to just tepid.

Marlenheim Fruit Tarts

At Le Cerf in Marlenheim, where the Tartelettes Flambées (p. 91) also come from, they make these delicate, light fruit tarts with whichever fruit is in season and serve them on huge, icing sugar-dusted white plates with cinnamon or vanilla ice cream ovals. *For each person you need:*

puff pastry (p. 88) (count on 25 g (1 oz) per person)
a well-flavoured eating apple (e.g. Cox's)
or 2–3 plums
icing sugar
dots of butter

Roll out the puff pastry very thinly and cut out disc(s) 12 cm (5 inches) in diameter, using a plate or saucer as a guide. Prick all over with a fork. Peel, core and slice the apple VERY thinly, or stone and very thinly slice the plums.

Arrange the fruit on top of the pastry disc, fanning it out and doming it up in the middle. If not to be baked immediately, open-freeze on trays until needed.

About 15 minutes before serving time, preheat the oven to 220°C (425°F) mark 7. Sprinkle the tart lavishly with icing sugar and dot with butter. Bake for 10 minutes or until the pastry is golden and the top caramelized. (If the top is not nicely brown, put briefly under the grill.) Serve each tart on a large plate with whipped cream or real vanilla ice cream.

THEME 16

PHYLLO PASTRIES

for wrap-ups, triangles, pies and rolls

The terms phyllo and strudel tend to be used interchangeably in recipes and on packets of bought pastry, although in fact phyllo, Middle Eastern in origin, is flaky and fragile, while strudel (from central Europe) is a richer, softer variation on the theme, closer to a very fine pasta dough. Both are a sort of primitive puff pastry, the difference being that the butter is brushed on to the prepared pastry sheets, rather than being built in from the start.

Make your own phyllo (or the strudel variation) for a bit of a challenge, or use bought phyllo to create unusual savoury and sweet dishes.

WATCHPOINTS

As with pasta, strong flour gives more body and elasticity to the pastry, but if this is unobtainable, a proportion of fine semolina gives the necessary strength. The amount of water given is only an approximation and will vary depending on the flour you use, the room temperature, humidity, etc. Be prepared to add more flour, or more water, to arrive at a fairly firm, not excessively sticky dough, similar to pasta (p. 66).

Resting the dough after the initial kneading makes it easier to stretch out, by giving the gluten time to relax. Experts stretch the pastry and toss it around their heads with great nonchalance; I find it easier to start by rolling the dough out with a rolling pin, followed by a careful stretching out over the backs of my hands until it is a huge, nearly transparent sheet. When narrow sheets will do, the pasta machine produces excellent results.

BASIC

PHYLLO PASTRY

Makes about 400 g (14 oz),
enough for 2 dishes for 4–6

plain white flour	200 g (7 oz)
fine semolina	50 g (2 oz)
salt	a pinch
warm water	about 100 ml (4 fl oz)
oil	60 ml (4 tbsp)

Put the flour, semolina and salt into a food processor or mixing bowl. Mix together the water and oil and add it to the flour. Process or mix for 2–3 minutes to a sleek, smooth, satiny dough which does not stick to your hands. Add sprinkles of extra water, or extra flour as necessary to achieve this. Cover with a tea-towel and leave to rest for at least 1 hour.

Flour a tea-towel lavishly. Cut the dough in half and work with half at a time. Roll it out on the floured tea-towel with a rolling pin until it is as thin as you can get it; then lift it on to the backs of your hands and carefully stretch it, moving your hands slowly apart. Work all around the dough, moving your hands apart each time you work on a new patch, until it is evenly stretched to at least the size of the tea-towel. If you've made any holes, brush the edges of them with a little water and press them together again. Cut off the clumsy, thick edges, brush the dough with flour and leave in a cool place to dry out a little. It must not be sticky, but must still be supple, otherwise it will break when you use it.

Brush phyllo sheets with a film of melted butter or oil and use immediately; or brush with flour, lay greaseproof paper over the top of them, roll up rather carefully and freeze. Thaw in the fridge, then bring to room temperature before using, otherwise they will be very brittle and hard to work with. Unused fresh or thawed phyllo can be rolled up and put in a sealed polythene bag.

Bake all phyllo pastries in a preheated 200°C (400°F) mark 6 oven.

93

- If strong white flour is available, use 250 g (9 oz) instead of plain flour and semolina.
- Use flavoured oils for the pastry (olive, walnut, hazelnut, etc.), or flavour with spices (cayenne, nutmeg, cinnamon, etc.).
- *Strudel pastry*: substitute 1 egg or 2 yolks for the oil.

Phyllo triangles: cut 20 × 10 cm (8 × 4 inch) strips of pastry, brush with melted butter, fold in half lengthways and brush again with butter. Filling ideas include:

- cooked, well squeezed out spinach with quark or ricotta, beaten egg and Parmesan
- duxelles (chopped sautéed mushrooms), cream and egg
- sweetcorn and cream cheese
- forcemeat (p. 24).

To shape the triangles, put a teaspoon of filling at the end of the pastry strip nearest you and fold it over and over in triangles all the way up the length of the strip. Brush again with melted butter. Bake immediately at 200°C (400°F) mark 6 for about 20 minutes or open freeze and put in a bag later. Bake from frozen, increasing the baking time a little.

Phyllo rolls: cut pieces of pastry about 20 cm (8 inches) square, brush with melted butter, and use the same fillings as above (30–45 ml (2–3 tbsp)), or:

- a fillet of smoked trout, mackerel or kipper
- a roll of ham wrapped around a nugget of Boursin
- several lightly cooked asparagus spears
- lightly sautéed chicken breast and chutney

To shape the rolls, put the filling at the end of the pastry strip nearest you, fold in a border of 2.5 cm (1 inch) towards the middle and roll up. Brush with melted butter and bake for 10 minutes or until golden and crispy.

Phyllo spirals: use the same fillings as for triangles, but be very mean with the filling. Roll up not more than a finger thick, coil them round in a spiral, brush

with butter and bake as before.

Phyllo-topped pies: make a meat or fish pie in the usual way, and top with several layers of buttered phyllo instead of shortcrust pastry or mashed potato. Bake for about 20 minutes or until golden and crisp.

Phyllo pastry shells: (instead of puff or shortcrust): butter 4 sheets of phyllo, lay them over an upturned container (a scallop shell, small round cast-iron dish, tartlet tin, etc.). Tuck or pleat as necessary to give a good shape. Bake for 8–10 minutes or until golden brown and crisp. Lift out and fill with fish, shellfish, mushrooms, sweetbreads in a sauce; or fruit with pastry cream, yogurt, sabayon, etc.

Phyllo fruit parcels: brush 2 large squares of pastry with melted butter and layer them together, top with a skinned peach or peeled, poached pear or apple, bring the edges of pastry up to make a purse-like parcel. Tie the neck loosely with string, brush with more butter and bake in a 200°C (400°F) mark 6 oven until golden brown and crisp. Remove the string before serving.

Strudel, sweet or savoury: make the strudel variation (p. 94), roll and stretch out half of it to the size of a tea-towel. Brush all over with melted butter, sprinkle two-thirds of the surface with breadcrumbs and fill with:

- finely chopped apples and sultanas with cinnamon sugar
- chopped cooked vegetables

Roll up fairly tightly, starting from the end with the filling on it. Brush with more melted butter and bake until golden and crispy: 20–30 minutes.

Greek Lamb Pie with Phyllo Pastry

A delicious and unusual dish for a buffet lunch, this can be prepared well ahead and refrigerated.

Serves 12

2 kg (4½ lb) trimmed shoulder or
leg of lamb, boned weight
olive oil
2 medium onions, finely chopped
2 garlic cloves, mashed
salt and pepper
a pinch of sugar
30 ml (2 tbsp) plain white flour
500 ml (18 fl oz) lamb or beef stock
4–5 large tomatoes, about 450 g
(1 lb), peeled and chopped, or a
400 g (14 oz) can peeled tomatoes
a 1 cm (½ inch) piece of cinnamon
stick
lots of chopped parsley and mint
4–6 eggs, lightly beaten
60–75 ml (4–5 tbsp) grated
Parmesan (optional)
a handful of pine nuts or black
olives
12 sheets basic phyllo pastry
dough (p. 93)

Cut the lamb into fairly small cubes and dry them well: soggy meat will not brown. In a large casserole sear the meat in several batches in 30 ml (2 tbsp) olive oil until lightly browned. Do not crowd the pan. Remove as ready to a side dish and continue with the rest. In the same fat, soften the onions and garlic without browning.

Return the lamb to the casserole and toss with the salt, pepper, sugar and flour until evenly coated. Pour on the stock, add the tomatoes and cinnamon, cover and cook at a very gentle simmer on top of the stove, or if you prefer in a 150°C (300°F) mark 2 oven for about 1½ hours or until tender. (The stew can be prepared ahead up to this stage and refrigerated for a couple of days.)

Reheat the stew gently, without boiling, then stir in the parsley and mint, the eggs, Parmesan and pine nuts or olives if used. Check the seasoning.

Lightly brush a large roasting tin (about 40 × 28 × 8 cm (16 × 11 × 3 inches) with some olive oil, then put one sheet of pastry in the bottom of the tin. Brush this with oil and layer 5 of the remaining pastry sheets on top, brushing each one with oil. Spoon in the filling and repeat the oiling process with the remaining 6 sheets of pastry. Brush finally with oil, trim the edges to leave 5 cm (2 inch) border all around, and fold or tuck this border snugly inside the tin. (The pie can be prepared ahead up to this point, covered with foil and kept in a cool place.)

Sprinkle or spray the pie with water to prevent the pastry from curling up and bake in a 200°C (400°F) mark 6 oven for 30–40 minutes or until the top is crisp, flaky and golden. Let it rest a little before cutting – it will keep happily in the turned off oven for at least an hour.

Phyllo Fish Rolls with Lemon and Chive Butter Sauce

A creamy mousseline of white fish is flecked with pieces of pink salmon fillet, rolled up in finest phyllo and baked golden.

Serves 12 as a starter,
6 as a light main course

200 g (7 oz) salmon fillet, skinned and cubed
salt and pepper
juice of 1 lemon
30 ml (2 tbsp) cognac or armagnac
400 g (14 oz) fresh white fish fillets such as whiting, monkfish, pike, well-chilled
a pinch of allspice
2 eggs
250 ml (9 fl oz) double cream
12 sheets basic phyllo pastry dough (p. 93) each about 18 cm (7 inches) square
melted butter
1 shallot, finely chopped
125 ml (4½ fl oz) dry white wine
250 ml (9 fl oz) fish stock
50 g (2 oz) butter
15 ml (1 tbsp) chopped chives

Marinate the salmon cubes in the salt, pepper, half the lemon juice and half the cognac or armagnac.

Purée the chilled white fish with 5 ml (1 tsp) salt, the allspice, eggs and the remaining cognac or armagnac in the food processor or blender until smooth, then work in the cream in short bursts until amalgamated. Do not overblend or it may separate. Stir in the salmon cubes and chill again.

Heat the oven to 200°C (400°F) mark 6 . Lay out the phyllo sheets stacked one on top of the other. Brush the top one with melted butter, fold it in half and brush again with butter. Put about 30 ml (2 tbsp) of the fish filling at the end, turn in the sides a little and roll it up like a cigar. Repeat the procedure with the remaining sheets. Put them on a greased baking sheet and bake for 10–15 minutes or until golden.

Boil together the shallot and wine until reduced to a tablespoon. Add the fish stock and reduce by half. Remove from the heat and whisk in the butter in bits. Stir in the remaining lemon juice and the chives, check the seasoning and serve a little sauce with each roll.

Mushroom Strudel

A rich strudel pastry is filled with oyster mushrooms, quark and walnuts for a bit of crunch, and served with a sorrel sauce.

Serves 4 as a starter or 2 as a supper dish

⅔ quantity (about 250 g (9 oz)) strudel pastry dough (p. 94)
250 g (9 oz) oyster or other mushrooms, finely chopped
1 shallot, finely chopped
25 g (1 oz) butter
chopped fresh herbs to taste
125 g (4½ oz) semi-skimmed quark
60–75 ml (4–5 tbsp) chopped walnuts
salt and pepper
melted butter
sesame seeds

SAUCE
a handful of sorrel leaves (about 100 g (4 oz))
200 ml (7 fl oz) vegetable or chicken stock
salt and pepper
60 ml (4 tbsp) double cream
green food colouring (optional)

Roll and stretch out the pastry as instructed on p. 93 and leave to dry out a little while you make the filling. Stew the mushrooms and shallot gently in the butter until the juices render. Then raise the heat and cook uncovered to evaporate the juices. Add chopped fresh herbs to taste, and stir in the quark and walnuts. Check the seasoning.

Brush the pastry sheet with melted butter and fold it over in half. Brush again, and spread the mushroom filling over two-thirds of the surface. Roll it up fairly firmly, starting at the end where there's some filling. Brush finally with melted butter and sprinkle on the sesame seeds. Heat the oven to 200°C (400°F) mark 6 and bake for about 20 minutes or until golden and crispy.

Meanwhile, strip the central ribs from the sorrel leaves and discard. Put the trimmed sorrel in the liquidizer. Reduce the stock by half by fast boiling, cool a little, then pour on to the sorrel and blend until smooth. Return to the pan, add cream and a little food colouring, if a heightened colour is wanted. Season to taste. Boil briefly and serve with the strudel.

A loving variation
on Tarte Tatin is this Upside Down Cox's
Apple Heart with Orange Pastry
(page 84)

*L*ight and *flaky* Puff
Pastry Poisson with Monkfish and Mushrooms
advertises its fishy contents most attractively
(page 90)

*L*ittle *parcels bursting*
with flavour, Phyllo-Wrapped Chicken Breasts
with a Sharp Green Sauce also contain avocado
and cheese (page 97)

*B*lackberry and Quark
Choux Poppadums are an adventurous occidental
dessert of crumbly pastry sandwiches with a
luscious filling (page 102)

Phyllo-wrapped Chicken Breasts with a Sharp Green Sauce

Chicken breasts are seared, split and filled with Mozzarella, topped with a quartered avocado, baked in phyllo and served with a sharp yogurt and parsley sauce.

Serves 4

8 chicken breasts, each about 75 g (3 oz)
salt and pepper
juice of 1 lemon
50 g (2 oz) butter
150 g (5 oz) Mozzarella, cut into 8 slices
2 avocados, quartered
8 sheets basic phyllo pastry dough (p. 93), each about 18 × 25 cm (7 × 10 inches) or 16 sheets bought
30–45 ml (2–3 tbsp) ground almonds

Season the chicken breasts with salt, pepper and lemon juice and sear them briefly in a little of the butter until lightly golden: about 3 minutes each side. Remove and let them cool a little. (Melt the rest of the butter in the same pan for brushing on the phyllo.)

With a sharp knife, cut a slit down the length of each chicken breast to form a pocket and put the Mozzarella inside. Season the avocado quarters and give them a squeeze of lemon juice too; press them down on top of the chicken to lodge them firmly.

Keep the phyllo sheets in a stack so they don't dry out. Brush the top sheet (or two, if using the finer bought pastry) with melted butter, put a chicken breast at the narrow end nearest you, turn in the edges and roll it up to form a bolster. Brush again with melted butter, sprinkle with ground almonds and put on a greased baking sheet. Continue with the rest of the chicken and phyllo. Keep the packets in the fridge if you are not ready to bake them yet.

Heat the oven to 200°C (400°F) mark 6 and bake the rolls for 15 minutes or until golden and hot.

SAUCE
10 parsley sprigs
50 g (2 oz) butter, softened
150 ml ($\frac{1}{4}$ pint) natural yogurt
1 egg
5 ml (1 tsp) cornflour
salt and pepper
150 ml ($\frac{1}{4}$ pint) well-reduced chicken stock

Liquidize together all the ingredients for the sauce until quite smooth. Whisk over moderate heat until light, frothy and thoroughly hot but NOT boiling. Serve at once with the phyllo rolls.

CHOUX PASTRIES

for savoury puffs, gnocchi, gougères, pie toppings and tarts

This is one of the most amusing sorts of pastry to make, not least because although it's simply a very thick white sauce with added eggs to give it a bit of propulsion, people tend to be inordinately impressed by it. While you're at it, you might as well make a good batch, and then use it in a number of different ways: instead of sticking to the conventional, smug little puffed up profiteroles, you could spread the mixture out flat to make a cross between a poppadum and *millefeuilles*, or branch out into more interesting variations, such as gnocchi. Or you can pipe choux over the top of a piece of fish or meat, or a pie, for something between a potato topping and a conventional pastry.

W A T C H P O I N T S

For choux pastry to succeed, it must be firm and glossy, not running about the place in an undisciplined sort of way – hence the apparently vague '3–4 eggs' in the ingredients for the basic recipe here. Add the first 3 eggs to the mixture, but whisk the final one in a cup and add only gradually, keeping the pastry stiff enough to hold its shape on a spoon. In an emergency, beat in sprinkles of flour through a sifter to give the necessarily fine upstanding texture.

Choux buns and profiteroles are nicest freshly baked, but the pastry does not have to be baked immediately; it will keep in the fridge for a day or two and still perform as required, or it can be frozen, ready-shaped on to non-stick baking paper for baking straight from the freezer.

B A S I C

CHOUX PASTRY

Makes about 700 g (1½ lb)

water	250 ml (9 fl oz)
butter	75 g (3 oz)
salt	a pinch
plain white flour, sifted	150 g (5 oz)
eggs	3–4

Place the water, butter and salt in a medium-sized saucepan and bring to a bubbling boil. Remove from the heat and add all the sifted flour at once. Mix until the splodges of white disappear, then return to the heat and stir for a minute or so to cook the flour and drive off any excess moisture. The mixture should form a very thick paste and there will be a slight film over the bottom of the pan.

Turn it into a food processor or electric mixer bowl and allow to cool a little. Add the first 3 eggs one by one and process or beat well; mix up the fourth egg in a cup and add it gradually, keeping the mixture very stiff. (Any surplus egg can be used to glaze the pastry before baking, or added to fillings.) Continue beating the mixture until stiff and shiny – about 2 minutes.

To shape choux buns (or profiteroles), line a heavy baking sheet with non-stick baking paper and spoon or pipe out the pastry into blobs (tiny for appetizers, larger for puffs (savoury) and profs (sweet)), well spaced apart. Use any leftover egg to paint the tops. Bake all choux pastry at 200°C (400°F) mark 6. Allow 20–25 minutes for choux buns until well risen and nicely golden and firm. Resist the temptation to remove choux too soon: if it is still on the pale side, it will collapse in a heap on exit.

When ready, puncture with a skewer to release air and, return to the turned off oven to dry out. Or keep the raw pastry in the fridge, covered with clingfilm, for a day or two for later use as suggested. Or freeze, either in a lump, or ready to bake: shape the puffs on to a tray lined with non-stick baking paper and open freeze them; then tip them into a bag once frozen hard and bake from frozen, increasing the baking time by a few minutes.

● *Savoury puffs*: use stock as your liquid and add interesting flavourings such as cayenne, garlic granules, dehydrated onion, cubes of cheese or herbs to the basic pastry. Fill with cream cheese and chutney, creamed shellfish, poultry or game, etc.
● *Sweet puffs (profiteroles)*: add a little sugar or honey if wished, and flavour with a little grated orange or lemon zest, ground nuts or praline. Shape and bake as above. Fill with ice cream (especially lemon or hazelnut), fresh fruit sorbet (for an even lighter effect) or pastry cream; with whipped cream or egg whites (p. 139), etc.

Savoury gougère(s): grease a shallow, ovenproof dish or individual dishes or shells. Pipe or spread the pastry in a ring around the base of the dish(es). Fill with creamed shellfish, mushrooms, sweetbreads, etc. or raid the fridge for interesting and presentable leftovers (meat, cheese, mushrooms, vegetables) and sauces. Bake for 30–35 minutes (for a large one) or 20–25 minutes (for individuals).

Toppings and casings: pipe little blobs or a lattice of choux pastry on top of meat or fish pies instead of mashed potato or shortcrust. Or use to cloak a chicken breast or piece of fish. Bake as usual.

Gnocchi: add to the choux pastry its own weight in stiff mashed potato, form egg shapes and poach in barely simmering water for 3–4 minutes. Put in a greased gratin dish, sprinkle with cheese and butter and bake at 200°C (400°F) mark 6 until golden.

Choux blinis: spread dollops of the same mixture on a greased baking sheet and bake at 200°C (400°F) mark 6 for 10–15 minutes or until golden and firm. Serve with smoked fish, sour cream and lemon wedges. Or top with a poached egg, sliced ham or cheese.

Sweet gougère(s): pipe or spread the sweet choux pastry as above and bake until firm and well risen; fill the hole with poached or fresh fruit, sitting on a bed of pastry cream, or covered with a fresh fruit yogurt.

Ice cream bases: spread the pastry out very thinly into discs on non-stick paper and bake as usual until golden and crispy; dredge with icing sugar and serve with ice cream.

Walnut and Cheese Gougères with Bacon and Mushroom Filling

Make these small (teacup saucer size) for an informal first course, or a large one for supper for the family.

Serves 4–6

½ **quantity (about 350 g (12 oz)) basic choux pastry (p. 98)**
45 ml (3 tbsp) finely chopped walnuts
30 ml (2 tbsp) grated Parmesan
6 rashers bacon, rinded and snipped into pieces
1 shallot, finely chopped
250 g (9 oz) mushrooms, sliced
2 celery sticks, chopped
45–60 ml (3–4 tbsp) single or double cream
salt and pepper
15 ml (1 tbsp) finely chopped chives

Make up the choux pastry as described in the basic recipe on p. 98, adding the walnuts and Parmesan after the eggs. Set aside. Fry the bacon snippets gently in a heavy pan until the fat runs. Add the shallot, mushrooms and celery, cover and cook until the mushroom juices are rendered. Raise the heat and cook until the juices evaporate and the celery is crisp-tender. Stir in the cream to bind the mixture and season to taste. Bubble up and stir in the chives.

Lightly grease 4–6 individual 10 cm (4 inch) ovenproof dishes (or a 23 cm (9 inch)) quiche tin or other dish). Pipe or spread the pastry around the edge and fill the hole with the bacon mixture. Bake in a 200°C (400°F) mark 6 oven for about 25 minutes (individuals) until well risen and golden (a bit more for a big one).

Basil Gnocchi

Gnocchi can be made on a semolina base, or as here on a choux pastry base with instant mashed potatoes, made up with rather less liquid than the packet stipulates to keep them very stiff. They make the perfect foil, fluffy and light, for rich, warming stews on winter days.

Serves 4 as an accompaniment

½ **quantity (about 350 g (12 oz)) tepid basic choux pastry (p. 98)**
300 g (11 oz) stiff mashed potatoes
salt and pepper to taste
30 ml (2 tbsp) chopped basil
30 ml (2 tbsp) grated Parmesan
melted butter

Make up the choux pastry as described in the basic recipe on p. 98 and mix with the stiff mashed potatoes – do not process or the potatoes will turn to glue. Season to taste with salt and pepper. Add the basil and Parmesan.

Bring a large, shallow pan of water to a gentle simmer. Using 2 wetted spoons, form egg-shaped gnocchi and slide them into the pan without crowding – you will have to do at least 2 batches, and should get 18–20 gnocchi out of this quantity. They will float to the top and roll over. Cook for about 5 minutes in all. Lift them out with a slotted spoon and put them in a large greased ovenproof dish which will take all the prepared gnocchi in one layer. Poach the rest in the same way. (They can be prepared ahead up to this stage and refrigerated in the ovenproof dish.)

Heat the oven to 200°C (400°F) mark 6. Drizzle a little melted butter (or juice from a stew or roast) over the top of the gnocchi and bake them for about 10 minutes, or until golden and sizzling hot.

Orange Choux Shells with Ice Cream and Chocolate Sauce

Just a few twists to the basic model make this into a bit more than the run-of-the-mill profiteroles with chocolate sauce.

Makes about 16 filled shells

½ **quantity (about 350 g (12 oz)) basic choux pastry (p. 98), grated zest of 1 orange**
5 ml (1 tsp) orange-flower water
450 ml (¾ pint) orange or lemon ice cream or sorbet
30–45 ml (2–3 tbsp) praline (p. 153)

SAUCE
150 g (5 oz) best-quality plain chocolate
250 ml (9 fl oz) water
100 g (4 oz) sugar
30 ml (2 tbsp) orange liqueur
juice of 1 orange

Make up the choux pastry as described in the basic recipe on p. 98, and add the grated zest and the orange flower water as well.

Put tablespoons of the pastry on a wetted baking sheet and flatten them into rounds with the back of a wet spoon. Make tracings with a fork to simulate the ribs of a shell. Bake as described on p. 98, remove from the oven when cooked through, cut open, leaving a hinge, and scoop out any soft middles – the orange juice tends to give a rather softer pastry than usual. Return the shells to the oven to dry out.

Cool on a rack, then open and fill each one with a scoop of ice cream, making them look like half-open cockle shells. Put in the freezer until needed.

For the sauce, melt the chocolate in the water with the sugar and simmer steadily until thick and syrupy – about 10 minutes. Stir in the orange liqueur and juice and serve warm with the choux shells (removed from the freezer shortly before serving), sprinkled with the praline.

Blackberry and Quark Choux Poppadums

The basic pastry is spread very thinly into discs, baked crisp and sandwiched with fruit and quark – they set out to be a sort of choux *millefeuilles*, but were aptly christened poppadums by a visiting guinea pig. Lemon or lime ice cream could be used instead of the cream and quark filling.

Serves 6

½ quantity (about 350 g (12 oz))
basic choux pastry (p. 98)
400 g (14 oz) blackberries or other soft fruit
sugar to taste
200 ml (7 fl oz) whipping cream
100 g (4 oz) quark
30–45 ml (2–3 tbsp) crème de cassis
mint sprigs

Draw twelve 11 cm (4½ inch) diameter circles on non-stick baking paper, as many as you can fit on your baking sheet. Preheat the oven to 200°C (400°F) mark 6. Make up the choux pastry as described in the basic recipe on p. 98 and put about 15 ml (1 tbsp) into each of the circumscribed shapes, using the back of the spoon to spread it about very thinly. You will probably need to do 2 batches of 6, unless you have a huge oven and/or can cook on several levels. Bake for about 10 minutes or until lightly golden, slightly puffed up and crispy.

Use half the blackberries to make a coulis: cook them very briefly with a little sugar until the juice runs, then liquidize or process them and push through a sieve. Slacken if necessary with a little water to give a light coating consistency.

Whip the cream until it stands in soft peaks, stir in the quark and sweeten to taste. Spread a little pool of blackberry coulis on to each serving plate, put a choux 'poppadum' on top, add some whipped cream and quark and some blackberries, sprinkle with the crème de cassis, follow with more cream/quark and top with a second poppadum. Decorate with spare blackberries and a mint sprig.

RAISED BREADS

for loaves, buns, baps, pitta and pizza

Your kitchen may be regularly filled with tempting smells and the bustle of living organisms (some of them to do with breadmaking); on the other hand, the very idea of yeast heaving around the place may make you nervous. Whether you're lucky enough to live in a country where the variety and quality of breads is sensational, or whether you're forced into breadmaking out of necessity, getting to grips with dough is one of the most creative, therapeutic and satisfying branches of cookery that exists.

Once you've mastered the dough, it's fun to discover that what you thought was only for bread can also be made into baps, pitta, pizza, or wrapped interestingly around a home-made sausage or pâté mixture. Afterwards you can try out the rich doughs (p. 113) and their variations.

W A T C H P O I N T S

450 g (1 lb) flour gives a nicely manageable quantity of dough, easily kneadable by hand or by machine, giving 1 large or 2 small loaves, or 16 rolls. For a bigger batch (or if you want to make bread and one of its variations), double everything but the yeast, which stays the same.

If, as some insist, good bread can only be made from 'strong' flour milled from hard wheat, how then to account for the wonder of Swiss bread, made largely from European-grown, soft wheat flours? And how to explain the awfulness of most English bread, which uses a high proportion of imported hard wheat flour? The process counts for more than the raw materials and you can make a good loaf out of many different sorts of flour in different proportions and combinations (see Variations) if you follow the instructions given here. Brown and white bread are equally nutritious and not all of the extravagant claims made on fibre's behalf are proven, so concentrate on making well-risen, tasty bread that you and your family actually enjoy eating.

Rye flour is a bit low in the gluten needed to make the bread rise, and oatmeal, cornmeal, soya, barley, potato flour, etc. have no gluten but give interesting flavours, added in moderation (see Variations).

The amount of salt recommended presupposes that you eat bread mainly unbuttered and as a complement/mopper for savoury dishes. If you regularly plaster your bread with salted butter, you may want to reduce the salt.

Instant-blending dried yeast is a bit slower to work than fresh, but gets there in the end. Contrary to popular belief (a tip from Monsieur Marchand, my friendly baker over the border in Alsace), it is not necessary to dissolve fresh yeast beforehand: simply crumble it into the flour like the instant dried variety. Avoid the little grey granules, which are a bore to dissolve and require sugar to get them going, undesirable in bread.

It's not only unnecessary to heat the liquid, but also risky: you can make it too hot and kill off the yeast prematurely. The quantity of liquid you use can vary, depending on your flour, kitchen temperature and humidity, how much you knead it, and other variables. The trick is to know what you're after: a sleek, supple, springy ball of dough which does not stick to your hands and which feels as though it has a life of its own. Good kneading distributes the yeast and exercises the gluten, the element in flour which gives dough its elasticity and bread its structure.

Two rises are essential, one in the bowl and another in the shaped state; three are better still (especially for free-formed loaves and rolls). Don't worry about how long it takes for the dough to rise, which may be anything from 1–3 hours, depending on the temperature at which it is working, the proportion of yeast it contains and other factors. The important thing is volume: the dough must double in bulk. The slower the rise, the better the flavour, which even includes allowing one rise in the fridge.

Black tins give a better all-round crust than bright shiny or glass ones. Oil tins before and after use; don't ever wash them or your bread will stick and the tins will rust. Or use non-stick loaf tins.

Put risen, shaped dough into a cold oven, then switch it to the required heat. The gradual increase in temperature gives it a useful final boost until full heat is reached and the yeast (no longer needed) is killed off. Spraying the loaf once or twice with water (use a plant sprayer) when the oven is really hot gives an approximation of what goes on inside bakers' ovens as well as a good crust.

If you don't want to use some or all of the dough immediately, knock it down after the first rise and freeze it, weighted down, before it has the chance to perform again. Freezing seems to deal dough something of a cruel blow: it seldom recovers enough strength to make a well-risen loaf, but will be fine for pizza or for wrapping around meat or a sausage. Freshly baked loaves seldom have the chance to get as far as the freezer, but they do say they freeze well, except for crusty varieties whose crust crumbles on thawing.

BASIC

BREAD DOUGH

Makes about 1 kg (2 lb 2 oz), enough for 1 large or 2 small loaves, or 16 rolls

flour	450 g (1 lb)
salt	10 ml (2 tsp)
instant-blending dried yeast	1 sachet 7 g ($\frac{1}{4}$ oz)
or fresh yeast	20 g ($\frac{3}{4}$ oz)
water	about 300 ml ($\frac{1}{2}$ pint)
oil	30 ml (2 tbsp)

Use an electric mixer with a dough hook if you have one; otherwise hands, plenty of elbow grease and good tummy muscles. In a large bowl mix together the flour and salt. Sprinkle or crumble the yeast over the mixture and work it in with an electric mixer or with your fingertips. Add the water and the oil and see what that gives you: if the mixture is too dry and flaky to come together at all into a dough, add more water by droplets until it does. If too slack and sloppy, work in sprinkles of flour, until it tightens up enough for you to be able to knead it without too much mess. It's easier to add too much water and then adjust with flour, than to start with too tight a dough in the first place.

Turn it out and knead for at least 10 minutes by hand, or leave in the bowl and knead for 5 minutes with the mixer and dough hook, to a firm, springy ball which does not stick excessively to your hands: add sprinkles of flour as necessary.

Oil the mixing bowl and return the dough to it. Cover it with a damp cloth and leave it alone for as long as it takes to double in bulk (1–3 hours). Knock it back and EITHER allow it a second rise in the bowl (for a finer-textured loaf), at room temperature (1–2 hours) or in the fridge (3–4 hours, or leave it overnight). OR shape it after only one rise.

Grease a 1.4 kg (3 lb) loaf tin (or 2 × 700 g (1½ lb) tins). Flatten the dough out to a rectangle the length of the tin and about 3 times its width. Fold it over into 3 as if folding a business letter, press the seams well together, then roll it firmly round and round to form a bolster which will fit snugly inside the tin(s). Place it in, seam side down, sprinkle or spray with water and leave to rise until it reaches the top of the tin(s) (at least another 30 minutes).

Put all breads (except pitta, pizza and turnovers (see pp. 106, 107 and 108)), into a cold oven, set the temperature to 200°C (400°F) mark 6 and bake for 25–30 minutes, or until golden brown and hollow-sounding when tapped.

VARIATIONS

● For flour, use plain white, or a combination of white and any of the following:
wholemeal (not more than ⅓ of total flour used)

rye
oatmeal
soya   (not more than
potato   ¼ of total flour used)
cornmeal

● Use celery, garlic or herbal salt for a change from plain salt.
● Add to the dry ingredients:
fresh or dried herbs
garlic powder or dehydrated onion flakes
spices (ground or whole)
grated Parmesan
● Instead of water, use in addition to a proportion of beer, milk (fresh or soured), buttermilk or yogurt. The acidity of beer and sour milk gives a particularly good rise and flavour.
● Substitute 25 g (1 oz) butter, margarine, lard or peanut butter for the oil.

Loaf finishes (instead of water):
● egg yolk with water (golden shiny crust)
● egg yolk with milk or thin cream (softer, golden, shiny crust)
● egg white (superbly crunchy crust)
● milk (soft crust)
● Add any of the following optional extras, either to the flours before making the dough, or sprinkled on top after shaping and spraying/glazing:
sesame, poppy, cumin, fennel or linseeds
coarse oatmeal
cracked wheat
chopped walnuts

Some favourite flour/liquid combinations:

Rich brown
350 g (12 oz) plain white + 150 g (5 oz) wholemeal flour
300 ml (½ pint) canned evaporated milk

Oatmeal
400 g (14 oz) plain white + 100 g (4 oz) wholemeal flour + 50 g (2 oz) fine oatmeal
200 ml (7 fl oz) milk + 150–175 ml (5–6 fl oz) water

Buttermilk white
450 g (1 lb) plain white flour
200 ml (7 fl oz) buttermilk + 100 ml (4 fl oz) water

Rye
300 g (11 oz) plain white + 100 g (4 oz) wholemeal + 100 g (4 oz) rye flour
150 ml (¼ pint) water + 150 ml (¼ pint) buttermilk or natural yogurt

Free-form loaf: make up the dough (any flavour) as described in the basic recipe on p. 104, but allow it two rises in the bowl, one at room temperature and one in the fridge. Knock it back, flatten out to a rectangle, fold over into 3 and roll it over and over to make a fat sausage. Put it seam side down on a greased baking sheet, spray with water, sprinkle with any of the optional extras (p. 105) and leave to rise until doubled once more in size. Bake as usual.

Plaits: make up the dough (any flavour) as described in the basic recipe on p. 104 and allow it two rises in the bowl. Cut it into 3 equal-sized pieces, flatten, fold and roll each one to a long sausage as above. Plait them together, spray with water, sprinkle with any of the optional extras (p. 105) and let rise until doubled once more. Bake as usual.

Rolls: make up the dough (any flavour) as described in the basic recipe on p. 104 but allow it two rises in the bowl. Knock it back, flatten, fold and roll up into a sausage as above. Cut into equal-sized pieces each weighing about 75 g (3 oz). Working on an unfloured marble slab or stainless steel work top, roll the pieces around under your slightly cupped hand, 2 at a time, in a circular movement until a nice plump ball is formed. Put on a greased baking sheet, sprinkle with any of the optional extras (p. 105), spray with water and allow to rise again.

Party breads (as made by Swiss bakers): place the shaped rolls side by side in a lightly greased quiche tin or springform tin, spray with water and allow to rise again. When baked, the rolls spread out and run into one another to form 'kissing crusts'. The whole bread comes to the table and guests break off rolls themselves. Same principle for harvest breads, only the rolls are made smaller and assembled into the form of a huge bunch of grapes, with stalk and leaves.

Baps: use all white flour, or a mixture of white and wholemeal, and milk and water (for a soft crumb and crust). Make up the dough as usual and allow to rise once in the mixing bowl. Grease and flour a heavy baking sheet. Flatten, fold, roll up and divide the dough as above, roll into balls, then squash down to flatten slightly. Place them on the prepared baking sheet, brush with milk, dust with flour and leave to rise until doubled. Bake in a 200°C (400°F) mark 6 oven for 20–25 minutes. Remove and cover with a damp tea-towel to prevent a crust forming.

Pitta: make up the basic dough with olive oil. Allow it one rise at room temperature and one in the fridge. Preheat the oven to 250°C (475°F) mark 9. Flour a heavy baking sheet. Flatten, roll up and divide the dough as above, roll into balls, then with a rolling pin, roll them out to large pancakes about 5 mm ($\frac{1}{4}$ inch) thick. Bake them 4 at a time for about 2 minutes only: they should be billowy and beautiful, still soft and pliable with a useful little pocket inside, ready to be filled with something interesting.

Herby spiral bread: make up any of the doughs, allow to rise once in a bowl, then flatten out and spread generously with a herby garlic butter. Roll up like a Swiss roll, press the ends together firmly and allow to rise again. Bake as usual.

Wholemeal Bread with Wholewheat Kernels

Granary bread must be about the only sort of bread not readily available in Switzerland, so here's my version in case you also hanker after something like it. The plaited top makes it a nice bread to give away.

Makes 2 loaves

100 g (4 oz) wholewheat kernels
625 ml (22 fl oz) water
50 g (2 oz) unsalted butter
600 g (1$\frac{1}{4}$ lb) plain white flour
400 g (14 oz) coarsely ground wholemeal flour
1 sachet (7 g ($\frac{1}{4}$ oz)) instant-blending dried yeast or 20 g ($\frac{3}{4}$ oz) fresh yeast
15 ml (1 tbsp) salt
250 ml (9 fl oz) milk

Cook the wholewheat kernels in 375 ml (13 fl oz) water until all the liquid is evaporated and the kernels are tender. Stir in the butter and leave to cool. Mix together the two flours, yeast, salt, milk, remaining 250 ml (9 fl oz) water, and cooked kernels and make up a firm dough as described in the basic recipe on p. 104. Knead well and leave to rise in the bowl. Knock back and cut off a 200 g (7 oz) chunk. Cut the remaining dough in two and shape these pieces into loaves as described on p. 105. Put in 2 × 900 g (2 lb) loaf tins and press a fairly deep valley down the centre of each with the side of your hand. Spray with water.

Cut the reserved chunk of dough into 6 pieces for the plaits and roll each of them out to a thin sausage the length of the loaf tins. Make 2 plaits, lay them in the valleys on top of the loaves and tuck the ends down the side of the tin to secure them, otherwise they'll topple off in the baking. Spray again with water. Leave to rise for about 30 minutes or until doubled in bulk once more. Bake as described at 200°C (400°F) mark 6 for 25–30 minutes or until golden brown and hollow-sounding when tapped with a knife.

4-Tastes Family Pizza

If you have the sort of family (who doesn't?) where one likes tuna and despises olives, another loves anchovies and gags on capers, a third loathes mushrooms but dotes on peppers, and the last couldn't care less as long as it's pizza, here's a 4-in-1 recipe with something for everybody. Make your own substitutions for topping ingredients, depending on the family's likes and dislikes, and the contents of the store cupboard.

Serves 4

1 quantity basic bread dough, white or brown, risen once (p. 104)
500 ml (18 fl oz) well-flavoured tomato sauce (p. 149)
225 g (8 oz) mushrooms, sliced and sautéed
3 slices ham, cut into strips
45–60 ml (3–4 tbsp) ratatouille
1 small can tuna, flaked
200 g (7 oz) thinly sliced cheese (Mozzarella is best; Cheddar, Gruyère, goat or Raclette are also good)
a handful of olives

Knock back the dough and divide it in half. Use one half for the pizza and the other half to make a loaf or other shapes (or freeze the raw dough for a later use).

Heat the oven to 220°C (425°F) mark 7. Lightly grease a huge baking sheet (mine is 36 × 38 cm (14 × 15 inches)) and press and push the dough out thinly to cover the whole sheet. Spread the tomato sauce thinly over the dough almost to the edges. Mentally divide the pizza into 4 quarters and arrange the 4 different chosen toppings in the quarters. Scatter the thinly sliced cheese all over the top and scatter the (optional) olives around.

Bake the pizza in the preheated oven for about 15 minutes – it should be crusty and brown underneath, but still quite supple and bendy.

Salami and Cheese Turnovers with Tomato Sauce

Discs of rye dough are filled with salami and cheese, folded over like pasties, brushed with olive oil and baked until billowy. Vary the dough and the fillings too, depending on what you have to hand.

Makes 6 turnovers

1 quantity rye bread dough (see favourite combinations, p. 105), or other dough of your choice, risen once
150 g (5 oz) salami, very thinly cut, skin removed
150 g (5 oz) Mozzarella, sliced
50 g (2 oz) Parmesan, grated
200 g (7 oz) cottage cheese
olive oil
tomato sauce (p. 149), to serve (optional)

Knock back the risen dough and use half for the turnovers and the other half to make a loaf or other shapes (or freeze the raw dough for another use).

Heat the oven to 225°C (425°F) mark 7. Lightly oil a heavy baking sheet. Divide the dough into 6 equal-sized pieces, roll them into balls, then flatten them a little and roll them out to thin ovals.

Put a layer of salami slices to one side of each oval, overlapping the slices slightly. Follow with some pieces of Mozzarella, a sprinkle of Parmesan and a mound of cottage cheese, leaving a 1 cm (½ inch) border all around. Brush the border with water and fold over the turnover, like a pasty, sealing the edges well with the fingers or a fork.

Brush with olive oil and bake in the preheated oven for 10–12 minutes or until golden brown. They will puff up rather dramatically. Serve with tomato sauce (p. 149) if wished, and a salad.

Herby Mince Plait

Another approach to hamburgers, the herby dough is spread out flat, filled with a minced meat filling, and the sides of the dough cut in strips which are crossed over the top.

Serves 4

1 quantity bread dough of your choice (pp. 104–5), risen once
45 ml (3 tbsp) finely chopped mixed parsley and chives
450 g (1 lb) minced beef
salt and pepper
3 eggs, 2 of them hard-boiled

Knock down the dough and divide in half. Add 30 ml (2 tbsp) of the herbs to one half for this recipe, and make the other half into a small loaf or rolls.

Beat or process together the minced beef, salt and pepper, the remaining herbs and most of the raw egg (keep back a little to glaze the plait). Wrap the mixture round the 2 hard-boiled eggs to make a sausage shape.

Pat out the herby dough on a floured board to a rectangle the same length as the 'sausage' and 3 times its width. Put the 'sausage' in the middle. Make cuts in the exposed dough at right angles to the meat and at 2 cm (¾ inch) intervals. Lift up the strips and cross them alternately over the meat at a slight angle to make a plaited effect. Brush with the remaining egg and leave the plait to recover its form a little for about 30 minutes.

Bake in a 200°C (400°F) mark 6 oven for 40 minutes, or until golden brown and puffy and a skewer stuck in the middle feels quite warm to the cheek. Serve with chutney, mustards and a salad.

FLAT BREADS

for tortillas, chapatis, enchiladas, quesadillas and pies

Most countries have their own flat breads, whether it's yeast-leavened pitta from the Middle East, French crêpes made with eggs and milk, baking powder-leavened drop scones or pancakes from England and America, or unleavened tortillas and chapatis from Mexico and India. The object was the same wherever it came from: to provide a way of eating your food without the need for knives or forks. Later, as we all became a bit fastidious and lost the art of eating with our fingers, flat breads developed into a sort of edible plate on which to set delicious titbits, or for layering with other ingredients in a big dish. The basic recipe is for wheat tortillas or chapatis, followed by plenty of ideas to rekindle enthusiasm for finger food.

W A T C H P O I N T S

The fat in the dough softens it and makes it easy to roll out into discs. As with all breadmaking, the amount of water you add to make flat breads varies depending on the type of flour used. The point is to achieve a fairly firm, springy dough which does not stick to your hands. It benefits from good kneading, followed by a rest to relax the gluten. (*Tortillas de maíz* need a special flour and slightly different handling, so are not included here.)

The dough can then either be rolled out to a big sheet and circles cut out around a plate; or divided up into balls, and each ball rolled out to a circle. It is important to cook the rolled out tortillas or chapatis immediately (otherwise they will dry out) and briefly (otherwise they will become hard, instead of supple and bendy) on a very hot cast-iron griddle or ungreased frying pan.

B A S I C

WHEAT TORTILLAS OR CHAPATIS

Makes about 20

plain flour (white, wholemeal or a mixture)	350 g (12 oz)
vegetable shortening, lard, butter or ghee	100 g (4 oz)
salt	5 ml (1 tsp)
warm water	about 150 ml ($\frac{1}{4}$ pint)

Using a food processor, mixer or the fingertips, mix together the flour, fat and salt as if making pastry. Add only enough water to make a supple dough which does not stick to your hands. Process or knead really well, then rest the dough for 30 minutes.

Heat a griddle or ungreased cast-iron frying pan rather ferociously: sprinkle in a few drops of water – they should dash about and disappear almost immediately. Divide the dough into 18–20 pieces and roll between the hands to balls the size of golf balls. Lavishly flour a large board or rolling pin and roll out one of the balls of dough to a circle about 15 cm (6 inches) in diameter. (Or divide the dough in half, roll each half out as thinly as you can and cut discs using a plate as guide.)

Cook briefly on the griddle or pan, pressing down with your fingers or a spatula until the tortilla or chapati is just firm enough for you to turn it over, but still supple and bendy, and the underside slightly spotty. Turn and cook the other side. Stack them up in a tea-towel as they are ready and continue with the rest. Serve the whole bundle, still cloth-wrapped, in a basket.

Rather than serving them as a bread at table (when most people don't know what to do with them), concentrate on the pan-to-mouth aspect of this sort of eating. Gather everybody in the kitchen or around the barbecue, offer a selection of fillings and use tortillas and chapatis as follows:

Turnovers: fill with slices of quick-melting cheese, avocado, ham (alone or in combination), and return to the griddle. Press down with a spatula and turn several times to make sure the filling is heated through, but the tortilla or chapati still bendy.

Sandwiches: sandwich two tortillas or chapatis together with the same filling(s) as above and heat through in the same way; or wrap in foil and bake in the oven until hot.

Alternative fillings:
- cooked, puréed beans and chopped chilli
- firm scrambled eggs with chilli and tomato
- cooked, shredded meat bound with raw egg
- interesting leftover meat, fish or vegetables bound in a sauce
- crumbled, fried sausage and bean purée

Roll up cigarwise, fasten with a toothpick and shallow fry.

Or make thicker than usual, and ensure that the griddle is very hot, so that they puff up, like pitta. Catch them before they subside, make a slit in the side and fill with any of the above. Serve immediately, or reheat on griddle or shallow fry.

Sincronizadas

Tortilla sandwiches with ham and cheese

Wheat tortillas are filled with ham and a quick-melting cheese, reheated in a frying pan or griddle and served with a sharp tomato sauce for an ultra-rapid snack.

Makes 6

SAUCE
1–2 fresh green chillis, or to taste
$\frac{1}{2}$ onion
1 beefsteak tomato, about 150 g (5 oz)
chopped fresh coriander to taste
5 ml (1 tsp) salt
a little lime juice (optional)

SINCRONIZADAS
12 cooked tortillas (p. 109)
6 slices ham, roughly the size of the tortillas
12 slices quick-melting cheese such as Raclette or Cheddar

De-seed the chillis, using rubber gloves if you have sensitive skin, otherwise your fingers will burn for hours afterwards.

In a food processor, or using a sharp knife, chop the onion and chilli very finely. Chop the tomato a bit more coarsely and put in a little serving bowl with coriander to taste, the salt and lime juice if used.

Get a heavy ungreased frying pan or griddle really hot – splash some water at it and it should protest rather fiercely. Sandwich two tortillas with 1 slice of ham and 2 of cheese and press them down in the pan with your fingers or a fish slice, turning once or twice until the cheese is melted and the tortillas nice and hot. If they get hard before the cheese has melted, splash or spray them with a little water – they should be supple and bendy. Serve as they are ready with the tomato sauce.

Budin Norteno

A bit like a Mexican version of lasagne, tortillas are layered with a spicy tomato sauce, meat, corn and cream and baked in the oven for a super buffet dish.

Serves 8–10

800 g (1¾ lb) cooked pork
shoulder, boneless
salt and pepper
2 large green peppers, de-seeded
and cut into strips
2 onions, finely sliced
45 ml (3 tbsp) oil
20 cooked tortillas (p. 109)
400 g (14 oz) frozen or canned
sweetcorn
200 ml (7 fl oz) soured cream
100 g (4 oz) grated Cheddar
cheese

SAUCE
800 g (1¾ lb) can peeled plum
tomatoes
2 garlic cloves
1 onion
2 fresh green chillis, de-seeded
and roughly chopped

Shred or chop the pork finely and season it well. Stew the pepper strips and onion slices in 15 ml (1 tbsp) oil until soft. Set them aside.

Make a spicy tomato sauce by liquidizing or processing together the tomatoes, garlic, onion and chillis until quite smooth. Heat the remaining 30 ml (2 tbsp) oil in a large, heavy pan until smoking, then throw in the puréed tomato mixture and cook, stirring from time to time, until rich and syrupy.

In a large, round ovenproof dish, arrange a layer of 4 tortillas, slightly overlapping. Spread with a little sauce, some of the sweetcorn, some pork, a smear of soured cream and some cheese. Continue in this way with the remaining tortillas and other ingredients until all are finished up, making sure that the last layer is of cream and cheese.

Bake in a 180°C (350°F) mark 4 oven for about 30 minutes or until golden brown and bubbly, and a skewer stuck in the middle feels rather warm to the cheek. Serve with a huge, sharply dressed salad.

Chapati Pie with Curried Chicken

A spicy dish for supper, the chapatis are layered with chicken in a curry sauce and topped with soured cream.

Serves 4

5 ml (1 tsp) oil
1 onion, finely chopped
1 garlic clove, mashed
1 Granny Smith apple, unpeeled, grated
15 ml (1 tbsp) curry powder
300 ml ($\frac{1}{2}$ pint) chicken stock
350 g (12 oz) cooked chicken, shredded
salt
200 ml (7 fl oz) soured cream or yogurt
6 chapatis (p. 109)

Heat the oil in a frying pan and fry the onion, garlic, apple and curry powder gently until soft. Add the stock and simmer for 10 minutes until quite thick and reduced. Stir in the shredded chicken, season to taste and cook for a few minutes.

In a deep ovenproof dish the same diameter as the chapatis, layer them with chicken and sauce and a splash of soured cream or yogurt. Finish with a little soured cream or yogurt and bake in a 180°C (350°F) mark 4 oven for 25–30 minutes or until nicely hot through. Serve with a cucumber and yogurt salad.

Quesadillas with a Creamy Chilli Filling

Instead of making up the tortillas as usual, fill the raw dough with a creamy filling spiked with chilli, fold over and bake in a hot oven until golden.

Makes 12

2 green peppers
2–3 fresh green chillis, de-seeded
1 large onion, sliced
15 ml (1 tbsp) oil or lard
salt
250 ml (9 fl oz) double or soured cream
150 g (5 oz) Cheddar cheese, grated
$\frac{1}{2}$ quantity (about 300 g (11 oz)) basic tortilla dough

GUACAMOLE
1 garlic clove
2.5 ml ($\frac{1}{2}$ tsp) salt
1–2 fresh green chillis, de-seeded
5–6 sprigs fresh coriander
2 avocados
1 shallot and 1 tomato, finely chopped (optional)

Sear the green peppers over a gas flame or under the grill until thoroughly blistered. Put them into a polythene bag to sweat for a few minutes, then rub off the skin under running water. Tear or cut them into fine strips. Cut the chillis into fine strips also. Soften the pepper, chilli and sliced onion in the oil or lard without browning. Season with salt, stir in the cream and the grated Cheddar and allow it to melt. Cool the mixture a little.

Roll out the dough on a well-floured board to a large sheet and cut out 12 × 13 cm (5 inch) discs. Spoon a little filling on to each disc of dough, wet the edges, make a turnover and press the edges well together to seal. (The quesadillas can be prepared ahead up to this point and chilled or frozen.)

Heat the oven to 200°C (400°F) mark 6 and bake the quesadillas on a heavy baking sheet for about 10 minutes or until golden brown and lightly puffed up.

Meanwhile, make the guacamole: mash together the garlic, salt, chillis and coriander to make a paste. Mash in the avocados and sprinkle on the shallot and tomato if used. Serve with the quesadillas.

RICH YEAST DOUGHS

for brioches, kugelhopfs, *pie doughs and wrap-ups*

A true brioche dough (where the weight in butter is equal to that of the flour, not to mention a few dozen eggs) is a tough proposition on most counts, needing careful handling (and careful digestion). Here is a slightly less rich basic dough which can be made up with a savoury or sweet emphasis – sweet brioches are a rare treat for breakfast, and savoury ones go well with potted meats, terrines or *foie gras*.

If you've never worked with rich doughs before, start with a batch of brioches which can double up as edible containers for shellfish or fruit – and keep back a little of the dough, maybe, to serve as yeast pastry for a fruit tart. Then when you get a bit braver, you can add a few interesting optional extras and turn the dough into *kugelhopf* or hot cross buns, or wrap it around interesting sausages or forcemeats (pp. 24–5).

W A T C H P O I N T S

All the same rules apply to brioche as to plain doughs, plus the following additional points.

Although French bakers often recommend allowing a brioche dough its second rise in the fridge, I've had mixed success with this, and find it works better with a margarine dough (see Variations) than with a butter dough. Try it for yourself and see: if the rise seems very slow, transfer the dough to room temperature and it will continue rising as usual.

Because of its high proportion of fat, eggs and milk, this is a very soft and sticky dough (far more so than a simple bread dough), so a heavy-duty mixer and dough hook (Kenwood or similar) is ideal, though if you're prepared to beat and slap the dough very vigorously for about 10 minutes with your hands in a large bowl, you'll get good results too. The food processor is not a success: by the time you've unglued the blade, extricated the dough and cleaned the bowl, you'll be wishing you'd done it by hand.

The butter should be soft but not melted. Beat it about a bit with a rolling pin if it's very firm.

Rich doughs (unlike puff pastry, p. 88) should not be egg-glazed until just before going into the oven, when their rise has been completed, otherwise they will be anchored down and unable to perform.

| B A S I C |

RICH DOUGH RECIPE

Makes about 1 kg (2 lb 2 oz)

	SAVOURY	SWEET
plain white flour	450 g (1 lb)	450 g (1 lb)
salt	5 ml (1 tsp)	a pinch
sugar	a pinch	45–60 ml (3–4 tbsp)
yeast, instant-blending, dried	1 sachet (7 g ($\frac{1}{4}$ oz))	1 sachet (7 g ($\frac{1}{4}$ oz))
or fresh	20 g ($\frac{3}{4}$ oz)	20 g ($\frac{3}{4}$ oz)
butter, unsalted	150 g (5 oz)	150 g (5 oz)
eggs, size 1 or 2	2	2
milk	about 200 ml (7 fl oz)	about 200 ml (7 fl oz)

Put the flour, salt and sugar into the bowl of an electric mixer with a dough hook fitted. Mix them together well and sprinkle or crumble on the yeast.

Beat the butter with a rolling pin a little if very cold and hard, then cut it into pieces and work it into the dry ingredients, as if making pastry. Whisk together the eggs and milk with a fork and add them too, mixing them in well. At this stage, the dough should be rather soft; if not, add a tiny bit more milk (too firm a start and the brioches will be dry).

To start with, the dough will look hopelessly unpromising, but continue to beat it at medium speed for 5–10 minutes, and gradually, as the gluten gets busy, it will tighten up and will finally start, miraculously, to come away from the sides of the bowl. If, after 10 minutes' beating, this does not happen, add sprinkles of flour until it does. Switch off, and lift out dough hook.

Use a dough scraper or spatula to clean off any excess dough. Lift and turn the dough. Cover with a damp cloth and leave to rise at room temperature until doubled in bulk – about $2\frac{1}{2}$–3 hours.

Knock back the dough, and for individual, top-knotted brioches, grease the number of brioche or other tins required (the total quantity makes 16). Divide the dough into 50 g (2 oz) pieces. Tear a little bit off each dough piece and roll it into a ball, then squash one end of it a bit to make it teardrop-shaped. Put the larger pieces in the prepared tins, poke a hole in the middle with a floury finger and post the little teardrop down the hole. Leave to rise once more until doubled in bulk (about 30 minutes at room temperature, longer in the fridge).

For round brioche loaves, divide the dough in two and do the above procedure; use 2 well-greased fluted brioche tins or charlotte moulds.

For 8-piece rectangular brioche

loaves, divide the dough up into 50 g (2 oz) balls, grease 2 × 1 kg (2 lb) loaf tins and put 8 in each tin. Leave to rise again until doubled in bulk.

Glaze all brioches with beaten egg yolk just before baking and put in a cold oven. Turn the temperature to 180°C (350°F) mark 4 and bake until golden brown and hollow-sounding when tapped: 15–20 minutes for small brioches, 35–40 minutes for large ones (rectangular or round).

Brioche dough can be frozen successfully, but like plain dough never quite musters sufficient strength to rise to the challenge of a loaf or individual brioches: use for wrapping around a sausage, piece of meat, etc. (see Further Ideas). Ready-baked brioches freeze well – warm them up to give the illusion of freshly-baked.

| V A R I A T I O N S |

● Substitute a well-flavoured (would you eat it?) unsalted margarine for butter. It gives a lighter – but less tasty – result, good for first attempts as less extravagant.

● To the basic sweet dough, risen once and knocked back, add any of the following:
a few soaked raisins, sultanas, currants, prunes or dried apricots (chopped small)
chocolate chips
chopped almonds, hazelnuts or walnuts
chopped candied peel

● Or to the basic savoury dough:
dehydrated onion flakes
chopped walnuts
chopped fresh or dried herbs

● Shape into brioches or loaves as instructed, allow to rise until doubled once more in bulk, glaze and bake as usual.

Hot cross buns: add 7.5 ml (1½ tsp) mixed spice to the dry ingredients at the beginning, make up the sweet dough, leave to rise and knock it back. Add 75 g (3 oz) soaked sultanas and 25 g (1 oz) chopped candied peel. Shape into buns, cut a cross on the tops (or stick on two thin strips of pastry, crossed), and leave to rise again until doubled in bulk. Brush with sugared milk and bake for 20–25 minutes.

Sweet kugelhopf: make up the sweet dough, allow to rise, knock it back and work in 75 g (3 oz) sultanas. Well grease a *kugelhopf* mould and place an almond in each runnel. Put in the dough and leave it to rise until it reaches the top of the mould. Bake for 40–45 minutes, or until it is golden brown and sounds hollow when tapped. (See recipes for a savoury version.)

Sausage in brioche: make up the savoury dough and allow it to rise once in the bowl. Knock it back, and wrap an interesting (probably foreign) sausage in it. Seal the joins with egg, place seam-side down on a greased baking sheet, and glaze with remaining egg. Allow it to rise again for about 30 minutes then bake for 20–25 minutes or until golden brown.

Open-faced fruit tarts: press one-third of the knocked-down sweet dough into a quiche tin, fill with fruit, dot with butter and sprinkle with sugar. Bake until the pastry is firm and golden and the fruit cooked.

Mariners' Brioches

Little savoury brioches are hollowed out and filled with monkfish, prawns and mushrooms, for a fairly rich starter.

Serves 6

6 individual savoury brioches (p. 114)
1 shallot, finely chopped
25 g (1 oz) butter
5 ml (1 tsp) olive oil
200 g (7 oz) tiny button mushrooms
250 g (9 oz) trimmed monkfish, cubed (buy 400 g (14 oz) on bone)
100 g (4 oz) shelled uncooked prawns
salt and pepper
200 ml (7 fl oz) dry white wine
100 ml (4 fl oz) sherry
200 ml (7 fl oz) fish stock
250 ml (9 fl oz) double cream
15 ml (1 tbsp) chopped tarragon

Cut the tops off the brioches, hollow out the crumb and freeze for breadcrumbs; keep the hats. Soften the shallot in the butter and oil without browning. Add the mushrooms and cook gently until the juices are rendered. Raise the heat to drive off excess moisture, then add the monkfish cubes and prawns. Season lightly and toss over moderate heat for 2–3 minutes until barely cooked. Lift out on to a side dish and keep warm.

Deglaze the pan with the wine, sherry and stock and reduce by half over lively heat. Meanwhile, put the hollowed-out brioches in a warm oven for 5–10 minutes to heat through.

Whisk the cream and tarragon into the reduction in the pan and simmer for a few minutes more. Check the seasoning. Fold in the reserved monkfish, prawns and mushrooms.

Put a warmed brioche on each serving plate, spoon in some filling and put the hat on top. Serve at once, with any extra sauce poured around.

Kugelhopf au Lard

Bacon, onion and walnut loaf

Less well known than the sweet *kugelhopf*, and infinitely more interesting, is the savoury version with bacon, onion and walnuts demonstrated to me by Monsieur Marchand, my friendly Alsatian baker. Failing the traditional mould, use a 1.8 kg (4 lb) loaf tin or charlotte mould.

Makes 1

125 g (4½ oz) smoked streaky bacon in one piece
1 small onion, chopped (or 30 ml (2 tbsp) freeze-dried onion flakes)
8 walnut halves
1 quantity basic savoury brioche dough (p. 114), risen once
45 ml (3 tbsp) finely chopped walnuts

Remove the rind from the bacon piece and cut it into little dice. Sweat gently in a small pan until the fat runs, but do not allow to become crisp, or it will turn into horrid little stones in the finished bread. Remove with a slotted spoon and in the rendered fat, gently fry the onion until lightly golden and the moisture evaporated. (If using onion flakes, add later on.)

Grease really well a 1.8 kg (4 lb) metal or ceramic *kugelhopf* mould, paying special attention to the central 'stalk' or funnel, where the dough tends to stick, and put the walnut halves in the runnels at the bottom. (Alternatively, use a similar-sized charlotte mould or bread tin.)

Knock back the risen dough and work in the bacon cubes, fried onion or onion flakes and chopped walnuts. Make a hole in the middle of the dough and slide it down into the mould, with the 'stalk' coming up through the middle. Put to rise, covered with a damp cloth, until it climbs up to the top of the mould (anything from 1–3 hours at room temperature, or try this rise overnight in the fridge).

Put in a cold oven and turn the temperature to 180°C (350°F) mark 4. Bake for 40–45 minutes. It will continue to rise above the rim as the oven gets warmer, and is done when the crust is a rich brown and the loaf sounds hollow when tapped. Turn it out and if still rather pale on the inside, return it to the oven for a few minutes more to bake to a good golden colour. Cool on a rack.

Kugelhopf Club Sandwich

Savoury kugelhopf layered with cream cheese and prosciutto

Thin slices of the preceding *kugelhopf* are spread with cream cheese, overlaid with prosciutto, cut in wedges and then reassembled. This makes a delicious light lunch or supper dish. Accompany with a creamy soup and/or a crisp salad.

Makes 16

1 *kugelhopf au lard*, preferably 1 day old
150 g (5 oz) Boursin cheese with garlic and herbs
300 ml (½ pint/11 oz) soured cream, *fromage blanc* or quark
200 g (7 oz) wafer-thin raw ham (e.g. prosciutto)

Take a thin slice off the top of the *kugelhopf*, complete with its walnuts, and set it aside. Slice the rest of the loaf horizontally into 10 thin slices, but be sure to leave a base (about 2 cm (¾ inch) thick) on which to sit it all. Pair up the slices in the order in which they were cut.

Mash the garlic and herb cheese into the soured cream, *fromage blanc* or quark and spread a thin layer on to one of each pair of *kugelhopf* slices. Top with some ham, spread a little more cheese on top and then sandwich it with its partner slice.

Put the reserved base on a serving plate. One by one, starting with the biggest, put the assembled slices back on to the base. Continue in this way to build up the *kugelhopf* to its former glory, and place the nutty crown on top. Cut evenly into 16 wedges.

It can be prepared one day ahead, completely covered with clingfilm and refrigerated until just before demolishing.

Apple Tart in Yeast Pastry

The old practice of keeping back a piece of sweetened bread dough to use instead of pastry in fruit tarts is, I think, a nice one, especially for very juicy fruits. Here, the little halved apples sit cut side down and the dough billows up rather agreeably around them.

Serves 4–6

450 g (1 lb) small eating apples (e.g. Cox's Orange Pippins)
juice of ½ lemon
5 ml (1 tsp) ground cinnamon
15 ml (1 tbsp) sugar
⅓ quantity (about 300 g/11 oz) basic sweet brioche dough (p. 114), risen once in the bowl and knocked back
25 g (1 oz) butter, cut into little dots

Peel the apples and cut them in half. Scoop out the cores with a melon baller and put the apple halves in a bowl with the lemon juice, cinnamon and sugar.

Spread out the dough, using the palms and knuckles, to fit a 25 cm (10 inch) quiche tin and raise it up the sides a bit. Bury the apple halves, cut side down, into the dough and pour over any exuded juices.

Leave for a few minutes to allow the tart to recover itself, then dot with butter and bake in a 180°C (350°F) mark 4 oven for 30–35 minutes or until the dough has puffed up all around the apples, and the edges and underside are a nice golden brown. Serve with (home-made) vanilla or cinnamon ice cream, or whipped cream.

GENOESE SPONGES

for layered, filled, rolled or frozen cakes

The idea of making a cake fills some people with dread and despair, so here is a recipe which is simplicity itself: whole eggs are beaten with sugar until light and fluffy, then flavourings, starch and optional melted butter are carefully added. By itself, it makes a fairly dull little sponge, but allow it a little leeway and it provides an excellent base from which to set off in various directions: delicious teatime cakes or delectable dinner party desserts, whether baked in rounds (for dusting, layering, filling or icing) or rectangular sheets (for filling and rolling, or cutting in strips or shapes and layering).

W A T C H P O I N T S

An egg will aerate its own weight of sugar and flour (e.g. a 60 g (size 4) egg to 30 g (1 generous oz) each of sugar and flour) without the need for baking powder (or self-raising flour, which has its own built in), always provided the eggs are really well beaten with the sugar until tripled in bulk before the flour is folded in. If you don't have a powerful electric mixer on a stand, beat with a hand-held mixer or whisk in a metal bowl over hot, not boiling water to get the required volume. Or separate the eggs and beat together first the yolks and half the sugar; then fold in the flour; then stiffly whisk the egg whites with the remaining sugar (as for meringues) and fold them in at the end.

Once the eggs and sugar are in the bowl together, resist all other distractions and get on and beat them immediately, otherwise the sugar will 'cook' the eggs into an ugly, immutable heap in the bottom of the bowl.

The flour must be folded in quickly and carefully; no more beating at this stage or the cake will be tough. The addition of butter gives a moister cake with better keeping qualities; without butter, your sponge will be finer and lighter, but quicker to stale. If you add the butter, make sure it is liquid but cool, otherwise the batter will collapse in disarray.

BASIC

GENOESE SPONGE

	3-egg sponge: 20–23 cm (8–9 inch) cake or a 20 × 30 cm (8 × 12 inch) sheet	4-egg sponge: 23–25 cm (9–10 inch) cake or a 30 × 40 cm (12 × 16 inch) sheet
eggs	3	4
caster sugar	90 g (3½ oz)	125 g (4½ oz)
plain white flour, sifted	90 g (3½ oz)	125 g (4½ oz)
salt	a pinch	a pinch
butter (optional)	50 g (2 oz)	60 g (2½ oz)

Heat the oven to 180°C (350°F) mark 4. For round cakes, grease and flour the sides of the appropriately sized tin and cut a disc of non-stick paper for the bottom; for sponge sheets, cut a sheet of non-stick paper 2.5 cm (1 inch) larger all around than the finished dimensions. Fold over a 2.5 cm (1 inch) border all around. Clip the corners, superimpose one cut piece over the other and fix with staples. Put the paper case on a baking sheet.

Beat together the eggs and sugar at high speed for 5–10 minutes until very pale, mousse-like and tripled in volume. Meanwhile sift the flour and salt together several times. Melt the butter, if used, and allow to cool; it should remain liquid. Sprinkle some of the flour over the egg mixture and use a balloon whisk to incorporate the flour: lift the mixture up on the whisk, shaking in the flour as you go. Continue with the rest of the flour until it is all added. Dribble the butter, if used, down the inside edge of the bowl and fold and cut it quickly into the mixture with a spatula.

Pour the batter into the prepared tin or sheet, bang it down sharply on the work surface and smooth the top with a baker's spatula to get a really even surface. Bake round cakes for 25–30 minutes and rectangular sheets for 10–12 minutes in the preheated oven. The sponge is done when pale golden, springy to the touch and a skewer inserted in the middle comes out clean, not gooey.

Invert round sponges (or release the spring from the tin) and leave them on a cake rack to cool; turn sponge sheets out on to non-stick baking paper, peel off the backing paper (spray or splash with water if difficult) and cover with a tea-towel. Proceed to roll or layer the sponge as soon as it is cool, so it doesn't dry out and become brittle.

The plain sponge is fairly ordinary, and really designed to go on to greater things; if you want a sponge to eat on its own, make any of the Variations, sprinkle with icing sugar and serve for tea.

VARIATIONS

● Flavour the sponge with any of the following, beaten in with the eggs and sugar:
grated zest of ½ lemon, lime or orange
5 ml (1 tsp) orange-flower water
5 ml (1 tsp) triple strength rosewater
a pinch of mixed spice, or cinnamon alone
5 ml (1 tsp) vanilla essence
15 ml (1 tbsp) coffee essence or very strong coffee

● For an even finer, lighter sponge, use half and half plain white flour and either: cornflour, potato flour (fécule) or rice flour.

● *Almond, hazelnut or walnut sponge*: use half plain white flour and half ground nuts of your choice. The nuts flavour as well as moistening the sponge. Don't use all nuts at the expense of flour or the sponge will be heavy.

● *Chocolate sponge*: remove 30 ml (2 tbsp) flour from the measured ingredients, and substitute 30 ml (2 tbsp) cocoa powder. Sift together and add to the beaten eggs.

● You can make a cake without any flour at all, but it will be more like a pancake than a sponge cake.

Further
IDEAS

Frozen ice cream cake: cut a round sponge in thin layers; or a rectangular sheet in strips. Spread all but the top layer thinly with sieved jam or jelly to match your ice cream flavour, then sandwich the whole lot with good ice cream (or several contrasting colours and flavours), wrap in foil and freeze.

Fruit mousse cake: cut a round sponge in 2 horizontally; or a sponge sheet in strips. Sandwich either sort with an almost-setting fruit mousse (p. 124) or bavarois (p 139). Wrap in foil and chill until needed.

Swiss rolls (which the Swiss call roulades): use plenty of variety in flavourings and fillings, for instance:
- orange/lemon-flavoured sponge spread with lemon curd/ marmalade
- chocolate sponge spread with chocolate nut spread
- cinnamon sponge spread with apple purée, etc. etc.

Fruit roll: proceed as for a Swiss roll but fill with fresh fruit and lightly sweetened whipped cream or *fromage blanc*. Roll up and serve chilled.

Frozen Swiss roll: spread with ice cream, roll up and freeze. Serve straight from the freezer and cut with an electric carving knife.

Chocolate Hazelnut Zebra Cake with Nutella Filling

A light, quick and easy teatime cake, great for children – let them help make it, so they have a vested interest. Substitute chocolate spread if you can't find Nutella.

Serves 4–6

4 eggs
125 g (4½ oz) caster sugar
50 g (2 oz) ground hazelnuts
60 g (2½ oz) plain white flour, sifted
15 ml (1 tbsp) cocoa powder
30–45 ml (2–3 tbsp) Nutella or chocolate spread
1 egg
cocoa powder and icing sugar

Prepare 2 × 15 cm (6 inch) springform cake tins (or a 23 cm (9 inch) one) and heat the oven to 180°C (350°F) mark 4.

Whisk together the eggs and sugar as described in the basic sponge recipe on p. 119, fold in the ground hazelnuts, flour and cocoa powder. Pour into the tin(s) and bake for 25 minutes or until just firm and springy to the touch and a skewer inserted in the middle comes out clean. Cool on a rack.

Whisk together the Nutella and the egg until light and creamy, and of a spreading consistency. Spread the underside of one of the cakes (or split the larger one in two and spread half of it) with the Nutella. Top with the other cake or half.

Cut strips of greaseproof paper 1 cm (½ inch) wide and lay them over the top of the cake, spaced 1 cm (½ inch) apart. Sprinkle the cake with icing sugar, then carefully lift off the strips of paper and shake off the excess sugar. Put them back on top of the icing sugar strips, and sprinkle the remaining spaces with cocoa powder, shaken through a tea strainer, to give a zebra-striped effect.

*T*his 4-Tastes Family
Pizza has something for everyone and the
variations are infinite
(page 107)

Kugelhopf Club
Sandwich transforms what is more commonly
encountered as a sweet into a delightful savoury
for a drink's party (page 116)

*C*hocolate Mousse
*Gâteau Tricolore combines three flavours of
chocolate with rich coffee-soaked sponge layers*
(page 123)

F or Strawberry
*Charlotte, a featherlight mousse is encircled by
hazelnut biscuits and crowned by ripe red fruit*
(page 126)

Mineola or Tangerine Charlotte with Sponge Spirals

A featherlight mineola or tangerine mousse is held in check by a corset of apricot jam-spread sponge spirals. If you don't feel in the mood for Swiss roll-playing, you can substitute boring old sponge fingers, but I think you may regret it.

Serves 6

a 3-egg sponge (p. 119) baked in a 30 × 40 cm (12 × 16 inch) case
45–60 ml (3–4 tbsp) apricot jam or marmalade, sieved
zest and juice of 2 mineolas or 4–5 tangerines (175 ml/6 fl oz juice)
juice of 1 lemon
15 ml (1 tbsp) powdered gelatine or 6 sheets
3 whole eggs
2 egg yolks
75 g (3 oz) caster sugar
150 ml (¼ pint) whipping cream
chocolate curls or leaves

Bake the sponge as described in the basic recipe on p. 119, turn it out on to non-stick baking paper, cover with a tea-towel and leave it to cool slightly. Trim all the edges and spread the sheet thinly with the jam or marmalade. Roll it up tightly and put it in the freezer for about an hour to facilitate slicing later on.

Put the mineola or tangerine juice with the lemon juice in a pan and sprinkle on the powdered gelatine. Alternatively soak the sheet gelatine in cold water until floppy, then squeeze it out and add it to the juice in the pan. Dissolve the gelatine over gentle heat without boiling.

Beat the whole eggs, egg yolks, sugar and mineola or tangerine zest at high speed in the mixer (or by hand over a bowl of not quite simmering water) until featherlight, very fluffy and at least tripled in bulk. Reduce the speed and dribble the warm gelatine mixture down the side of the bowl. Continue beating until just mixed. Put the mixture into the fridge, stirring once or twice to prevent uneven setting. When it begins to thicken, whip the cream until the beater leaves soft tracks, then fold it gently into the fruit base. Make sure there is not a layer of jellied juice in the bottom – if there is, stir it gently around to distribute it.

Take the cake out of the freezer and cut it into thin even slices. Use them to line the bottom and sides of a 23 cm (9 inch) springform cake tin. Pour the nearly setting, but still pourable mousse into its corset and put it in the fridge to set.

To serve, release the spring from the tin, set the charlotte on a beautiful plate, garnish with chocolate curls or leaves (paint melted chocolate on to rose leaves, let it harden, then peel away the leaf) and serve extra mineola/tangerine slices around. Turn the slices over on their side to serve, otherwise the point of the sponge layer on the bottom is rather lost.

Citrus Almond Roulade

The straight sponge is made richer and more interesting with the addition of ground almonds, spread with a lemon curd or marmalade filling and rolled up. Almost too good for tea, so try it for dessert with a dark chocolate sauce.

Serves 4–6

3 eggs
90 g (3½ oz) caster sugar
grated zest and juice of ½ lemon or 1 lime
40 g (1½ oz) ground almonds
50 g (2 oz) cornflour
150 g (5 oz) *fromage blanc* or quark
30 ml (2 tbsp) lemon curd or fine-cut marmalade

CHOCOLATE SAUCE (optional)
150 g (5 oz) plain chocolate
300 ml (½ pint) water
100 g (4 oz) sugar

Prepare a sponge sheet paper case 20 × 30 cm (8 × 12 inches) as described in the basic recipe on p. 119 and heat the oven to 180°C (350°F) mark 4.

Whisk together the eggs, sugar and zest as described in the basic recipe on p. 119. Add the juice and shake in the ground almonds and cornflour with a wire whisk. Spread this mixture into the prepared paper case and smooth the top with a dough scraper, making sure the batter goes right into the corners. Bake in the preheated oven for 12–15 minutes or until just firm and springy to the touch. Remove from the oven and let the sponge cool in its paper case on the baking sheet, with a tea-towel over the top. Invert on to a piece of non-stick baking paper, peel off the backing paper, trim the edges and cover with a tea-towel until ready to fill.

Mix together the *fromage blanc* or quark and lemon curd or marmalade and spread it quickly on to the sponge sheet. Roll it up as tidily as you can (it will be rather brittle and sticky, because of the almonds and juice in the sponge) and put it in the fridge.

If serving with chocolate sauce, melt the chocolate in the water with the sugar over gentle heat. Then raise the heat and boil steadily for about 10 minutes until syrupy and thick. Serve chilled with the cake.

Raspberry Mousse Layer Cake

The key to this delicate and delicious dessert is to spread the batter for the sponge sheets only 5 mm (¼ inch) thick, otherwise it becomes clumsy. The strips are spread with redcurrant jelly and layered with an almost setting fruit mousse.

Serves 10

a 4-egg sponge (p. 119) baked in 2 sheets, each 20 × 30 cm (8 × 12 inches)
450 g (1 lb) raspberries
60–90 ml (4–6 tbsp) caster sugar, or to taste
15 ml (1 tbsp) *crème de cassis*
15 ml (1 tbsp) powdered gelatine or 6 sheets
100 ml (4 fl oz) sweet white wine or water
450 ml (¾ pint) whipping cream
redcurrant jelly
mint sprigs

FRUIT COULIS
250 g (9 oz) raspberries or redcurrants
125 g (4½ oz) icing sugar

Trim the sponge sheets and cut each one in half lengthways to give 4 sheets approximately 10 × 30 cm (4 × 12 inches). Purée the raspberries with the sugar and *crème de cassis* in a blender or food processor, then push through a sieve. Return the purée to the blender or food processor.

Sprinkle the powdered gelatine on to the wine, leave until spongy, then dissolve it in the wine without boiling. Or soak the gelatine sheets in a large bowl of cold water; squeeze them out to remove excess water and then dissolve them in the wine or water. Add the gelatine liquid, still hot, to the purée. Blend again. Check for sweetness, adding more sugar if necessary. Leave to cool, stirring from time to time to prevent uneven setting. Whip the cream until soft peaks form and fold it into the cool purée. Put it into the fridge until it is beginning to set, but is still spreadable.

Spread 3 of the 4 sponge sheets with a thin layer of redcurrant jelly, and put one of them on a large sheet of foil. Follow with a 1 cm (½ inch) layer of nearly setting mousse. If the mousse falls about the place instead of staying on the sponge sheet, return it to the fridge to firm up a little. Continue spreading mousse on to the jelly-spread sheets, to give 4 layers of sponge and 3 of mousse. Bring the sides of the foil up and around the cake and shut it all up in a parcel. Put into the fridge to set, along with any leftover mousse, which is served in ovals along with the cake.

Make a raspberry or redcurrant coulis by puréeing the fruit with the sugar, sieving, and diluting to a coating consistency with some water. Unpeel the foil and cut the cake in 1 cm (½ inch) slices. Pour a little fruit coulis on to each serving plate and lay 2 slices over it so the layers can be seen. Serve an oval of raspberry mousse in between, topped with a sprig of mint.

Chocolate Mousse Gâteau Tricolore

Strips of coffee-soaked sponge are layered with three different colours of chocolate mousse. Slice it and lay it out on the serving plates, so everyone can gasp in delight at the layering effect.

Serves 6–8

100 g (4 oz) each of white, milk and plain chocolate
200 ml (7 fl oz) double cream
2 egg whites
a pinch of salt
60 ml (4 tbsp) caster sugar
100 ml (4 fl oz) strong coffee
30 ml (2 tbsp) rum
a 4-egg sponge sheet (p. 91), baked in a 30 × 40 cm (12 × 16 inch) case
600 ml (1 pint) vanilla sauce, plain, coffee- or orange-flavoured (p. 138)

Choose 3 small bowls which will all fit together in a bain-marie and into each one put a different coloured chocolate. Bring the water to just below boiling and stir the chocolates gently until just liquefied. Remove and allow them to cool but not solidify.

Whip the cream until the beater leaves soft tracks, and divide it equally between the chocolates, folding it in carefully. Finally whisk the whites with the pinch of salt until in soft peaks, then add half the sugar and continue beating until just stiff but still creamy. Divide this also among the 3 chocolates and fold it in too.

Dissolve the remaining sugar in the coffee and stir in the rum. Trim the sponge sheet and cut into 4 strips each about 10 × 30 cm (4 × 12 inches). Brush 3 of them with the coffee syrup.

Spread each of the 3 layers with a different coloured mousse and stack them up, making sure the white one is in the middle. Top with the final layer of sponge and refrigerate until needed. Slice the cake rather thinly and give each person 2 slices, laid over a pool of vanilla sauce.

SWEET MOUSSES

fruit mousses, soufflés, charlottes and mousse cakes

Here is a basic mousse which can be adapted to include any fresh fruit you like (except fresh pineapple, papaya or figs, which all wreak havoc with gelatine), or interesting frozen or canned fruit. A mousse doesn't have to stay a mousse all its life: put it in a collared dish which is a bit too small for it and it becomes a 'soufflé'; mould it in a corset of sponge fingers or fine slices of Swiss roll and it turns into a charlotte; or layer it with fine layers of sponge and it takes on the guise of a *gâteau aux fruits de la saison.*

W A T C H P O I N T S

Powdered gelatine has a distinct flavour; sheet gelatine has none. While I don't think it matters which you use for savoury mousses, I do think the flavour is affected in a delicate sweet mousse, so try and find sheet gelatine if you can. To use it, soak in cold water until floppy, then lift out and squeeze, discard the soaking water and dissolve it in the liquid called for in the recipe. As with savoury mousses, 4 sheets or 10 ml (2 tsp) powdered gives a soft mousse and 6 sheets or 10 ml (2 tsp) powdered per 600 ml (1 pint) a slightly firmer one. How much you use will depend on the firmness of the fruit used, whether it's summer or winter, and whether or not you plan to unmould the mousse. It also helps to add the hot dissolved gelatine to the fruit, as in one fell swoop you purée the fruit and ensure even distribution of the dissolved gelatine and no 'jelly babies'.

* Gelatine figures:
6 sheets = 10 g = scant $\frac{1}{2}$ oz =
1 UK sachet = 3 level (5 ml)
teaspoons = 1 level (15 ml)
tablespoon

Some fruit will have to be sieved afterwards, some not. The lemon juice is a sort of seasoning, which brings out the flavour in the fruit, and the amount of sugar will vary depending on the type of fruit used.

You can use double or whipping cream, depending on purse or pocket. Whip it lightly and add to the cool mixture, otherwise it will collapse. Some fruit mousses include beaten egg whites at the end, but this gives a cotton-woolly, slightly bland result. Provided your cream is nicely whipped, this alone will give the light texture needed, while preserving all the taste of the fruit.

BASIC

FRUIT MOUSSE

Serves 4–6

gelatine, sheets	**4–6**
***or* powdered**	**10–15 ml (2–3 tsp)**
water, fruit juice or sweet white wine	**90 ml (6 tbsp)**
fruit, fresh, frozen or canned	**about 450 g (1 lb)**
lemon juice	**to taste**
sugar	**to taste**
cream	**250 ml (9 fl oz)**

If using sheet gelatine, soak the sheets in a large bowl of cold water until floppy. Squeeze them out and put them into a saucepan with the water, fruit juice or wine. (If using powdered gelatine, sprinkle it directly on to the 90 ml (6 tbsp) liquid in a small saucepan and leave it to sponge up.) Dissolve either sort of gelatine in the liquid over gentle heat without boiling.

Put the fruit in a liquidizer with the lemon juice and blend until quite smooth. Add the gelatine liquid and sugar to taste and blend again. Sieve the resulting purée if necessary to remove pips, fibres, etc.

Whip the cream until the beater leaves soft tracks, then fold this gently into the fruit purée. Pour the mousse into a serving bowl or into individual ramekins or coupes and put into the fridge for at least 3 hours to set; or leave it in the mixing bowl and use as suggested further on.

VARIATIONS

- For fruit use raw soft fruit (strawberries, mangoes, raspberries, passion fruit, peaches, black or redcurrants, etc.).
- Or use interesting canned fruit like papaya chunks, lychees, mango slices, kiwis, pineapple.
- Or cook rhubarb, cranberries, blackberries, black or redcurrants, stoned plums, apple slices, quince slices, etc. very briefly with sugar (no added water) until soft, then purée with the gelatine liquid as usual.
- You can substitute *fromage blanc* for the cream, but you end up with a sort of blancmange. (Maybe you like blancmange...)

Cold 'Soufflé': instead of serving in ramekins or coupes, tie a foil collar around a soufflé dish which is purposely too small for the mixture, pour it in and leave until set. Remove the foil collar, roll the exposed 'neck' in chopped nuts, praline, etc.

Charlottes: use variously shaped and sized containers (cake tins, *moules à manquer*, terrines, loaf tins, etc.), line the container with liqueur/water-splashed:
- sponge fingers
- ginger biscuits
- macaroons
- other interesting biscuits, bought or home-made
and pour in the mousse.

Chocolate-encased mousses: melt chocolate, spread it over the bottom and up the sides of a cake tin lined with non-stick baking paper and allow it to harden; pour in the mousse. Or do the same with paper fairy cake cases and make individual, chocolate-encased mousses.

Fruit mousse ovals: allow the mousse to set in its mixing bowl, then spoon out ovals and set them over a fruit coulis, a pool of yogurt or a vanilla sauce (p. 138). Or intersperse fruit mousse ovals with chocolate mousse ovals (p. 129).
Or use the nearly setting mousse for layering in sponge cakes (p. 119), meringues (p. 144); or pour into fragile pastry cases or tuiles (p. 153).

Mango Mousse Ovals with Yogurt Sauce

Scoops of basic mousse, mango-flavoured, are served in a fruity yogurt sauce.

Serves 6

2 ripe mangoes, each 300 g (11 oz)
juice of 1 lemon
6 sheets or 15 ml (1 tbsp)
powdered gelatine
90 ml (6 tbsp) water
45 ml (3 tbsp) caster sugar
250 ml (9 fl oz) double cream
juice of 1 orange
1 carton mango or orange yogurt
grated bitter chocolate

Embed a fork in the stalk end of each mango and peel away the skin, as if peeling a banana. Still with the fork embedded, slice off the pulp as close to the hairy paddle as you can decently get. Put the pulp in a liquidizer and blend with the lemon juice until smooth. Sieve to remove hairy fibres and return to the liquidizer.

Dissolve the gelatine with the water as described in the basic recipe on p. 124. Add this to the liquidizer with the sugar. Blend again until smooth. Allow to cool but not set, then add the lightly whipped cream. Chill in the bowl for at least 3 hours to set.

Whisk the orange juice into the yogurt and pour a pool of sauce on to each plate. Take a dessertspoon with a pleasing, oval shape and dip it into a cup of hot water. Shape good ovals of mousse on the spoon (3 per serving) and turn them over on to the sauce. Sprinkle with grated chocolate and serve.

Strawberry Charlotte

A featherlight mousse of strawberries and cream is kept in check by a corset of hazelnut biscuits or sponge fingers.

Serves 6

30 ml (2 tbsp) sweet white wine
60 ml (4 tbsp) water
about 40 hazelnut biscuits or sponge fingers
double quantity basic fruit mousse (p. 124) made with 900 g (2 lb) strawberries
30 ml (2 tbsp) kirsch or framboise (optional)
90 ml (6 tbsp) sugar
6–8 beautiful strawberries, unhulled and unwashed

Lightly oil a 23 cm (9 inch) springform cake tin. Combine the wine and half the water. Lay the hazelnut biscuits or sponge fingers out on a large dish and brush them with the wine and water mixture. Use them immediately, before they get too soggy, to line the springform tin, standing them upright side by side all around the inside wall.

Make a strawberry mousse as described in the basic recipe on p. 124 and stir in the liqueur if used. Pour the mixture into the lined tin and put in the fridge for at least 3 hours.

Make a caramel (see p. 153 for detailed instructions) by dissolving the sugar in the remaining water, gently at first until the liquid is clear, and then boiling to a light brown caramel. Remove from the heat and cool slightly. Hold the unhulled strawberries by the tail (or spear on a toothpick) and twirl them around carefully in the caramel. Set aside on non-stick baking paper to harden.

Release the spring from the cake tin and put the cake on a plain serving plate. Garnish with the caramelized strawberries. A bowl of *fromage blanc* and a coulis of strawberries goes nicely with this.

Terrine of Rhubarb with Syrupy Orange Slices

Really a sort of glorified rhubarb fool, the rhubarb mousse is moulded in a terrine lined with syrupy orange slices.

Serves 6–8

150 g (5 oz) sugar
100 ml (4 fl oz) water
600 g ($1\frac{1}{4}$ lb) well-trimmed fresh or frozen rhubarb
2 (blood) oranges, unpeeled, sliced thinly
6 sheets or 15 ml (1 tbsp) powdered gelatine
90 ml (6 tbsp) fruity white wine such as muscat
250 ml (9 fl oz) double or whipping cream

In a wide, heavy pan make a syrup with the sugar and water and simmer the rhubarb gently in it (plus rendered juice if using frozen rhubarb) for 4–5 minutes or until just tender. Remove the rhubarb with a slotted spoon and put it into a liquidizer.

Boil the residual juices until thick and well-reduced, then cook the orange slices in this syrup, turning them once or twice, until they are soft but not mushy. Fish them out with a skewer and use to line the base and walls of a lightly oiled 1.1 kg (2½ lb) terrine.

Soak the gelatine as described in the basic recipe on p. 124 and dissolve it in the wine. Add it hot to the rhubarb in the liquidizer and blend until smooth. Taste, adding more sugar if necessary. Let this mixture cool, then add the lightly whipped cream.

Pour the mousse into the orange-lined terrine, tap it down sharply to settle the contents and put it in the fridge for at least 3 hours to set. To serve run a knife round the edge and turn out. Remove the orange slices for easier cutting and lay them on top of each serving.

Blackberry Mousse Cake with Sponge Spirals

A blackberry mousse is poured into a cake tin lined with slices of blackberry jelly Swiss roll.

Serves 6–8

a 3-egg sponge (p. 119) baked in a 30 × 40 cm (12 × 16 inch) case
60–75 ml (4–5 tbsp) blackberry jelly
450 g (1 lb) blackberries
150 g (5 oz) sugar
6 sheets or 15 ml (1 tbsp) powdered gelatine
60 ml (4 tbsp) water
30 ml (2 tbsp) *crème de cassis*
250 ml (9 fl oz) double or whipping cream

Trim the sponge sheet, spread with jelly and roll up tightly. Wrap in foil and put into the freezer for about 1 hour to firm up and make slicing easier.

Put the blackberries into a large, non-aluminium pan, add the sugar and stew gently until the juices run – about 5 minutes. Put them with their juice in a liquidizer and blend until smooth. Push through a sieve to eliminate the pips and return to the liquidizer.

Soak the gelatine as described in the basic recipe on p. 124, then dissolve it in the water and *crème de cassis* and add it hot to the blackberry purée. Blend again until smooth and allow to cool, then add the softly whipped cream as usual.

Remove the sponge from the freezer and, still frozen, slice it very thinly. Arrange the slices on the bottom and around the sides of a 25 cm (10 inch) springform tin or *moule à manquer*, pour in the mousse and put in the fridge for at least 3 hours until set.

Release the spring from the cake tin (or invert the *moule à manquer*) and set the cake on a serving plate. Serve with vanilla sauce (p. 138).

THEME 23

CHOCOLATE MOUSSES

for chilled or frozen desserts, mousse cakes and nutty variations

There are almost as many different recipes for chocolate mousse as there are days in the year, and I tried out a fairly good proportion of them before settling for this one, an adaptation of Fred's (pastry chef at Le Crocodile in Strasbourg, who also gave most of the tips). In this recipe, whole eggs and extra yolks are whisked to a snow with a little sugar (a bit like a sabayon), combined with melted, cooled chocolate and lightened with whipped cream. Needless to say, it's only as good as the chocolate which goes into it, so if your chocolate is not one you would ordinarily enjoy nibbling, don't use it for a mousse.(Chocolate-flavoured cake covering will *not* do.)

Chocolate mousse is delicious in its own right, but as it is extremely versatile and lends itself to lots of other possibilities the recipe is quite a large one, enabling you to do at least two variations on the theme: freeze it and it becomes an ice cream, encase it in layers or walls of sponge, nut biscuits, tuiles, meringue layers or rolled up sponge sheets and you can create sophisticated and elegant puddings.

WATCHPOINTS

Chocolate mousse is a minefield of potential disasters: melting chocolate over too high heat, or the introduction of even the tiniest drop of moisture will cause it to tighten into an unusable mass. Melt it in a bowl suspended over (but not touching) nearly simmering water in a pan and take extreme care not to let in any drops of moisture. For the same reason, if adding a liqueur, now is *not* the moment to do it – add later when all is combined and the danger is over. If your chocolate should 'block', some people suggest adding a knob of margarine or butter; Fred shakes his head and says the only remedy is to add quite a lot of water, a little sugar, and boil it up to make a chocolate sauce (see Citrus Almond Roulade with chocolate sauce, p. 122); then start your mousse again with a fresh lot of chocolate.

Chill the bowl and the cream before whipping, for more volume and a quicker result; it should not be so stiff you could pipe it out, but should form soft peaks which should hold their shape. It will turn to butter if you do not watch it carefully and reduce the speed of whipping as it thickens. The whipped cream will give extra body (but an illusion of lightness, because of all the air you've beaten in) to the finished mousse.

BASIC

CHOCOLATE MOUSSE

Makes about 1 litre (1¾ pints), serving 6–8

best-quality plain chocolate	200 g (7 oz)
whole eggs	2
egg yolks	2
caster sugar	50 g (2 oz)
whipping cream, well-chilled	300 ml (½ pint)
rum (optional)	30 ml (2 tbsp)

Put the chocolate into a bowl over a pan of hot, not boiling water. Allow it to liquefy, then remove it from the heat. In an electric mixer at high speed (or with a hand-held mixer in a bowl over the pan of hot water) beat together the eggs, yolks and sugar until pale yellow, very light and tripled in bulk.

Fold in the melted, cooled chocolate with a wire whisk: the egg mixture will lose a lot of volume, which is normal, but keep going until the chocolate is evenly and smoothly mixed. Whip the cream to soft peaks, then fold it carefully with the optional rum into the cool chocolate and egg mixture.

Pour directly into a serving bowl or 8–10 individual dishes or coupes and chill in the fridge; or use as suggested right.

VARIATIONS

- Instead of plain chocolate, use milk, white, Toblerone or mint chocolate.
- Instead of rum, use strong coffee, or Grand Marnier, Cointreau, a fruit *eau-de-vie* (especially *framboise*), etc.
- Give extra flavour and texture to the mousse with crumbled macaroons, crushed meringues, peppermint essence, crunchy breakfast cereal (muesli), etc.

Further IDEAS

Bi-coloured chocolate mousses: use half white chocolate and half plain chocolate, and divide the remaining ingredients between the two chocolates. Or, for a larger quantity, double or triple the recipe, using 2 or 3 different types of chocolate. Layer in ramekins or a glass serving dish.

Mousse ovals: instead of pouring into a dish or ramekins, chill the mousse (any colour, or a selection) in the mixing bowl(s) until firm, spoon out mousse ovals with a wetted spoon and serve over a vanilla sauce (p. 138) or fruit coulis.

Chocolate 'soufflés': tie a collar of foil or greaseproof paper around the ramekins and pour in the mousse to come up into the collar. Chill until firm, remove collars, decorate and serve.

Or pour the mousse as usual into ramekins leaving a little head space; put in the fridge until firm, then pour over a thin layer of melted chocolate (same flavour, or contrasting) and return to the fridge until set hard. The contrast of the hard shell and soft mousse is rather pleasing.

Chocolate orange mousses: flavour the mousse with Grand Marnier and pour it into halved, emptied out oranges – use the flesh for an orange salad to accompany.

Layer the chocolate mousse (any colour), before it has set, with meringue discs (p. 145) or sponge sheets (p. 119). Or pour it into small sweet pastry cases (p. 83), or a sponge finger- or macaroon-lined springform tin.

White Chocolate Mousse in Minty Boxes

The extreme sweetness of white chocolate is nicely counterbalanced here by the bitter chocolate and mint of the After 8 boxes, with a good colour contrast.

Serves 8

32 After Eight mints
1 quantity chocolate mousse
(p. 129) made with white
chocolate
fresh mint leaves
200 g (7 oz) raspberries
100 g (4 oz) icing sugar
lemon juice to taste

Tear off strips of heavy duty foil and fold them over to make bands the same width as the mints. Put a piece of non-stick baking paper on a flat board which will fit in the fridge. Make eight 4-sided cases with the mints, using the doubled foil strips as a brace, and secure with pins or a stapler.

Make up the chocolate mousse as described in the basic recipe on p. 129, using white instead of bitter chocolate. About half will be needed for this recipe; the rest can be frozen or used in another dessert. Spoon about 45 ml (3 tbsp) mousse into each of the boxes. Put the whole business into the fridge to set firm.

Make a raspberry coulis by liquidizing the fruit with the icing sugar; push through a sieve to eliminate pips, sharpen with lemon juice to taste and thin with water to a pouring consistency. To serve, lift the boxes on to serving plates with a fish slice, release the foil corset, top each one with a fresh mint leaf and serve the coulis round about.

Iced Meringue Sandwiches with Chocolate Mousse

Plain meringue mixture is divided in half, one half to be flavoured with hazelnuts and the other with cocoa. Spread out wafer-thin and baked dry, the rounds are then sandwiched with a plain chocolate mousse.

Makes 6

3 egg whites
a pinch of salt
150 g (5 oz) caster sugar
5 ml (1 tsp) white wine vinegar
30 ml (2 tbsp) ground hazelnuts
15 ml (1 tbsp) cocoa powder
1 quantity plain chocolate
mousse (p. 129)
1 quantity orange-flavoured
vanilla sauce (p. 138) (optional)

Draw 12 circles on 2 sheets of non-stick baking paper, each circle 10 cm (4 inches) in diameter. Make up the plain meringue mixture with the egg whites, salt, sugar and vinegar as described on p. 144 and divide it in half. To one half add the ground hazelnuts and leave the other plain. Spread the meringue 5 mm ($\frac{1}{4}$ inch) thick into each of the 12 circles and sift the cocoa powder through a tea strainer over the top of the plain meringue discs. Bake the meringue discs for about an hour in a 120°C (250°F) mark $\frac{1}{2}$ oven until set but not coloured.

Make up the chocolate mousse as described in the basic recipe on p. 129, but do not chill it. You will need a little over half for this recipe; freeze the rest for ice cream or use in one of the other recipes in this section.

Set the 6 hazelnut meringue discs on a tray which will fit into the freezer. Make a doubled foil collar to fit around them, 3 cm (1$\frac{1}{2}$ inches) high and fix with a stapler. Spoon a 1 cm ($\frac{1}{2}$ inch) layer of mousse over each of the 6 hazelnut discs and smooth it in to make sure there are no air gaps. Put the cocoa-sprinkled meringue discs on top, pressing down gently to make sure they are flush with the mousse. Put in the freezer to harden.

Just before serving, remove the meringues from the freezer, peel off the foil collars and serve, if wished, with the vanilla sauce poured around.

Chocolate Mousse in Hazelnut Fingers or Macaroons

Plain chocolate mousse is layered with white and poured into a springform tin lined with hazelnut fingers or macaroons.

Serves 8–10

100 g (4 oz) plain chocolate
100 g (4 oz) white chocolate
2 whole eggs
2 egg yolks
50 g (2 oz) caster sugar
300 ml ($\frac{1}{2}$ pint) whipping cream
hazelnut fingers or macaroons
30 ml (2 tbsp) eau-de-vie de framboise (or other liqueur)
30 ml (2 tbsp) water
200 g (7 oz) redcurrants
100 g (4 oz) icing sugar

Melt the 2 sorts of chocolate in two different bowls. Then proceed as described in the basic recipe on p. 129: whisk together the whole eggs, egg yolks and sugar, and divide this mixture between the 2 bowls of melted chocolate. Whip the cream to soft peaks and divide also between the 2 mixtures.

Splash enough hazelnut fingers or macaroons to line a 23 cm (9 inch) springform cake tin with the mixed *framboise* and water and arrange them all around the sides. Pour in half the white chocolate mousse and put briefly in the freezer to firm it up a little. Then pour on the plain chocolate mousse and return to the freezer. Finally pour on the remaining white chocolate and put it in the fridge.

Release the spring from the cake tin, put the cake on a plain round plate and serve with a redcurrant coulis: purée the redcurrants with the icing sugar, sieve and dilute to a pouring consistency with water.

Chocolate Mousse Ovals in Almond Tuile Boats

Alternating ovals of dark and white chocolate mousse set sail in tuile boats.

Serves 6

100 g (4 oz) plain chocolate
100 g (4 oz) white chocolate
2 whole eggs
2 egg yolks
50 g (2 oz) caster sugar
400 ml (14 fl oz) whipping cream
30 ml (2 tbsp) orange liqueur

TUILES
2 egg whites
75 g (3 oz) sugar
50 g (2 oz) flaked almonds
30 ml (2 tbsp) plain white flour, sifted
grated zest of $\frac{1}{2}$ orange
5 ml (1 tsp) orange liqueur or orange-flower water

Make up the 2 colours of chocolate mousse as described in the basic recipe on p. 129: melt the 2 sorts of chocolate separately, whisk the eggs, yolks and sugar, divide in half and whisk the plain chocolate into one half and the white chocolate into the other. Whip the cream to soft peaks, divide in half and incorporate this also, along with 15 ml (1 tbsp) orange liqueur for each mousse. Chill the mousses well.

For the tuiles, mix gently together the egg whites, sugar, almonds, flour, orange zest and liqueur or orange-flower water. Use 2 baking sheets lined with non-stick baking paper and spread 6 teaspoons on to each, well spaced out. Flatten them with a wet fork – they should be very thin.

Heat the oven to 200°C (400°F) mark 6 and bake for about 8 minutes until golden brown. Remove, and while still warm and flexible, lift with a spatula and press them into a non-stick or greased ring mould to curve them up. On another sheet of baking paper, draw 12 sail shapes and fill them with the remaining mixture. Bake them too, then prise them off the paper and allow to cool flat on a rack.

Arrange two boats on each plate, fill with an oval of each sort of mousse and give each one a sail. Serve with slices of fresh fruit (strawberries, kiwis, mango, etc.), in season.

THEME 24

SABAYONS

for fruit gratins, ice creams, soufflés and mousses

A sabayon (zabaglione) is most commonly a simple egg mousse base where yolks are beaten to an ethereal foam with sugar and liqueur (or fruit juice) over heat. If you add a proportion of whole egg, the mixture is still lighter. I have an insomniac scientist friend who specializes in sneaking down to the kitchen at dead of night to whip up a sabayon for a quick midnight snack; his preference is to eat it all by itself, without further ceremony, but I think it really comes into its own when poured over fresh fruit and gratinéd, or when used as the base for a particularly light, soft ice cream (usually called a parfait), or as the departure point for iced 'soufflés' or gelatine-set desserts.

WATCHPOINTS

Many books recommend a double boiler for making a sabayon, but as this does not give you enough room in which to beat the yolks and sugar to the required volume, I think it's better to beat it in a metal bowl placed over nearly boiling water with a hand-held mixer or balloon whisk; or – easier still if you have one – use a powerful electric mixer on a stand, when no heat will be necessary. The point is that the mixture must triple in bulk and become very light and mousse-like. Beating is more important than heating: you're not trying to cook it (the eggs remain virtually raw and the sabayon is at most tepid), but to give it maximum volume and lightness.

The amount of sugar will depend on the sweetness of your tooth, and on the wine (or fruit juice, see Variations) and liqueur used – 20–30 ml (4–6 tsp) per yolk is the usual range.

BASIC

SABAYON

Makes about 1 litre (1¾ pints), serving 6–8

egg yolks	3
whole egg	1
caster sugar	75–100 g (3–4 oz)
sweetish wine	90 ml (6 tbsp)
liqueur (optional)	30–45 ml (2–3 tbsp)

Whisk together the egg yolks, whole egg, sugar, wine and liqueur if used until light, fluffy and tripled in bulk. Pour into glasses, coupes, brandy balloons, etc. and serve within the hour, before the mixture starts to liquefy again. Or put into a bowl or jug and serve with fresh fruit, ice cream, cakes, etc.; or pour over sliced, fresh fruit and put briefly under the grill to gratiner (or use a blow-torch). Or allow the sabayon to cool and proceed with any of the following suggestions.

VARIATIONS

Further IDEAS

● Beat into the yolks and egg any of the following for further flavour: lemon, orange or lime zest, a little ginger, vanilla or cinnamon, etc., depending on your taste and what the sabayon is to accompany/turn into.

● For wine, use a rich, fruity white (muscat, sauternes, etc.) or sherry, marsala or champagne; or substitute fruit juice (lemon, lime, orange, tangerine, mineola, grapefruit, or a mixture); or use strong coffee.

● For liqueur, use Grand Marnier, kirsch, fruit *eaux-de-vie*, rum, etc.

Ice cream (parfaits) (makes about 1.4 litres (2½ pints): add to the sabayon (in any of its variations) 300 ml (½ pint) softly whipped cream and freeze (in coupes, ramekins, tartlet tins, heart moulds, a terrine, etc.). Enrich if wished with any of the following, macerated in the liqueur used for the sabayon:

● raisins
● sultanas
● glacé cherries
● chopped candied peel
● dried apricots
● chopped stoned prunes

Or add crumbled meringues, macaroons, biscuits or praline (p. 153) for texture. Don't add cubes of fresh fruit, which freeze into little rocks in the finished ice.

Fruit ice creams: add 300 ml (½ pint) fruit purée sweetened to taste to the basic mixture, plus 300 ml (½ pint) softly whipped cream.

Layered ice creams: make 2 or 3 different flavours and layer them in a glass dish or coupes; or layer a parfait with a bought ice cream or sorbet.

Soufflé glacé: pour the parfait into a collared dish to come up inside the collar. Freeze until firm, then remove collar.

Vacherin glacé: make meringue rounds, squares, rectangles, etc. (p. 145), spread them with the well-chilled but still spreadable parfait, top with another meringue round and freeze.

Frozen ice cream cakes: spread parfait on to sponge sheets or rounds.

Mousse: dissolve 4 sheets or 10 ml (2 tsp) powdered softened gelatine (see p. 52 for detailed instructions on use of gelatine) in the liqueur or fruit juice and beat into the sabayon. Allow to cool, then fold in 300 ml (½ pint) softly whipped cream. Turn into moulds, ramekins, a terrine, etc. and chill until set.

Or line a charlotte mould or springform cake tin with:

● sponge fingers
● thin slices of Swiss roll
● non-stick baking paper spread with melted chocolate, and allowed to harden. Pour in the mousse.
● Or pour the mousse into little chocolate cups or almond pastry tartlets.

Sherry and Macaroon Parfait with Hot Berries

Ideal for using up that bottle of euphemistically named 'medium dry' (i.e. sickeningly sweet) sherry in the cupboard, a light parfait with crumbled macaroons is frozen in a loaf tin, cut into slices and served with warm, sharp red fruits for a good contrast.

Serves 6–8

3 egg yolks
1 whole egg
75 g (3 oz) sugar
90 ml (6 tbsp) medium dry sherry
300 ml (½ pint) whipping cream
45 ml (3 tbsp) crushed macaroons or sweet biscuits
250 g (9 oz) frozen raspberries or black or redcurrants
extra sugar to taste

Line a 1.4 kg (3 lb) loaf tin with foil. Make a sabayon as described in the basic recipe on p. 133 with the egg yolks, whole egg, sugar and sherry. Whip the cream to soft peaks and fold it in, together with the macaroon or biscuit crumbs.

Pour into the lined tin and freeze until firm. Shortly before serving (parfaits never freeze very hard, so there is no need to take it out much beforehand) lift the whole parcel out of the tin, peel away the foil and put the parfait on a serving plate.

Heat the raspberries or currants in a pan with sugar to taste – not too much, as the ice is very sweet and a contrast is important. Serve in a bowl to accompany.

Gratin of Pineapple with an Orange Sabayon

An orange/kirsch sabayon is poured over sliced fresh pineapple and put briefly under the grill at the last minute to dapple with gold.

Serves 8

1 medium pineapple, about 1 kg (2 lb 2 oz), to give 8 slices
3 egg yolks
1 whole egg
45 ml (3 tbsp) kirsch
90 ml (6 tbsp) orange juice
100 g (4 oz) caster sugar

Cut the skin off the pineapple and remove the eyes. Slice into 8 fairly thin slices, stamp out the cores with an apple corer and put the fruit to chill.

Whisk together the egg yolks, whole egg, liqueur, orange juice and sugar to make a sabayon as described in the basic recipe on p. 133. Set aside – it will remain stable for at least an hour. Shortly before serving, put the pineapple slices on plates which will stand a spell under the grill and cut each slice into wedges. Spoon the sabayon over and put briefly under a hot grill to dapple with golden flecks.

Chef Michel Husser uses the same system for segments of orange (navels or blood, or alternating) or grapefruit (plain or pink-fleshed, or alternating): peel the fruit *à vif* (to the quick) and cut out the segments, leaving behind the pith. Squeeze any excess juice into the sabayon in place of some of the orange juice, splay out the segments on a plate, cover with the sabayon and gratiner as usual.

Lime Mousse Gâteau with a Gelatine Mirror

A lime mousse on a sabayon base is poured over a layer of lightly set lime jelly and covered with a light sponge which, when the gâteau is inverted, becomes the base. A super-chic, sharp, light dessert – ideal after a rich meal. Lemons may be substituted for limes.

Serves 6

a 3-egg sponge (p. 119) baked in a 24 cm (9½ inch) tin
30 ml (2 tbsp) fresh lime juice
30 ml (2 tbsp) water
30 ml (2 tbsp) caster sugar
15 ml (1 tbsp) light rum

LIME JELLY
2 sheets or 5 ml (1 tsp) powdered gelatine
150 ml (¼ pint) fresh lime juice
45 ml (3 tbsp) water
100 g (4 oz) caster sugar
1 thin slice of lime

MOUSSE
3 egg yolks
1 whole egg
150 g (5 oz) caster sugar
100 ml (4 fl oz) lime juice
4 sheets or 10 ml (2 tsp) powdered gelatine
30 ml (2 tbsp) rum
300 ml (½ pint) whipping cream

Cut a 1 cm (½ inch) horizontal slice from the sponge, lay a 22 cm (8½ inch) Teflon-lined *moule à manquer* or similar sized glass or porcelain dish over it as a template and trim the sponge to fit. (Use the rest of the sponge for another purpose, or freeze.)

Make a thin syrup by simmering together the lime juice, water, sugar and rum and set aside to cool.

To make the lime jelly, soften the gelatine sheets in a bowl of cold water, squeeze out and dissolve in a pan with the lime juice, water and sugar, or sprinkle the powdered gelatine on to the water in a small pan, soften, then add the lime juice and sugar and dissolve. Brush the *moule à manquer* with a film of tasteless oil and strain in the jelly. Put in the fridge to set, and when almost set, put the lime slice on top. Return to the fridge.

Meanwhile, make a sabayon as described in the basic recipe on p. 133 with the egg yolks, whole egg, sugar and all but 45 ml (3 tbsp) of the lime juice. Soak sheet gelatine in cold water as above until floppy, then dissolve in the remaining juice and rum, or sprinkle powdered gelatine over remaining juice and rum, then dissolve. Whisk the liquid gelatine into the sabayon. Put in the fridge, stirring from time to time until it begins to thicken.

Whip the cream until soft peaks form. When the sabayon base begins to thicken and is almost the same consistency as the whipped cream, fold the two together. Pour this mousse over the set layer of jelly and return to the fridge until set.

Splash the sponge sheet with the syrup and lay it over the top of the mousse; return to the fridge and leave overnight. About an hour before serving, dip the bottom of the tin briefly in hot water and turn the gâteau out on to a serving plate.

Emile Jung's Iced Grand Marnier Bombs

From Le Crocodile in Strasbourg comes this light orange parfait covering a surprise nugget of sorbet or ice cream and served with a warm blood orange salad.

Serves 8

3 egg yolks
1 whole egg
200 g (7 oz) caster sugar
juice of 1 blood orange
30 ml (2 tbsp) Grand Marnier or Cointreau
300 ml ($\frac{1}{2}$ pint) whipping cream
8 scoops of ice cream or sorbet of your choice
6 blood oranges
150 ml ($\frac{1}{4}$ pint) water

Make a sabayon with the egg yolks, whole egg, 100 g (4 oz) of the sugar, the orange juice and Grand Marnier, as described in the basic recipe on p. 133. Allow it to cool. Whip the cream until in soft peaks and fold it carefully into the sabayon base.

Use 8 × 200 ml (7 fl oz) containers such as yogurt or cottage cheese cartons to mould this dessert. In the bottom of each one, place a rounded scoop of ice cream or sorbet. Pour over the sabayon to cloak it completely and put in the freezer to harden.

Peel the oranges, saving any juice, slice them rather thinly and halve the slices. Put the orange slices and the juice into a bowl. Make a caramel with the remaining sugar and 45 ml (3 tbsp) of the water. When it is a rich golden, remove it from the heat, cover your hand with a cloth to prevent splashing and add the rest of the water to liquefy the caramel again. Set aside.

Remove the bombs from the freezer, run a knife around the edge and turn them out on to serving plates. Surround with halved slices of orange, reheat the liquid caramel briefly and pour it over the oranges.

SWEET CUSTARDS

crèmes anglaise *and* pâtissière *for sauces,* bavarois, *ice creams and fillings*

Custard (bright yellow and out of a packet) belongs in the nursery. *Crèmes anglaise* and *pâtissière* are also custards, if the truth be told, but they're made on a base of egg yolks, milk and real vanilla and have graduated with honours to the dinner table: they sound much more fetching when translated as vanilla sauce and pastry cream respectively.

Vanilla sauce in its naked state lifts an otherwise fairly ordinary dessert into another class, and can be flavoured with coffee, orange or fruit juice instead of vanilla. With a little embroidery, it becomes a bavarois or Real Ice Cream. Pastry cream, that delectable rib-sticking confection found under those wicked strawberry tarts in French pâtisseries, can be used to fill profiteroles, millefeuilles and tartlet shells, and serves as a sweet soufflé base.

WATCHPOINTS

A vanilla pod or ground vanilla gives more flavour than the essence (which is often not even vanilla) and leaves tell-tale black specks. The pods can be used several times: rinse off after each use and bury in the sugar.

Vanilla sauce is very lightly thickened without additional starch to about the consistency of single cream, and on no account must boil or you will have scrambled eggs. If you're nervous, use a double boiler; if a little nonchalant, a heavy-bottomed saucepan will do.

Pastry cream, on the other hand, can (and must, to cook the starch) be boiled in order to thicken it correctly.

The obvious place for all the extra egg whites is the meringues (p. 144), but don't forget they can also be used in pastry (p. 81), pasta (p. 66) salad dressings (p. 76) and almond tuiles (p. 153).

BASIC

VANILLA SAUCE

Makes about 600 ml (1 pint)

milk	500 ml (18 fl oz)
vanilla pod, split lengthways	1
egg yolks	6
caster sugar	100 g (4 oz)

Heat the milk to boiling with the vanilla pod. Beat the yolks with the sugar to a very pale fluffy mass. Pour on the nearly boiling milk, return everything to the rinsed out pan and stir over gentle heat until wisps of steam are evident, a definite channel can be made on the spoon and the sauce is about the consistency of single cream.

Strain it into the mixing bowl, cover with clingfilm and leave to cool. (If left in the pan it will continue to cook on the bottom.)

Use chilled vanilla sauce to go with meringues, cakes, mousses, floating islands etc.

B A S I C

PASTRY CREAM

Makes about 600 ml (1 pint)

milk	500 ml (18 fl oz)
vanilla pod, split lengthways	1
egg yolks	6
caster sugar	100 g (4 oz)
plain white flour or cornflour	50 g (2 oz)

Heat the milk to boiling with the vanilla pod. Beat the yolks with the sugar and starch to a very pale fluffy mass. Pour on the nearly boiling milk, return everything to the rinsed out pan and stir over moderate heat until a boil is reached. Stir like crazy to prevent lumps forming and if it is thickening too fast and unevenly for your liking, remove it from the heat and whisk until smooth.

Return to the heat and simmer gently for 2–3 minutes to cook the starch. Rub a knob of butter over the surface to prevent a skin forming.

Use chilled pastry cream as a base on which to sit fresh fruit in a pastry case or as a filling for profiteroles, millefeuilles, brioches or dessert crêpes.

V A R I A T I O N S

● *An extra rich sauce (for crème brûlée)*: make a vanilla sauce with half milk and half cream, or all cream. (Sprinkle the set custard with sugar and caramelize under a grill for *crème brûlée*.)
● Instead of a vanilla pod, use 5 ml (1 tsp) ground vanilla (or essence). Or flavour the milk with mint leaves, blackcurrant leaves, lemon balm, scented tea, lightly crushed coffee beans or a piece of cinnamon stick, crumbled; then strain and use as before. Or make a caramel (p. 153), remove it from the heat and pour the milk on to it. Proceed as before.
● Or whisk any of the following alternative flavourings in with the yolks and sugar:
grated zest of an orange or lemon
30 ml (2 tbsp) strong coffee
30 ml (2 tbsp) cocoa powder
30 ml (2 tbsp) liqueur of your choice
● Or flavour the ready-made sauce or pastry cream with a little puréed fruit, or some praline (p. 153).

Using vanilla sauce
Bavarois (gelatine-set mousse on a vanilla sauce base): make a vanilla sauce (or any of its variations) and add to the still hot sauce 6 sheets soaked and squeezed gelatine (or 15 ml (1 tbsp) powdered, soaked and dissolved in 30 ml (2 tbsp) water). Stir to make sure the gelatine is well distributed and dissolved. Cool, then add 200 ml (7 fl oz) softly whipped cream. Chill until set.

Fruit bavarois: make a plain vanilla sauce, add 6 sheets or 15 ml (1 tbsp) powdered gelatine as above to the hot sauce, cool, then add 200 g (7 oz) puréed, sieved fruit and 200 ml (7 fl oz) softly whipped cream. Chill until set.

Ice cream: add 300 ml ($\frac{1}{2}$ pint) softly whipped cream to the cool sauce (in any of its variations) and freeze, stirring occasionally to prevent ice crystals forming.

Using pastry cream
Crème Chiboust: add 30 ml (2 tbsp) caster sugar to 6 stiffly whisked egg whites and fold them into the hot pastry cream, plain or flavoured.

Gâteau St. Honoré: make a sweet shortcrust pastry base, pipe a ring of choux pastry around for the wall and bake until the base is set and the choux firm. Fill the hole with Crème Chiboust.
Or spread Crème Chiboust over fresh or poached fruit and bake at 200°C (400°F) mark 6 until golden and puffy.

Graham Dunton (pastry chef at the Connaught)'s puits d'amour: load the Crème Chiboust into little tartlet shells and bake at 200°C (400°F) mark 6 for about 10 minutes or until golden and puffy.

Crème Chiboust soufflés: put the crème in well-buttered and sugared ramekins, or hollowed out fruit, and bake at 200°C (400°F) mark 6 for 7–8 minutes or until risen and golden.

Chocolate Almond Sponge with Raspberry Crème Anglaise

A raspberry-flavoured *crème anglaise* both complements and contrasts with a moist chocolate almond cake.

Serves 6–8

4 eggs
125 g (4½ oz) caster sugar
125 g (4½ oz) best plain chocolate
125 g (4½ oz) butter
75 ml (5 tbsp) ground almonds
50 g (2 oz) plain white flour, sifted
450 g (1 lb) raspberries
1 quantity basic vanilla sauce (p. 138)
icing sugar

Heat the oven to 180°C (350°F) mark 4. Grease and flour a 22 cm (8½ inch) springform cake tin and cut a disc of non-stick baking paper to fit the bottom. In an electric mixer beat the eggs and sugar together at high speed for about 5 minutes or until very light, pale and interesting. They should be tripled in bulk.

Melt the chocolate in a bowl sitting over a pan of hot, not boiling, water. Add the butter bit by bit, stirring to make a smooth paste. Cool to tepid.

Mix together the ground almonds and flour and fold them into the beaten eggs. Dribble the melted chocolate and butter around the edge and fold it in carefully but quickly. Do not overmix, otherwise everything will collapse in disarray. Pour into the prepared cake tin and bake for 35–40 minutes or until just risen, firm to the touch and a skewer inserted in the middle comes out clean. Remove from the oven and allow to cool a little before releasing the spring. Cool on a cake rack.

Set aside 9 beautiful raspberries for the top of the cake and purée the rest in a liquidizer. Push through a sieve and return to the liquidizer with the vanilla sauce. Blend until smooth.

Set the cake on your best white plate and pour a little sauce around. Sprinkle with icing sugar, arrange the reserved raspberries on top and serve the rest of the sauce separately.

Stripey Strawberry and Raspberry Charlotte

For people who enjoy a bit of a challenge, this recipe creates something amazingly elegant out of very simple beginnings. The basic vanilla sauce is flavoured with fruit, lightly set with gelatine and enriched with cream to give a bavarois. It is then moulded in a corset of stripey sponge strips which stand around the charlotte like railings.

Serves 8

a 3-egg sponge (p. 119) baked in a 28 × 38 cm (11 × 15 inch) case
redcurrant jelly
6 sheets or 15 ml (1 tbsp) powdered gelatine
30 ml (2 tbsp) sweet white wine
1 quantity basic vanilla sauce (p. 138)
200 g (7 oz) mixed strawberries and raspberries
200 ml (7 fl oz) whipping cream

GARNISH
extra fruit
lemon balm sprigs
borage flowers

Cut the sponge sheet in half lengthways and then cut each half into 4 equal long strips. Spread 7 of the strips with a thin layer of redcurrant jelly, top with the 8th and then stack them up one on top of another. Cut the stack crossways into 5 mm ($\frac{1}{4}$ inch) slices. Use them to line a lightly oiled 20 cm (8 inch) springform cake tin. Make sure the jelly lines are going vertically, like railings all around the edge, and trim the top edges so they are perfectly flush with the top of the tin.

If using sheet gelatine soak it in cold water until floppy, then squeeze it out and add to the wine. If using powdered gelatine, sprinkle it over the wine and leave until spongy. Dissolve either sort gently until clear. Make a vanilla sauce as described in the basic recipe on p. 138, then add the dissolved gelatine to the hot sauce, stirring to make sure it is thoroughly incorporated. Leave to cool.

Purée the fruit and sieve it to remove pips. Add this to the cool sauce. Whip the cream to soft peaks. When the fruit sauce is getting syrupy and is nearly set, fold in the cream. Pour it into the prepared tin, and chill until set.

Release the spring from the cake tin and set the charlotte on a serving plate. Arrange extra fruit, lemon balm sprigs and/or borage flowers on top.

Peach Chiboust

There's something wonderfully explosive about the name *Chiboust*, which refers to a pastry cream lightened with whisked egg whites. Here is a definitely explosive dessert: sharp, cool peaches cloaked in the lightened cream and baked to a warm golden halo.

Serves 8

8 ripe peaches
juice of 1 lemon
6 egg whites
a pinch of salt
30 ml (2 tbsp) caster sugar
1 quantity basic pastry cream (p. 139)
250 g (9 oz) raspberries
125 g (4$\frac{1}{2}$ oz) icing sugar

Skin the peaches by plunging them in boiling water for a few minutes, then peel. Put them on a lightly greased ovenproof dish and sprinkle with the lemon juice to prevent them from discolouring.

Beat the egg whites with the salt until stiff but still creamy, sprinkle on the caster sugar and continue to beat until stiff and meringue-like. Fold the meringue with a wire whisk into the hot pastry cream – it is important that the cream is hot, so reheat it if necessary. Spoon it carefully over the peaches. They can wait in the fridge for 2 or 3 hours, but not more or the cream will collapse.

Purée together the raspberries and icing sugar, push through a sieve and loosen with enough water to give a pouring consistency.

About 10 minutes before serving, heat the oven to 220°C (425°F) mark 7. Bake the peaches until the tops are golden brown and just firm to the touch. Serve at once with the raspberry coulis.

Bitter Chocolate Ice Cream

Any bitter chocolate that's good enough to eat is good enough for this.

Makes 1 litre (1¾ pints)

1 quantity basic vanilla sauce (p. 138)
150 g (5 oz) bitter chocolate
300 ml (½ pint) double or whipping cream

Make a vanilla sauce as described in the basic recipe on p. 138. Break up the chocolate and melt it in the hot sauce. Allow it to cool. Whip the cream until the beater leaves soft tracks and fold it into the cold sauce. Freeze in a metal bowl until semi-firm.

Stir up with a wire whisk and return to the freezer until hard. Serve in oval scoops over a coffee-flavoured vanilla sauce (see Variations) or orange-flavoured yogurt.

Blackcurrant Leaf Bavarois with Blackcurrant Ice Cream

Virginal white hearts of blackcurrant leaf mousse are served with home-made blackcurrant ice cream. Use ramekins if you don't have heart moulds.

Serves 8

20 blackcurrant leaves
500 ml (18 fl oz) milk
6 egg yolks
100 g (4 oz) caster sugar
6 sheets or 15 ml (1 tbsp) powdered gelatine
250 ml (9 fl oz) whipping cream
mint leaves, to garnish

ICE CREAM
450 g (1 lb) blackcurrants
225 g (8 oz) sugar
125 ml (4½ fl oz) water
3 egg yolks
300 ml (½ pint) whipping cream
30 ml (2 tbsp) *crème de cassis*

Rub the blackcurrant leaves between your hands a little to bring out the perfume and oil in them, then drop them into the milk in a saucepan. Bring to the boil, remove from the heat and let the leaves sit in the milk for at least 10 minutes to flavour it well. Strain, then use to make a *crème anglaise* with the egg yolks and sugar as described in the basic recipe for vanilla sauce on p. 138, but omitting the vanilla pod.

If using sheet gelatine, soak the sheets in cold water until floppy, squeeze them out and drop them in the hot *crème* when it is ready, stirring until dissolved. If using powdered gelatine, sprinkle it on to 45 ml (3 tbsp) water and leave until spongy. Stir into the hot *crème* until dissolved. Cool.

Whisk the cream until the beater leaves soft tracks, then fold this into the cool *crème*. Divide between 8 × 125 ml (4½ fl oz) Teflon-lined heart moulds (or other shape). Chill until set.

For the ice cream, cook the trimmed blackcurrants with half the sugar in a heavy saucepan for 4–5 minutes, just until the juice runs. Cool a little, then purée in a food processor or liquidizer and push through a sieve. Set aside.

Make a syrup to the thread stage: dissolve the remaining sugar in the water, then boil hard for about 10 minutes over moderately high heat until thick bubbles form. Dip a fork into the syrup and take a little between finger and thumb – a thread should form between them as you open and close them. Pour the syrup on to the beaten egg yolks and beat until very pale, mousse-like and doubled in volume.

Beat in the blackcurrant purée and allow it to cool. Whip the cream to soft peaks and fold it into the purée base with the *crème de cassis*. Freeze until firm.

Unmould the bavarois on to individual serving plates, garnish each with a mint leaf and serve a small oval scoop of ice cream to one side of each.

THEME 26

MERINGUES

for vacherins, toppings, layer cakes and meringue nests

There's more to meringues than meets the eye, and if you're
already an expert at making melting, gooey, marshmallowy
heaps, sandwiched together with whipped cream, you might
like to take your skills one step further: the basic proportions of
sugar to egg white (50 g (approximately 2 oz) sugar per white)
remain the same, but ground nuts, coffee, cocoa powder, lemon
or orange zest or even crunchy breakfast cereal can be
incorporated to give characteristic flavouring. You can make
discs, squares, rectangles (even heart shapes, if you're feeling in
the mood), and changes in the fillings can be rung almost
indefinitely.

WATCHPOINTS

Controversy rages as to whether your egg whites should be chilled or at room temperature before beating. I don't believe it makes any difference. Experts are, however, unanimous on the importance of a scrupulously clean, dry bowl, preferably metal. Copper bowls are seldom used even by top chefs nowadays, but while balloon whisks definitely are (and give the best volume and voluptuousness to whites), I find a powerful electric mixer on a stand is just as good; otherwise, place your bowl over a pan of nearly simmering water and use a hand mixer. Glass bowls are all right, plastic less good as they can harbour traces of grease.

A pinch of salt added to whites at the beginning gives them extra stability and volume; vinegar (or a pinch of cream of tartar) does the same, as well as giving them a melting, marshmallowy quality. If you like your meringues dry and

dusty, omit it. You can start beating whites slowly, to get them in the mood, then gradually increase the speed to maximum until really stiff, and finally add the sugar; or if you have a heavy duty mixer or are prepared to beat by hand for a long time, there's nothing to stop you putting whites, salt, sugar and vinegar all in together and beating until thoroughly stiff.

Stiffly whisked to a fine upstanding texture, the plain meringue is stable for at least an hour; if, however, you add any of the variants, most of which contain oil (nuts, cocoa powder, lemon zest), the meringue tends to go a bit runny and needs prompt shaping and baking. Always use non-stick baking paper for meringues and bake them at 120°C (250°F) mark $\frac{1}{2}$ for 1–1$\frac{1}{2}$ hours: you are really drying them out, rather than actually cooking them. They are done when firm

but not coloured, and can easily be lifted off the paper. People with Agas swear by them for meringues; I once made a batch in a hot air oven and the texture turned out like chewing gum, so don't recommend this type of oven for meringues.

Egg whites freeze well – some people claim they whip up better as a result. If you lose track of how many you have frozen, bear in mind that 1 egg white weighs 25–30 g (1 oz). I don't think there's any advantage in freezing meringues: too fragile and space-consuming.

BASIC

MERINGUE

	4-egg white quantity	6-egg white quantity
egg whites	4	6
salt	a pinch	a pinch
caster sugar	200 g (7 oz)	300 g (11 oz)
vinegar	10 ml (2 tsp)	15 ml (1 tbsp)

Beat the whites with the salt, slowly at first until foaming, then increase the speed to maximum and beat until in soft peaks. Still beating, sprinkle on the sugar and vinegar and continue to beat until the mixture is so stiff you could turn the whole bowl upside down without it falling out on to your feet. Shape the meringue(s) on to non-stick baking paper and dry out in a 120°C (250°F) mark ½ oven for about 1 hour, or until they will lift off the baking paper without opposition.

VARIATIONS

● Use soft light brown instead of white sugar for a rather different flavour and warm beige colour.

● To the stiffly whisked meringue, fold in any of the following:

4 egg white quantity		6 egg white quantity
75 g (3 oz)	ground almonds/hazelnuts	100 g (4 oz)
30 ml (2 tbsp)	sifted cocoa powder	45 ml (3 tbsp)
4	finely chopped After Eight mints	6
45 ml (3 tbsp)	crunchy breakfast cereal	60 ml (4 tbsp)

A contrast of tastes and
colours: White Chocolate Mousse in a Minty Box
surrounded by a crimson pool of raspberry coulis
(page 130)

A light orange parfait
enrobes a surprise nugget of ice cream in
Emile Jung's Iced Grand Marnier Bomb
(page 137)

*R*aspberry and chocolate
combine again, this time in a delicate confection,
Chocolate Almond Sponge in Raspberry Crème
Anglaise (page 140)

*F*inely-textured and
subtly-flavoured layers make Frozen Meringue
Torte with Rhubarb Ice Cream the ideal dessert for
a special dinner party (page 146)

Besides beautiful, billowy blobs, you can make layers for meringue cakes, shaped into:
- large discs
- small (individual size) discs
- rectangles
- ovals
- hearts (for anniversaries)
- diamonds (to be different)
- numbers (for children's birthday parties)

Draw the required shape on non-stick baking paper, fill with meringue, plain or in any of its variations (or 2 or 3 different sorts). Use a piping bag with plain 1 cm ($\frac{1}{2}$ inch) nozzle for quite thick layers, or spread very thinly (5 mm ($\frac{1}{4}$ inch)) with a dough scraper or the back of a spoon for thin, elegant layers.

Fill with:
- fruit purée
- ice cream
- whipped cream with praline (p. 153), toasted nuts or chocolate shavings;
- chocolate mousse (p. 129)
- fruit mousse (p. 124)
- Greek yogurt with sugar/jam/jelly/lemon curd, etc.
  with a preference for sharp fillings such as rhubarb or dried apricot purée, lemon ice cream, bitter chocolate or raspberry mousse, sliced kumquats, etc. to contrast with the sweetness of the meringue.

Or small meringue rounds can serve as the base for a wine-poached pear/peach/apple, sitting on a sharp raspberry coulis.

Or anoint a wine-poached pear/apple/peach with plain meringue, sprinkle with slivered almonds and bake at 220°C (425°F) mark 7 until lightly golden and set.

Pie toppings: spread the plain meringue mixture over an open-faced, ready-baked fruit tart. Bake in a 200°C (400°F) mark 6 oven just long enough to set the meringue and lightly colour it.

Pavlova: fold 20 ml (4 tsp) cornflour into the 4-egg white basic meringue on p. 144 (2 tbsp for 6-egg white quantity). Shape into a large round on non-stick baking paper and hollow out the middle a little. Bake as described on p. 144, fill with fresh fruit (passion fruit is practically mandatory) and whipped cream.

Floating islands (though why anyone would want to make such a deadly dull dessert, or eat it, is a mystery to me): make up the basic meringue mixture and poach great blobs of it in water or milk for 30 seconds on each side. Tradition dictates that they are then drizzled with caramel and sat on a pool of vanilla sauce (p. 138).

Soft Kiwi Ice Cream

A soft ice cream is made on a meringue base with kiwi purée and cream.

Serves 6

8 kiwis, to give about 300 g (11 oz) pulp
juice of 1 lemon
4 egg whites
200 g (7 oz) caster sugar
300 ml ($\frac{1}{2}$ pint) whipping cream
discreet drops of green food colouring

Peel the kiwis and purée to a smooth pulp with the lemon juice in a blender or food processor. Sieve to remove the black seeds.

Beat the egg whites and sugar as if making meringue (see p. 144). Lightly whip the cream to soft peaks. Fold the 3 preparations together and add a hint of green colouring if wished. Freeze until firm, and serve with almond tuiles (p. 153).

Frozen Meringue Torte with Rhubarb Ice Cream

The lint white of this meringue torte (very, very sweet), layered with the rhubarb ice and the carmine fruit sauce makes for an exceptionally beautiful and delicious dessert.

Serves 8–10

6-egg white quantity basic meringue (p. 144)
450 g (1 lb) rhubarb
150 g (5 oz) sugar
100 ml (4 fl oz) fruity white wine (e.g. muscat)
juice of ½ lemon
4 egg yolks
300 ml (½ pint) double or whipping cream
mint leaves

FRUIT COULIS
300 g (11 oz) raspberries or strawberries
lemon juice, to taste
icing sugar to taste

Draw 3 rectangles each 25 × 10 cm (10 × 4 inches) on non-stick baking paper and divide the meringue thinly and evenly between them, keeping back a little to pipe 8 tiny meringues. Bake as described in the basic meringue recipe on p. 144 at 120°C (250°F) mark ½ for about 1 hour or until just set but not coloured, and lift-off is obtained.

Cut the trimmed rhubarb into chunks and put into a heavy pan with the sugar, wine and lemon juice. Simmer gently for about 10 minutes until the juice runs. Lift the rhubarb out of the juice with a slotted spoon and purée until smooth. Boil the juice down until reduced by about half: you need 125 ml (4½ fl oz). Meanwhile, beat the yolks until creamy, then pour on the boiling rhubarb juice in a steady stream. Continue beating until thick and mousse-like. Fold in the purée and set aside to cool.

Whip the cream to soft peaks and fold into the cool rhubarb mixture. Freeze until semi-hard but still spreadable. Put one of the meringue strips on a large sheet of foil and spread it with a 1 cm (½ inch) layer of ice cream; follow with another meringue strip, more ice cream and the third strip. Bring the sides of foil closely up round the *torte*, fold over to make a tight parcel and put it in the freezer for several hours or overnight to firm up.

Make a raspberry or strawberry coulis: liquidize the fruit with the lemon juice, strain through a sieve, return to the liquidizer and sweeten to your liking with icing sugar. Blend again and loosen with a little water if it is too thick. Shortly before serving, remove the *torte* from the freezer and cut neat, even slices (an electric carving knife is good and doesn't squash things too much). On each plate put a little coulis and arrange two slices of torte on top. Garnish with the extra meringues and a mint leaf or two and take straight to the table.

Hazelnut and Almond Meringue Cake with Buttercream and Apple Filling

You need an apple with a little more character than a cooker for this gorgeous autumn cake – like a Cox, or Discovery, slightly under-ripe to give a tart contrast to the sweetness of the meringue and the buttercream. Prepare the cake the day before the party and it will be much easier to slice.

Serves 10

75 g (3 oz) shelled hazelnuts
75 g (3 oz) ground almonds
15 ml (1 tbsp) cornflour
6-egg white quantity basic meringue (p. 144)
1 kg (2 lb 2 oz) tart eating apples
25 g (1 oz) butter
60 ml (4 tbsp) apricot jam
grated rind and juice of ½ lemon
50 g (2 oz) sugar
30 ml (2 tbsp) calvados
30–45 ml (2–3 tbsp) chopped toasted almonds, to decorate

BUTTERCREAM
200 g (7 oz) unsalted butter
200 g (7 oz) icing sugar
2 egg yolks
5 ml (1 tsp) vanilla essence
45–60 ml (3–4 tbsp) calvados

Draw 3 × 20 cm (8 inch) circles on non-stick baking paper placed on baking sheets. Toast the hazelnuts in a 200°C (400°F) mark 6 oven until golden brown and fragrant. Reduce the oven to 120°C (250°F) mark ½.

Grind the cooled hazelnuts (husks and all) in a processor or nutmill and mix them with the ground almonds and cornflour. Make up the basic meringue as described on p. 144, fold in the nuts and cornflour and divide the mixture equally among the 3 circles. Smooth the tops with a palette knife or dough-scraper and bake them for about 1 hour or until they are firm and can easily be lifted off the paper. Lift them with a spatula on to a cake rack and leave to cool.

Peel, core and roughly chop the apples. Melt the butter in a non-aluminium pan (aluminium would discolour the fruit) and stew them gently until tender, stirring and squashing with a potato masher as they soften. Add the jam, lemon juice, rind and sugar. Raise the heat and cook, stirring, until really thick and syrupy. Cool.

Cream together the butter and icing sugar for the buttercream until light and fluffy. Add the egg yolks, vanilla and calvados and continue beating until mixed.

To assemble the cake, place a layer of nut meringue on a serving plate and spread with about one-third of the buttercream. Smooth over the top of it about half the apple mixture, then follow with another layer of meringue, more buttercream and apple and the final layer of meringue. Spread any remaining buttercream around the sides and press the toasted almonds against them. Put in the fridge to firm up.

If the top is very cracked, sieve a little icing sugar over it and decorate with a sprig of blackberries-with-their-leaves, if you happen to live conveniently near a hedgerow.

Caramel Meringue Cake with Lemon Curd Filling

The plain meringue is spread in two large discs, one over a layer of caramel which, after baking, softens into a delicious toffee layer, crowning the creamy, lemon curd-filled cake; a caramel sauce accompanies it.

Serves 8–10

250 g (9 oz) sugar
90 ml (6 tbsp) water
200 ml (7 fl oz) single cream
6-egg white quantity basic meringue (p. 144)
300 ml (½ pint) whipping cream
90 ml (6 tbsp) lemon curd
a little praline (p. 153)

Line two 30 cm (12 inch) cake tins or quiche tins with non-stick baking paper and grease and flour the sides. Make a caramel with the sugar and water (see p. 153) and drizzle about half of it in criss-crossed lines into one of the tins. Immediately pour the single cream on to the remaining caramel in the pan, and whisk it in vigorously. Set aside this sauce.

Make up the meringue as per the basic recipe on p. 144 and divide it between the two tins. Place the tin with the caramelized meringue in a bain-marie; bake them both in a 120°C (250°F) mark ½ oven for 1¼–1½ hours.

Whip the cream to soft peaks and stir in the lemon curd. As soon as the meringues are ready, remove them and put the uncaramelized disc of meringue on a large plate. Spread with the cream and lemon curd and immediately invert the caramelized disc over it, carefully peeling away the paper. Provided you do this while the caramel is still a little warm, it should not be difficult to remove the paper.

Refrigerate the cake for at least 6 hours or overnight. Serve the cake in slices laid over a pool of caramel sauce and sprinkle with a little praline.

PRESERVES

no jam, no marmalade, lots of chutney and tomato sauce

It's a source of continual disappointment to me that as a family, we don't eat much jam or marmalade. My preserving instincts are satisfactorily met, however, by the making of industrial quantities of chutney and tomato sauce.

Chutneys as we know them must, I think, have been adopted (if not actually invented) by grateful British nation to give flavour to our own national dishes which would otherwise have been terminally bland. This all-purpose recipe can be adapted to include whatever you have in the garden, larder or fridge, and which will vary according to the season, and to where you live. Chutneys should not be confined to cold meats and curries: many a dreary fish pie has been cheered by their company, and they can be used in stuffings for bland meats such as chicken or veal, or spread a thin layer over the bottom of quiches as a waterproof layer between filling and pastry. Give them attractive pots, hats and labels and keep a few for presents.

As for the tomato, if the Mexicans invented it, then the Italians patented the invention. Both of them seem to understand tomatoes, and make properly rich and wonderful sauces. Flavoured with basil, marjoram, oregano and olive oil, the sauce becomes Mediterranean; fried in lard with chillis, cuminseed or a pinch of cinnamon, there's more of a Mexican feel to it. Make up a good batch and freeze in 300 ml ($\frac{1}{2}$ pint) cartons.

W A T C H P O I N T S

Don't chop the ingredients too finely for chutneys: they should have a bit of character. Brown sugar will give a darker and slightly less sweet result than white in both chutney and tomato sauce. Boil down really hard to thicken and concentrate matters. It's impossible to be rigid about the cooking time, which will depend on your pan (a proper preserving pan, wide at the top, aids evaporation and speeds things up), your heat source and your choice of vegetables and fruits (the juicier they are, the longer it will take). The point is to reduce the mixture by about half and to achieve a rich, syrupy confection.

Chutney

BASIC

INGREDIENTS

For about 10 × 450 g (1 lb) jars

fruit, vegetables or a mixture	**3 kg (6$\frac{1}{2}$ lb)**
onions	**450 g (1 lb)**
chillis, fresh or dried, red or green	**4**
vinegar	**1 litre (1$\frac{3}{4}$ pints)**
sugar	**1 kg (2 lb 2 oz)**
raisins or sultanas	**400 g (14 oz)**
salt	**30 ml (2 tbsp)**
pickling spice (or make your own blend of mustard and coriander seeds/chillis/cloves/allspice)	**30 ml (2 tbsp)**
ground ginger	**30 ml (2 tbsp)**

Roughly chop or process the fruit, vegetables, onions and chillis, and put them in a large (e.g. preserving) pan with the remaining ingredients. Bring to the boil and simmer steadily for at least 1$\frac{1}{2}$ hours, or until thick and syrupy and there is no longer a watery layer floating about on top. Cool a little. Wash and dry in the oven 10 × 450 g (1 lb) jam jars with non-corroding lids. Pour the chutney through a funnel (or use a small jug with a good lip) into the hot jars, cover at once and label the jars. Cut discs rather larger than the lids out of some cheerful material, put them on top and secure with an elastic band. Leave for a good 6 months before broaching.

For fruit, use apples, plums, pears, apricots, mangoes, peaches etc. For vegetables, use tomatoes, carrots, peppers, courgettes, marrows etc., in different proportions and combinations.

2 kg (4½ lb) tomatoes + 200 g (7 oz) plums + 800 g (1¾ lb) apples
2 kg (4½ lb) apricots + 1 kg (2 lb 2 oz) apples
1 kg (2 lb 2 oz) tomatoes + 1 kg (2 lb 2 oz) apples + 1 kg (2 lb 2 oz) peppers
2 kg (4½ lb) pears + 450 g (1 lb) tomatoes + 450 g (1 lb) peppers
2 kg (4½ lb) green tomatoes + 1 kg (2 lb 2 oz) apples
2 kg (4½ lb) plums + 450 g (1 lb) apples + 450 g (1 lb) carrots

Tomato Sauce

Fresh, big beefsteak tomatoes give a wonderful sauce in high summer when they're really sun-ripened, but in deepest winter it's best to use tinned tomatoes, topped up with a pinch or two of sugar. Blend the raw ingredients to a rough purée, then cook until rich and syrupy, and sieve them after cooking; that way you avoid the tedious skinning and de-seeding process. Get the fat or oil for frying the sauce really hot and cook the sauce briskly to concentrate the flavour and to achieve a good consistency.

INGREDIENTS

Makes about 600 ml (1 pint)

tomatoes, quartered	**1 kg (2 lb)**
or tinned peeled tomatoes	**800 g (1¾ lb)**
onions, roughly chopped	**2**
garlic, peeled and chopped	**2 cloves**
salt	**10 ml (2 tsp)**
sugar	**to taste, depending on the tomatoes**
herbs, spices, chillis etc.	**to taste**
oil or lard	**15 ml (1 tbsp)**

Put all the ingredients except the oil or lard in the blender or processor and blend to a rough purée. Heat the fat until smoking and throw in the purée, stirring like mad until the worst of the bubbles subside. Lower the heat and cook, stirring from time to time, until a rich, syrupy consistency is achieved. Push the sauce through a sieve to eliminate pips and skin, and either serve at once with pasta or freeze in pots for later use as suggested.

Vary the herbs and spices depending on what you plan to use the sauce for:
● chopped red or green chillis, seeds removed
● cinnamon
● basil
● marjoram
● cuminseed
● aniseed

Mexican eggs: poach or scramble eggs directly into a simmering sauce (highly spiked with chilli) and serve with tortillas (p. 109) for brunch.
Creamy tomato sauce: whisk 200 ml (7 fl oz) double cream into half the basic sauce and use with stuffed peppers, chicken breasts, fish, shellfish etc.
Quiche filling: add 3 eggs to 300 ml (½ pint) basic tomato sauce, dot with olives and anchovies and bake in a pastry shell until set and golden brown.

Chicken Breasts with Chutney and Breadcrumb Stuffing

Chicken breasts are beaten out flat, spread with a chutney, butter and breadcrumb paste and baked *en papillote.*

Serves 4

**4 skinless, boneless chicken breasts (about 100 g (4 oz) each)
garlic salt and pepper
60 ml (4 tbsp) fresh breadcrumbs
25 g (1 oz) butter
30 ml (2 tbsp) well-ripened chutney (apricot is very good)
oil for frying**

Beat out the chicken breasts as thinly as you can without splitting the flesh and season with garlic salt and pepper. Mash or process together the breadcrumbs, butter and chutney and spread it on the chicken pieces. Fold them over or roll them up and fry them very briefly in hot oil just until lightly golden (maximum 2 minutes each side).

Put each one on a sheet of buttered foil, close the foil into an airtight parcel and bake at 180°C (350°F) mark 4 for 15 minutes. Remove from the oven and leave to rest for a few minutes in their packages before unwrapping, slicing and serving with extra chutney and crunchy cooked cabbage.

Savoury Choux Bites with Meat and Chutney Filling

Nice for pre-dinner nibbles.

Makes 12 mouthfuls

**150 g (5 oz) cooked ham, tongue, chicken or corned beef
30 ml (2 tbsp) chutney, any flavour
50 g (2 oz) butter
salt and pepper
16 bite-sized choux pastry puffs (see p. 98)**

Blend or process together the meat, chutney and butter and season to taste with salt and pepper. Fill the choux puffs shortly before serving, otherwise they go soggy.

Stuffed Peppers with Sweetcorn and Creamy Tomato Sauce

Grilled, peeled peppers are filled with a sweetcorn mixture, covered with a creamy tomato sauce and baked in the oven. A good vegetarian dish for 6.

Serves 6

6 small green peppers
1 onion
1 clove garlic
1–2 fresh green chillis, seeded and chopped
15 ml (1 tbsp) oil
2 corn cobs (or 350 g (12 oz) frozen corn kernels)
75 g (3 oz) Philadelphia cream cheese
salt
200 ml (7 fl oz) soured cream
½ quantity basic tomato sauce with chilli (p. 149)

Grill and peel the peppers until blistered and blackened all over, put them in a plastic bag and retrieve them 10 minutes later, when they will be easy to peel under running water. Cut a slit down the side of each of them and carefully take out the seeds, leaving the stalk and top intact.

Soften the onion, garlic and chillis in the oil without browning. Cut the kernels off the corn cobs and mix them (or the frozen kernels) with the cream cheese and softened vegetables. Season quite highly with salt – the corn seems to absorb rather a lot.

Stuff the peppers with the corn cheese mixture and put them in a lightly greased ovenproof dish. Whisk most of the soured cream into the tomato sauce and pour it over. Splash the rest of the cream on top. Bake in a 180°C (350°F) mark 4 oven for about 20 minutes or until golden brown on top and bubbling hot.

Mussel and Mango Chutney Quiche

Chutney has a nice, slightly sweet-sour flavour which goes well with the mussels.

Serves 4

450 kg (1 lb) fresh mussels (to give 200 g (7 oz) shelled)
½ quantity (about 225 g (8 oz)) basic shortcrust pastry (p. 81)
45 ml (3 tbsp) mango chutney, pushed through a sieve
150 ml (¼ pint) double cream
3 eggs
pepper

Clean the mussels and put them in a large pan with a lid. Cook over high heat for a couple of minutes until they open. Discard any that don't after 5 minutes' cooking. Place a colander over a bowl and line it with a nappy liner or muslin. Tip the mussels into the colander, remove them from their shells and set aside 150 ml (¼ pint) of the strained juice.

Roll out the pastry to fit a 25 cm (10 inch) quiche tin and spread it thinly with the mango chutney. Scatter the mussels on top. Mix together the reserved juice, the cream and the eggs. Salt will not be necessary but pepper may be: taste and see. Heat a heavy baking sheet in a 200°C (400°F) mark 6 oven and put the quiche on top of it. Reduce the heat to 180°C (350°F) mark 4 and bake for 35–40 minutes until golden brown and puffy.

THEME 28

ODDS AND ENDS

A Good Stock

Not for nothing are stocks called *fonds de cuisine* in French: the basis of your cooking. It's unlikely that you'll make a really fine sauce without a good base, so wherever possible, buy your meat and fish on the bone, butcher or fillet it yourself and use the bones for stock for its accompanying sauce.

Do not add salt to stock: that way you know where you are when you come to make a sauce and can season from scratch. Cook stocks at the barest simmer, otherwise the fat particles will cloud the issue. Meat stocks can be simmered for several hours, fish and vegetable only 30 minutes otherwise they will become bitter. Always reduce stocks after straining to concentrate the flavour. From a freezing point of view, it makes more sense to have small pots of well flavoured stock than gallons of faintly coloured water taking up space. Use within 2–3 days or freeze in 300 ml (½ pint) pots (a good quantity for sauces).

Makes about 1 litre (1¾ pints)

1 kg (2 lb 2 oz) bones: veal/beef/ lamb/game/chicken/fish
1 onion, halved
1 carrot, quartered
2 celery sticks with leaves
1 leek, trimmed and halved
1 bouquet garni (thyme, parsley and bay leaf)
10 peppercorns
300 ml (½ pint) wine, red or white (optional)
2 litres (3¼ pints) water

For a robust meat or game stock, roast the relevant bones and vegetables in a hot oven with a little fat until well browned; for a light meat, chicken or fish stock, omit the browning step; for a vegetable stock, omit the bones altogether.

Put bones, vegetables, herbs, peppercorns, wine, if used, and water in a huge pan and bring to the boil, skimming off the scum as it reaches a boil. Reduce the heat so that the water is barely trembling and simmer gently: 3–4 hours for meat or game stocks; 30 minutes only for fish or vegetable stocks.

When cooking time is up, strain the stock, discard the débris and return to the pan. Reduce to about 1 litre (1¾ pints) by fast boiling.

A Good White Sauce

Probably the reason why flour-based sauces have acquired such a bad name is because the *roux* is often insufficiently cooked in the first place, and the sauce not allowed a good long simmer to cook out the floury taste. Take care of these two points and don't make it too thick, and you'll have a useful sauce for everyday.

Makes about 500 ml (18 fl oz)

25 g (1 oz) butter
25 g (1 oz) plain white flour
500 ml (18 fl oz) milk, *or* half and half milk and stock
1 bay leaf
salt and pepper

Melt the butter and stir in the flour. Cook over gentle heat for 5 minutes – do not allow it to colour more than a pale gold. Remove from the heat and pour on the milk or milk and stock.

Return to the heat and whisk back to a boil with a wire whisk. Turn down the heat, add the bay leaf, with salt and pepper to taste, and leave to simmer gently for at least 20 minutes (30 is better still). Fish out the bay leaf, check the seasoning and thickness: if too thick, thin with a little milk or cream; if too thin, boil the sauce down a bit to evaporate the liquid until it reaches the right consistency.

Home-made Yogurt

Yogurt is endlessly useful, but not everyone is near a supply of natural yogurt, so here is a recipe for making your own. No complicated gadgetry or sinister bacteria required for this, just a large pot or pan and a ready made yogurt. The powdered milk gives a thicker result, a bit like a Greek yogurt.

Makes 7 × 150 ml ($\frac{1}{4}$ pint) cartons

1 litre (1$\frac{3}{4}$ pints) milk
150 ml ($\frac{1}{4}$ pint) yogurt cartonful powdered milk
30 ml (2 tbsp) natural yogurt (bought, or from the last batch)

Bring the milk to just below the boil, remove from the heat and leave uncovered at room temperature for 15 minutes. Put 7 empty yogurt cartons in a large casserole with a lid. Whisk the powdered milk and yogurt into the cooled milk and divide it among the yogurt cartons. Cover and leave in a warm place overnight, or for however long it takes for the yogurt to set – it varies, depending on the season, temperature of the kitchen, etc. and sometimes it doesn't set at all – in which case use it for breadmaking (pp. 104–5).

Caramel

Great for crunchy toppings, or diluted for fruit salads and sauces, or mixed with toasted nuts for praline. Adding lemon juice and not allowing the water to boil until the sugar is dissolved helps to reduce the danger of crystallization.

Makes about 150 ml ($\frac{1}{4}$ pint)

100 g (4 oz) granulated sugar
45 ml (3 tbsp) water
5 ml (1 tsp) lemon juice

Dissolve the sugar in the water with the lemon juice over moderate heat without boiling, until no longer cloudy. Boil until thick and bubbly, then allow it to turn through golden to a rich brown. Be careful not to let it burn – if things start to go a bit fast for your liking, take the pan off the heat and dunk the base in a sinkful of cold water. Use immediately, while still liquid, to coat the inside of dishes or moulds, e.g. for crème caramel.

Praline: add 100 g (4 oz) toasted almonds, walnuts or hazelnuts to the hot caramel and stir until well coated. Turn out on to an oiled piece of paper and leave to harden. Grind to a powder in a food processor or nutmill and use for sprinkling over ice creams, profiteroles, etc.

Liquid caramel: cool the caramel a little, dilute with 100 ml (4 fl oz) water, chill and use for fruit salads (especially orange).

Caramel sauce: whisk 200 ml (7 fl oz) single cream into the hot caramel, cool and serve with ice creams, etc.

Almond Tuiles

Lacy almond biscuits to serve with ice creams and mousses.

Makes about 18

2 egg whites
75 g (3 oz) caster sugar
50 g (2 oz) flaked almonds
30 ml (2 tbsp) plain white flour, sifted
grated zest of $\frac{1}{2}$ orange
5 ml (1 tsp) orange liqueur or orange-flower water

Mix gently together the egg whites, sugar, almonds, flour, orange zest and liqueur or orange-flower water and spread teaspoons on non-stick baking paper, well spaced out. (Bake the tuiles in several batches if necessary.) Flatten the tuiles with a wet fork – they should be very thin.

Heat the oven to 200°C (400°F) mark 6 and bake for about 8 minutes until golden brown. Remove, and while still warm and flexible, lift with a spatula and press them into a non-stick or greased ring mould to curve them up. Continue with the rest of the mixture.

INDEX